IRELAND: TOWARDS NEW IDENTITIES?

THE DOLPHIN

General Editor: Tim Caudery

29

IRELAND: TOWARDS NEW IDENTITIES?

Edited by
Karl-Heinz Westarp
and Michael Böss

AARHUS UNIVERSITY PRESS

AARHUS UNIVERSITY PRESS
Building 170
University of Aarhus
DK-8000 Aarhus C, Denmark
Fax (+45) 8619 8433

73 Lime Walk
Headington
Oxford OX3 7AD
Fax (+44) 1865 750 079

Box 511
Oakville, Conn. 06779
Fax (+1) 860 945 9468

Editorial address:
The Dolphin
Department of English, Building 326
University of Aarhus
8000 Aarhus C, Denmark
Fax (+45) 8942 2099
E-mail engtc@hum.aau.dk

Published with financial support from the Aarhus University Research Foundation.
The editors want to thank Tim Caudery, the general editor of *The Dolphin*, for his untiring and meticulous help, and the technical editor, Vibeke Kjær, for her professional help and her patience.

Cover photo of The Giant's Causeway by Michael Böss.

The cartoon on p. 82 is reproduced with the kind permission of *The Irish Times*.

Contents

5

Introduction: Towards New Identities?

In an essay in *The Irish Times*, celebrating the Peace Agreement of 10 April 1998, the poet Seamus Heaney described the agreement as a result not of a 'revolution' but rather of an 'evolution'. For Heaney, however, this did not keep him from feeling a biblical sense of wonder over what had been created on this latter-day Good Friday. For whereas a revolution was the kicking down of a rotten door, evolution was like 'pushing the stone from the mouth of a tomb':

> There is an Easter energy about it, a sense of arrival rather than wreckage, and what is nonpareil about the new conditions is the promise they offer of a new covenant between people living in this country. For once, and at long last, the language of the Bible can be appropriated by those with a vision of the future rather than those who sing the battle hymns of the past.

What the agreement offered, Heaney went on, was a northern Irish world where a phrase like 'the people of Ulster' would have to include both majority and minority; both the unionist majority and the nationalist and republican minority. One should not conclude, however, that a new regional identity was in the making. Northern Ireland would remain a place of many and complex identities, but at least 'Ulsterness' would now be a 'shared attribute' for the minority: 'Ulster will remain a site of contention, politically and culturally, but at least the contenders will have assented to play on the same pitch and by agreed rules'.[1]

The new political and institutional framework, it is to be hoped, might gradually lead to a broader acknowledgement of Ulster's – and Ireland's – evolving identities, past and present, in the same way as has happened south of the border.

1. Identity

Identities are the ways in which individuals and groups understand and create meaning and value for themselves in interaction with other individuals and groups, constructing, by means of metaphor and image, symbolic orders by which they represent themselves and others, past and present, in given historical contexts. Given the constraints of the situational context – interacting with the ideas, volitions and motivations of the social actors – identities are not static, simple and unalterable but, as expressions of a continuous process of self-interpretation, multidimensional, dynamic and changing.[2]

7

The dynamic nature of identity is testified to by a number of studies of national and ethnic identity that have been made in Northern Ireland since the 'Troubles' started in the late 1960s. For instance, an attitude survey conducted in 1968 by the political scientist, Richard Rose, gave the following responses from Protestants when asked, 'Which of these terms ["British", "Irish", or "Ulster"] best describes the way you usually think of yourself?': 'British' (39%), 'Ulster' (32%) and 'Irish' (20%).[3] Ten years into the 'Troubles', when the survey was repeated by Edward Moxon-Browne, the answers deviated widely from those given in 1968. Now 67% answered 'British', and only 20% and 8% 'Ulster' and 'Irish'. There were no similar changes among Catholics, of whom 76% called themselves 'Irish' (69% in 1978), 15% 'British' (both years) and 5% 'Ulster' (6% in 1978). Edward Moxon-Browne interpreted the decline in Protestants' identification with the 'Irish' label as their 'rejection of the policies followed by certain groups in the name of "Irish unity" or "Irish nationalism"'. The decline in the percentage identifying with the Ulster label was explained as a result of a loss of faith among Protestants in the strength of Ulster as a political unit that could protect them against the threat posed by Northern Irish nationalists. It was evidence of a 'need to seek emotional refuge in a grouping large and powerful enough (even if occasionally unreliable) to withstand the inroads of Irish nationalism'.[4]

The history of national and ethnic identities in the island of Ireland should be seen against the background of prolonged attempts by settled and incoming groups to either defend themselves or extend their political dominance, both through physical force and, culturally, by labelling and defining themselves as different from the 'others'.

Issues of ethnic and national identity may be seen as subordinate aspects of a more general problem, namely the social, economic, political and cultural power relationships between minorities and majorities both within individual states and between states and 'cultures'.[5] This perception is reflected in the so-called 'double minority model', which has often been applied to explain the ethnic and national conflicts in the island of Ireland. The model assumes that a minority will always feel a degree of threat from a majority and therefore be likely to be extremely sensitive to words and behaviour by which the majority attempts to dominate them – or is perceived to do so.[6] Thus, the actual behaviour of individuals, subgroups and political parties associated with the two major groups – nationalists/'Catholics' and unionists/'Protestants' – can be interpreted as a result of the fact that they both experience themselves as minorities.[7]

Since the plantation of Ulster in the 17th century, Irish Catholics have been a minority in the North of Ireland. Until the partition of the island in 1920, however, they were part of an overall Catholic majority in the island. Partition put an end to this situation and reduced them to a permanent minority within the boundaries of the Northern Irish state, since southern nationalists soon resigned themselves to a *de facto* if not a *de jure* recognition of the new border. This policy caused bitterness and a considerable degree of alienation among Northern Catholics towards the South, and in this way contributed to giving Northern nationalism its own character and to developing a more 'reactive' sense of national identity than in the South.

On the other side of the ethnic boundary, unionists/'Protestants' have long felt threatened by the prospect of becoming a discriminated minority in a united Ireland. For although, today, they make up a majority of 58% of the population of Northern Ireland, they would be a minority of 25% in the event of Irish unity. In 1992 a British journalist, Tony Parker, registered this minority fear among Northern Protestants in a book of interviews. In one of them, a female former lecturer from The Queen's University in Belfast says, 'I was born British and I want to live British. I feel under threat from those Irish people in the south, and if the border went I'd be terrified, because I feel the south is a male-dominated and church-dominated country'.[8]

In 1985, the British and Irish governments signed the Hillsborough Agreement. The 'Anglo-Irish Agreement' was an international treaty which amounted to a *de jure* recognition of Northern Ireland by the Irish government. It stated that future changes in the constitutional status of Northern Ireland could only be made on the basis of 'the consent of the majority of the people of Northern Ireland', but it also recognised the legitimacy of an Irish dimension by giving the Republic a consultative status through the intergovernmental ministerial conference and its permanent secretariat in matters regarding the accommodation of the two communities of Northern Ireland. Finally, it expressed an intention on the part of both governments to continue and enhance cross-border cooperation on matters of security, economy and social policy.

Since unionist politicians had not been included in the negotiations, they saw the agreement as an opening to a future in which they could not expect their voice to be heard. They therefore launched a campaign of non-cooperation with British ministers and called loyalists to the streets in violent and non-violent protest. For the rest of the decade, loyalist paramilitary organisations were able to recruit on the basis of a substantial degree of alienation among unionists, and the violence of these groups soon exceeded that of the IRA. Past arrogance was increasingly replaced by a feeling of having been relegated to the loser's side. Such feelings were sometimes enhanced by reports documenting growing emigration of young people to England or predicting an 'outgrowing' of the unionist majority in Northern Ireland within a generation.

Such reactions may seem to reflect a simple story of continued confrontations between the majority and the minority in Northern Ireland. But this would be to belie other important evidence that points in the direction of shifting identities in both communities in recent decades. The way collective identities are often conveyed politically may not truthfully represent or determine the way individuals understand themselves or the stands they take towards practical issues.

A study from 1987, for example, revealed a complex picture of the political aspirations of the 'Catholic' minority with regard to the question of Irish unity. 42% of those identifying themselves as 'Catholics' were for, 16% were against and 41% were undecided.[9] An opinion poll taken in 1996 for *The Irish Times* –

9

which offered more options for the 'undecided' – showed that within the previous 10 years there had apparently been a slight drop in the number of Northern Catholics in support of Irish unity: 39% were now for, 12% supported 'a local Parliament for NI within the UK with power-sharing between local parties', 23% favoured 'a local Parliament for NI within the UK with power-sharing and North-South links', 3% 'NI becoming more fully part of the UK', 3% 'NI as an independent state', and 16% were for 'NI under the control of both the British and Irish Governments'. 2% per cent even preferred 'a return to majority rule'![10] The indication that the goal of Irish unity was only an absolute good for a minority within the minority was confirmed in 1997 in *The Belfast Telegraph*/Queen's Survey.[11]

Studies of attitudes to, for instance, integrated schools and political violence seem to indicate that such nuanced attitudes may reflect the fact that the relationship between group identities and individual identity is a more complex matter than can be measured by mere poll taking. Not surprisingly, it took a journalistic study – Fionnuala O Connor's portraits of Northern Catholics in *In Search of a State: Catholics in Northern Ireland* – to document shifting attitudes in identity formation among members of the minority.[12]

But why did it take a journalist to more fully document the complex, floating and emotional character of Northern nationalist identities than had ever been done by a social scientist? O Connor herself found fault with the traditional method of using questionnaires to study the way people understand themselves. She suspected that a set number of prefabricated answers cannot adequately reflect the fluid state of many people's opinions. This can only be borne out 'by the twists and turns of conversation', she concluded (2).

O Connor's suspicion raises a general methodological question: how do we develop the right methods to register and interpret the complex process by which individual subjectivities are not only affected by but also, in turn, contribute to the revision of collective identities and the social and cultural structures to which they may give rise?[13]

The anthropologist Anthony P. Cohen once said that focusing on individual self-consciousness, reflexiveness and motivation in the study of culture does not imply that we should deny the existence of common and collective forms and significations in a given society. The study of subjectivities, however, will reveal the 'problematic' – i.e., indeterministic – character of the interaction between individual and society; and it will show that it is often from individual agents that society may derive as much of its dynamism as it will from its collective, institutional, and structural levels.

It is this very multiplicity and the motivational – and thus structurally productive – character of individual self-interpretations that make ethnicist and nationalist ideologues and politicians wish to inform and control individual attitudes and states of mind through their 'politics of identity' by, for example, creating, encouraging and maintaining symbols, rituals and ideas that define and preserve (or seek to destroy) national and cultural borders, where – from the individual viewpoint – only vague and shifting boundaries between themselves and 'others' may be perceived.

Cohen's view of the problematic relationship between social and cultural constraints and the way in which the individual understands himself or herself has strong implications for our understanding of the way individuals develop a sense of their own ethnic and national identities. But, perhaps more importantly, it has implications for an understanding of how such identities change and evolve under the impact of new political, social and cultural contexts.

Cohen's considerations tell us that only by studying the subjectivities of the past and the present will the cultural historian be able to develop a sophisticated understanding of the nature of identity, and of the role that individual and collective identities play for social, political, and cultural processes. This also means that a variety of methods and disciplines from the human and social sciences must be applied in order to draw a full picture. This perspective adds to the methodological reasoning behind 'Irish Studies' as an interdisciplinary scholarly effort.[14] Political scientists, historians, cultural anthropologists and literary scholars all have something to contribute.

The rise and fall of Gaelic-Catholic nationalism in Southern Ireland is a case in point.

2. Literature and Identity

The construction of the images that fed nationalist ideology at the end of the 19th century can be traced back to individual intellectuals and writers responding creatively to ideological, social and political circumstances of their own time. In many cases the biographies of such writers became chapters in the history of the formation of an Irish national identity at the turn of the century.

But after 1922, Irish writers also became instrumental in breaking down these very same images.

Discussing in 1990 with Julia Carlson why writers in the Republic until recently suffered under some of the severest censorship laws in Europe, the novelist John McGahern said that the writer in Ireland has always been feared because 'he's one of the only uncompromised moral authorities'.[15]

The sharpest critic of the Censorship of Publications Act, 1929, Sean O'Faolain, who, like McGahern, was one of the victims of censorship and the codified public prudery it represented, saw Irish literature since 1920 as a voice of 'realism' fundamentally critical of the romantic notions of Ireland that influenced nationalist ideology and politics. In his portrait of the Irish from 1947, O'Faolain wrote:

> In the most creative period of Anglo-Irish literature (from about 1890 to about 1920) the writers saw Irish life, in the main, romantically. ... Towards the end of the period a satirical note made itself felt, and in the plays of Sean O' Casey – all the natural wonder being

11

removed, for they are set in the Dublin slums – we were left with an unassuaged realism. The Novel, budding from the work of George Moore and James Joyce, and profoundly affected by French and Russian realists, likewise began to hold a far from indulgent mirror up to nature. When the revolutionary period of 1916-1922 ended miserably in a civil war, romance died completely. Most Irish literature since 1922 has been of an uncompromising scepticism, one might even say ferocity.[16]

Since the Literary Revival, Irish literature had been a crucial part of the process of giving the Irish new images of themselves. Literature, as O'Faolain saw it, was more than a mirror – or a 'summary' – of collective identities. It was itself 'an active agent'. The Literary Revival, for example, had been far more than a number of isolated writers 'expressing themselves': 'It was a whole people giving tongue, and by that self-articulation approaching nearer than ever before to "intellectual and imaginative freedom"' (*ibid.*, 129). What Irish writers had done ever since, by virtue of this sense of freedom, was to force 'a concentration of power to expose itself' (*ibid.*, 142).

Looking back 30 years later, the literary and cultural historian Terence Brown saw a line from modernist and realist writers – and enemies of the Censorship Act (Joyce, Beckett, O'Faolain among others) – to the debates about Irish identity and its political, cultural, and constitutional implications from the 1960s onwards:

> The critics of the censorship policy in the 1940s were in fact, it can be argued, the vanguard of the intellectual and cultural changes that were to take place in Ireland over the next thirty years. For it became an aspect of their critique of censorship that not only was it a manifestly absurd policy but that Ireland, in crisis as the flight from the land accelerated, could not adapt to save itself if it did not open windows to influences from abroad. They reckoned that Ireland would have to abandon its obsessive absorption with its own past and its own diminished cultural forms and adapt to the world about it, openly accepting what energy and diversity it could find as a modern nation. Censorship was a dangerously inhibiting check on such necessary adaptation. Their attacks on censorship were therefore only a part of a larger ideological conflict in the country that in the 1940s was manifested most obviously on this issue, but which was to be expressed increasingly in various social and cultural debates in the subsequent decades.[17]

The attempt to define an Irish national identity culminated in the latter half of the 19th century. In this period, for the first time in the history of Ireland, a modern nationalist movement laid claim to territorial and political independence with the argument that the Irish made up a nation with their own cultural and mental characteristics. The notion about this alleged national identity bore the marks of the social, economic and cultural transformations that Ireland was going through in this period; to some extent it appeared as a reaction to 'modernity' – seen as an 'English' phenomenon – in the various aspects of the concept. This was to be an important factor in the struggle for Irish national independence. At the same time, however, it had the effect of exacerbating the old religious and social conflict between descendants of 'Gaels' and 'Planters' in Ulster at a time when the former Protestant Ascendancy in the South were becoming more 'Irish'.

The result of this conflict was the partition of Ireland in 1920 and the creation of two states, each with its own semi-official identity – one Irish-Catholic, the other British-Protestant – which from now on were used to justify the suppression of the right of minorities and individuals to freely express their own identities.

As said above, all the great violent conflicts in the history of Ireland – the post-Reformation wars, the rising in 1798, the rising of Young Ireland, the War of Independence, the Civil War, and the so-called Troubles – have partly been conflicts over what it means to be Irish (or non-Irish) in the island of Ireland. Because of the large minority of Irish Catholics in the northern state, this conflict of identity has been carried on here. In the South, however, the conflict has abated significantly, to the degree of non-existence. Also the old antagonism between 'Irish' and 'English' seems obsolete or deviant when, occasionally, it is evoked as a reaction to events in Northern Ireland.

This has been the result of a process in which the United Kingdom, from being a colonial power, the dominant partner of a political union and, eventually, a military enemy, moved to becoming a partner in a larger European context and in the joint effort to solve the ongoing conflict in Northern Ireland.

Another decisive factor in the process has been the growing criticism of the unofficial political role of the Catholic church in the first 50 years of the southern state. Voices critical of the Catholic identity of the state, codified in the 1937 Constitution, came from liberal intellectuals, academics, bureaucrats, business-men, politicians, and writers.

Thirdly, the return of militant republicanism in Northern Ireland after 1969 threw southern nationalism, with its own roots in physical force republicanism, into a political credibility crisis, and gave rise to public debates on the need to revise Irish national identity and stereotyped views of the 'others' in newspapers, news-magazines, cultural periodicals and intellectual pamphlets – such as *The Irish Times, Magill, The Crane Bag*, and *Field Day Pamphlets*.

Finally, through the mass media, the educational system, book stores, theatres and mass culture, the new images and stories of Ireland began to spread into the Irish population at large in the 1980s, gradually changing the political culture of the Republic. The political results are evident, culminating with the legal reforms of the 1990s and the revision of Articles 2 and 3 of the Constitution endorsed by 95% of the voters in the referendum of 22 May 1998. A more informal evidence of a people undergoing radical changes in its perception of itself is that it is no longer *comme il faut* to talk about Irish identity in the singular.[18] The South has already moved in the direction of new identities.

After the Peace Agreement of Easter 1998, the great question now begging an answer is: has Northern Ireland now set out on a similar voyage towards new identities? The essays of this volume will follow some of the steps that have taken Ireland, North and South, to a point of arrival, as Seamus Heaney described it in his essay. With the aid of metaphor and symbol, it may also turn out to be a point of a new embarkation.

Notes

1. *The Irish Times*, 11 April 1998.
2. Liah Greenfeld, *Nationalism: Five Roads to Modernity* (Cambridge: Harvard University Press, 1992), 19; Fredrik Barth (ed.), *Ethnic Groups and Boundaries* (Boston: Little, Brown and Company, 1969); Andrew M. Greeley, *Ethnicity in the United States* (New York: John Wiley, 1974); Herbert J. Gans, *Ethnic Identity and Assimilation* (New York: Praeger, 1974); Zdzislaw Mach, *Symbols, Conflict and Identity: Essays in Political Anthropology* (Albany: State University of New York Press, 1993), 3-21.
3. Richard Rose, *Governing Without Consensus* (London: Faber, 1971), 208.
4. Edward Moxon-Browne, *Nation, Class and Creed in Northern Ireland* (Aldershot: Gower, 1983), 5-6.
5. Cf. Elizabeth Tomkin (ed.), *History and Ethnicity* (London: Routledge, 1989); Karen Fog Olwig, 'Etnicitet og kulturel identitet', in Helen Krag and Margit Warburg (eds), *Minoriteter: En grundbog* (Copenhagen: Spektrum, 1992), 60-74; and George A. de Vos and Lola Romanucci-Ross, 'Ethnic Identity: A Psychocultural Perspective', in de Vos and Romanucci-Ross (eds), *Ethnic Identity: Creation, Conflict, and Accommodation*, 3rd edition (Walnut Creek and London: Altamira Press, 1996), 349-73.
6. See for example A.T.Q. Stewart, *The Narrow Ground: Aspects of Ulster, 1609-1969* (London: Faber and Faber, 1977), 162; Rona Fields, *Society under Siege: A Psychology of Northern Ireland* (Philadelphia, Pa.: Temple University Press, 1977), 196; Ed Cairns, 'Intergroup Conflict in Northern Ireland', in Henri Tajfel (ed.), *Social Identity and Intergroup Relations* (Cambridge: Cambridge University Press, 1982), 277-97; and Brian Lennon, *After the Ceasefires* (Dublin: Columba Press, 1995), 18-21.
7. The terms 'Catholic' and 'Protestant' should be understood as so-called ethnic markers, not as necessarily denoting denominational affiliation.
8. Tony Parker, *May the Lord in His Mercy Be Kind to Belfast* (London: Jonathan Cape, 1992), 130.
9. David Smith, *Equality and Inequality in Northern Ireland, Part 3: Perceptions and Views* (London: Political Studies Institute, 1987).
10. To this should be added that about 11% (1991 census) of the population in Northern Ireland choose not to state any religious denomination when asked. See *Irish Almanac and Yearbook of Facts 1997* (Speenoge: Artcam Publishing, 1997), 123.
11. *Fortnight*, May, 1997.
12. *Fortnight*, September, 1993. See also Kevin Boyle and Tom Hadden, *Northern Ireland: The Choice*, 62-63; and Fionnuala O Connor, *In Search of a State: Catholics in Northern Ireland* (Belfast: Blackstaff Press, 1993).
13. Cf. Liah Greenfeld, *Nationalism: Five Roads to Modernity* (Cambridge, Mass.: Harvard University Press, 1992), 20.
14. Cf. Joep Leerssen, *Mere Irish and Fíor-Ghael: Studies in the Idea of Irish Nationality, its Development and Literary Expression prior to the Nineteenth Century* (Cork: Cork University Press, 1996), 4-5.
15. Julia Carlson, *Banned in Ireland: Censorship and the Irish Writer* (London: Routledge, 1990), 64.
16. *The Irish* (Penguin: West Drayton, Middlesex, 1947), 137-38.
17. Terence Brown, *Ireland: A Social and Cultural History 1922-79* (Glasgow: Fontana, 1981), 198-99.
18. See Michael Böss, *Den irske verden: Historie, kultur og identitet i det moderne samfund* (København: Samleren, 1997).

Part I

Irish Identities:
Historical Considerations

The Slow Triumph of Politics: Irish Endgame

Tom Garvin

The resurgence of popular nationalism in eastern Europe and elsewhere in the world, often accompanied by horrific violence, has stunned many observers. This reemergence of hitherto smothered collective identities has obscured the fact that the general upheavals of the past decade have had little impact on analogous collective identities in western Europe. In the British Isles, Germany, France, Iberia and Italy, the minor nationalities have tended toward a guarded acceptance of existing state structures, usually accompanied by a willingness of the existing states to modify those structures to accommodate the susceptibilities of the minorities. Ireland would seem to offer a serious exception to this generalisation, although even this exception may be more apparent than real.

Arguably, the nationalist explosions in what were the Communist Party states of eastern Europe have been particularly violent precisely because communism repressed them so determinedly over the decades; by contrast, in western Europe, local particularisms have tended to gain authentic institutional recognition in pragmatic, piecemeal ways. Politics has tended to replace insurrectionism, with South Tyrol being one of the earlier of such piecemeal solutions.[1] Such solutions are rendered easier to achieve by the curious alliances that have been evolving between the inter-state agencies of Brussels and the sub-state representative systems that sometimes express regional or national identities. The classic European nation-state is being increasingly bypassed in ways that offer opportunities for political self-expression to local particularisms and nationalisms.

In Ireland, however, the problem historically has been that Irish separatist nationalism received full recognition in the form of an independent Irish state two generations ago, while that same nationalism was refused recognition in the pro-Britain 'unionist' area of Northern Ireland. This was so despite the existence of a large pro-separation minority in that region. This uneasy stand-off has begun to change. Whilst efforts to resolve the stalemate by armed conflict have failed, the growing importance of the European Union, the emergence of a Northern Irish Catholic and nationalist middle class that favours prosperity over strife, and the new strategic unimportance of the island of Ireland have introduced a new dynamic into the Irish national question. The effect of these developments is likely to have far-reaching implications not only for the Irish quarrel but also for the character of Irish nationalism more generally.

1. Irish Divisions

To understand the Irish situation and the features of its nationalism today, one must appreciate that the Irish have always been the outlier among the nations of the British Isles; they are the least British of the British, or, as they would put it themselves, the non-British of the Isles. Ireland is, most obviously, a separate island, and was the centre of a distinctive Gaelic-Christian culture during the first millennium A.D. Furthermore, after the Norman and English invasions of the medieval and early modern period, whereas the bulk of the land passed into the hands of newcomers from Britain, the majority of the population clung to a separate identity. Assimilation to English culture, or even acceptance of a common 'British Isles' identity, did not occur, although it may have been a close-run thing.[2] Rather, in the twentieth century the bulk of the Irish opted for separation, and despite its costs, have never really regretted the decision.

There are many reasons why the Irish chose to assert a national identity distinct from, and opposed to, English or British identity, and why that distinctiveness persists today. From the start, religion has been the key to Irish national consciousness. As already suggested, the defeated majority of the indigenous Irish remained Catholic after the defeat of the Irish Catholic aristocracy at the hands of English, Scottish and Irish Protestants in 1690. This was due mainly to the missionary efforts of a well-organised counter-Reformation Catholic Church with secure bases in France and Spain, safe from English power. A further reason for the survival of Irish Catholicism was the underdevelopment and weakness of purpose of Irish Anglican Protestantism, which did not proselytise very effectively among the general population.

The Irish majority was not only Catholic, it was also dispossessed. Its lands passed, as swordland, into the hands of the Protestant minority on the island. Dispossession and faith (and later nationalism) thus reinforced one another. If one was Protestant, one had more civil rights, including the right to own property. Education, where it existed in any formal fashion, tended to be a Protestant preserve, as Catholic schools were discouraged by law and public policy.

Scotland and Wales, where separatism has never become as strong in modern times as it did in Ireland, afford revealing contrasts. Scotland accepted integration with the larger English nation as something positive, and thus became a relatively satisfied 'national sub-state' within the United Kingdom, retaining its national Kirk, its universities and its legal system. Scottish members of Parliament constituted a determined and successful team of defenders of Scottish national interests. Wales, more closely linked to England, never had its own independent or quasi-autonomous state, unlike either Scotland or Ireland. Its nationalism has usually confined itself to demands for religious rights and linguistic self-expression. The success of the Welsh approach can be witnessed by the continuing survival, and relative prospering, of the Welsh language.

Irish nationalism has, by contrast, always been confronted by Irish unionism, or the wish to be united with England or Britain. The Irish members at Westminster between 1801 and 1922 tended to be spokesmen for one Irish interest at the expense of the other: landlord versus tenant in the early years of the Union with Britain, unionist versus nationalist in the latter years. No common Irish interest was expressed at Westminster, particularly because the Irish unionist minority had powerful friends in the Conservative Party. The failure to achieve successful integration with England – the 'Scottish' solution – was a consequence of these divisions, exacerbated by Irish religious fanaticism and an equally rabid English political and religious bigotry. The Irish union with Great Britain was crippled from the start.

The sharpest Irish division has been between the Protestant northeast of the island and the Catholic remainder. Unequal economic development, favouring the northeast, aggravated this division and laid the foundations for the partition that is the focal point of much of Ireland's contemporary agitations. During the nineteenth century, restrictions on Catholic land ownership were relaxed and, in a slow, profound historical shift, the land of Ireland passed back from the mainly Protestant landlord class to its mainly Catholic tenantry.[3] This process was accompanied by a gradual democratisation, so that by the end of the nineteenth century a bastard feudalism was replaced by a free-farmer democracy in embryo.

However, whereas Britain was now a mature industrial democracy, Ireland had been de-industrialised by the Union; local small manufacturers had been wiped out by British competition.[4] Only one area on the island experienced a different development in the era after 1690: the northern province of Ulster, geographically and culturally close to Scotland and subject, in the 17th century, to widespread colonisation by Protestant settlers from Britain.

Ulster shared in the British industrial revolution, and Belfast, the capital of the northeast, mushroomed as an important industrial city in the 19th century, with linen, shipbuilding and ironworking being the most important activities. The rest of the island stagnated while Ulster prospered. A huge famine in the 1840s killed one million of the island's inhabitants, out of a total population of over eight million. Another million fled the Great Hunger, as it was called, to the United States, there to nurse their hatred of England. Fairly or otherwise, the British were perceived as watching the catastrophe with some complacency. The resultant bitterness, as we will see, was to have repercussions for Irish nationalism that extend to the present. Millions more Irish people emigrated to America subsequently; by the end of the century the population of the island had halved to about four million, about one-third of this total being in the area that was to become the Protestant-dominated province of Northern Ireland ('Ulster') in 1920. This partition came after a protracted period of violence following on the North's refusal to join in a 'Home Rule' Ireland in 1912, a refusal which was backed up with guns. This defiance of the Irish majority was encouraged by strong elements in the Conservative Party, the British Army and the German Government.

In many ways, a huge mental gulf has grown up between North and South since then. Both North and South have had utterly different political experiences, the North that of a British province under local Protestant rule, the rest of the island as an independent democracy, earlier a British Commonwealth dominion *à la* Canada, latterly an independent republic. After 1945, the North clung on tightly to Britain while the Republic of Ireland forgot the British, focusing instead on its own economic and social development. It also went through a complex cultural transformation that the North did not share. Nowadays, Northerners are more religiously minded than Southerners; whereas neither part of Ireland is as post-Christian as the rest of western Europe, a secularisation process appears, paradoxically, to have moved further in the Republic than in the North.

In other noticeable ways the southern republic has been evolving away from the North, and for certain purposes out of the British Isles altogether. Up to 1960, most of the Republic's trade was with the United Kingdom, and culturally it remained, as it still does, a province of the Isles. Since 1960, however, trade with the rest of the world has increased markedly, and this tendency has accelerated since both islands joined the European Community in 1973. The Republic has substantially succeeded in exchanging its historical economic dependence on Britain for a more diversified dependence on the continental mainland. This ties in rather well with the culture's longstanding Catholic links with the mainland; faith and wallet have joined forces and produced a marked, and very un-British, Europhilia in the Republic. Europe has thus become a counterweight that Dublin can use for leverage against the otherwise overwhelming weight of Britain.[5] For one example among many, the British could once put tariffs up against Irish goods; that power is now gone.

The upshot of these trends is that the Republic has essentially gone post-nationalist and consequently has dropped most of the fundamentalist rhetoric of the early period after independence, most notably its rhetorical claims for a united independent all-Ireland state. By contrast, nationalism of a traditional 'faith and fatherland' kind has remained strong in parts of Catholic areas in Northern Ireland. The Republic has developed its own, almost 'national' identity, whilst many Northerners are unsure, and often confused, as to whether they are British, Irish or both. This confusion has provided fertile ground for the pursuit of political ends through violent means.[6]

2.   A Question of Violence

Long before independence and partition, Irish nationalism contained within it a minority tradition of armed violence, fed in particular by the Irish-American diaspora. As I have suggested, it always had to compete with a dominant tradition of democratic compromise, symbolised best by the early 19th century figure of

Daniel O'Connell. However, occasionally the violent tradition 'got lucky' and bested the dominant tradition, as it did in 1912-13 and in Northern Ireland between 1969 and 1994.

In general, violence and nationalism seem to combine most explosively when the actual existence of the *ethnie* seems to be threatened, as in modern Yugoslavia. Alternatively, the combination thrives when a vital economic interest, such as control of land, seems to be involved and reinforces nationalist sentiment. A real or imagined assault on a central set of ethnic or religious values or symbols, held to be vital to the collective well-being, can also spark off extraordinary violence.

The Irish minority tradition of violence dates from the eighteenth century. Since the end of that century there have been three great armed campaigns against British rule in Ireland and, at times, against local supporters of that rule. The first, culminating in the Rising of 1798, was inspired by the French and American revolutions, and involved a southern Catholic and Ulster dissenter alliance against the small Anglican landed class and their British patrons. The insurrection was put down with great brutality, perhaps 50,000 people being killed.

The second era of armed resistance, the 'Troubled Times', was that of 1912-13, culminating in partitioned independence. In reaction to Ulster's *defi* of 1912, a rebellion took place in Dublin in 1916. The leaders were executed, and the British attempted to conscript Irishmen for the Great War. The result was a hugely popular general rejection of British rule. In these years, perhaps 6,000 people were killed on the island. British forces and Irish guerrillas fought a small war, mainly in the extreme south of the island and in Dublin.[7] In the North, sectarian pogroms occurred with British toleration, the Protestant side doing the majority of the killings.

After partition and independence in 1920-22, Protestant and British forces suppressed the large Catholic minority in Northern Ireland. In the Catholic south, the guerrillas of the Irish Republican Army (IRA) split and fought a short internecine civil war over the issue of Irish sovereignty and membership of the British Commonwealth. The forces of the democratic majority won, and the South settled down to construct a liberal democracy.[8] However, in the North, the two religious groups remained in a sullen stasis, Protestants wielding a local hegemony over the Catholic minority with British acquiescence. Northern Ireland remained part of the United Kingdom, but London did not supervise the local rulers. Catholics were not disenfranchised, but were shorn of all real political power and discriminated against heavily. The Protestants had a built-in majority, and gerrymandered the local council electoral constituencies so as to expand their natural majority in Northern Ireland even further.[9]

In return, the Catholics battened down the hatches and built a counter-culture centred around their Church and Catholic/nationalist institutions. Catholics and Protestants lived cheek-by-jowl, commonly cooperated politely with each other, but did not socialise much and rarely intermarried. The two communities constructed totally distinct cultural worlds, each only half-aware of the complexities inside the other. The Canadian writer Hugh MacLennan, in the context of the Quebec national question, has accurately called this a situation of 'two solitudes'.[10] Protestants saw Catholics as allied with the Catholic Republic in the South, as being in league with it to take over the Protestant homeland of Northern Ireland and, perhaps, to drive Protestants out: 'back to Scotland'. They commonly saw Catholicism as a superstitious and even evil religion. Catholics, for their part, saw Protestants as richer than themselves, as bigoted, and as having the might of Britain, the local superpower, behind them. Catholics developed a victim psychology, seeing their own woes more vividly than those of the other side. Protestants were commonly similarly blind to the condition of Catholics.[11] It is against this backdrop that the third era of armed resistance to Protestant and British rule began in the late 1960s.

Like so much else in modern Ireland, the political process that destabilised the post-1923 stand-off in Ireland was imported from America. It consisted of a series of campaigns mounted by young, mainly Catholic leaders and activists for civil rights, modelled on the black civil rights campaign of that time in the United States. In effect, the Catholics, echoing 18th century predecessors, said to the Protestant government of Northern Ireland: 'you say we are all British, you refuse to permit us to join the independent Republic, and you deny our Irish identity. Very well, then, give us the rights of Britons'.

This argument fell on sympathetic ears, particularly in Britain and the United States. London was belatedly embarrassed by the fruit of its own malign negligence and rushed to make amends. However, it was too late; Protestant terrorists tried to provoke action by the authorities against the Catholics by faking IRA bombings. Rioting in late 1969, in which an uncontrollable Protestant police took a major part, resulted in mass attacks by rioters and state forces on Catholic ghettos in Derry and Belfast. The British sent in the Army in an attempt, temporarily successful, to quell the fighting. In the Republic, pressure to intervene grew, but did not result in any incursions by the Republic's army into the North. In the North, distrust between the British soldiers and the Catholics grew, and, after a few years, the new Provisional Irish Republican Army (PIRA) started to murder soldiers, Protestant civilians and Catholic dissidents.[12] PIRA bombing and killing reached its height in 1972 and London, in response, abolished the Belfast Parliament and introduced 'direct rule' from London.

Direct rule did little to stop the violence in the medium run. Over 3,000 people have lost their lives in Northern Ireland in the past quarter of a century because of the Ulster Troubles. Most of the killing, however, has been concentrated in small areas inside Northern Ireland. Occasionally Protestant bombers made an excursion to Dublin, and similarly the PIRA made excursions to London. However, by and large the PIRA and its Protestant, notionally pro-British, equivalents, have killed civilians, car-bombed pubs and supermarkets, and murdered people going to work essentially because the assassins were certain, or thought they were certain, of the victims' politics and religion.[13] Each side tended to deny the centrality of religious denomination; in fact, it was commonly declared that to say the conflict in Northern Ireland was about religion was a gross oversimplification. In reality it is no oversimplification at all.

For many years Irish insurrectionists like the PIRA benefitted from the support of Irish-Americans, just as diaspora communities have supported more radical expressions of nationalism elsewhere in Europe; Croatia, the Baltic states and Armenia afford examples of this syndrome. PIRA propaganda to the effect that the Dublin government was a British puppet fell on uninformed but receptive ears in Boston and New York. Irish democracy had won the Irish Civil War of 1922-23 in Ireland, but it lost it in parts of Irish-America. After all, many emigrants from Ireland to the United States in the 1920s had been involved on the defeated side in the Civil War. The allegiance of the Irish-Americans has been gradually shifting to the constitutionalist cause represented by Dublin, as all parties to the conflict became slowly persuaded of the futility of seeking to resolve the Irish national question through violent means.

3. Hibernian Endgame

What is happening in Ireland today is a slow but relentless triumph of politics over physical force, as the PIRA and the British each realise what Dublin has long since understood: that there can be no victory in this apparently endless war. On the PIRA side, the demise of the Soviet Union has removed a potent ally; for years, the PIRA and other anti-British insurgency in Ireland were encouraged by Soviet psychological and financial support, usually wielded indirectly. This parallelled Soviet encouragement to Islamic and anti-Zionist groups in the Middle East and North Africa. Similarly, the shrinking of Irish-American support has been accelerated by the diplomatic offensives of the Republic. The PIRA has become increasingly isolated internationally; each time it killed someone, it lost political kudos.

Dublin and London nowadays do not look on Northern Ireland as a bone of contention, but rather as a common problem for which a political solution must be found. The British and Irish democracies have to deal with Ulster together and both now know this. The PIRA and the Protestant paramilitaries also, belatedly, have come to understand this.

It has become clear that the PIRA started to put out feelers to both the British and Irish governments in the mid-1980s, once it became clear that few on the island sympathised with the PIRA's characteristic fusion of violent means and political ends. The Anglo-Irish Accord of 1985 and the joint Dublin-London Downing Street Declaration of late 1993 both made it clear that the Republic wished no union with the North against the wishes of the Northern majority, and similarly, that London had no desire to hold on to the North against the wishes of that majority. In August and September 1994, the PIRA and the Protestant paramilitaries declared ceasefires after twenty-five years of violence. The PIRA ceasefire was called off after eighteen months, but an informal ceasefire still prevailed in Ireland, whereas a rather lame PIRA bombing campaign continued in Britain until July, 1997, when the ceasefire was resumed.

In the early years of the Ulster Troubles, there had been fears of an all-Ireland conflagration, and the danger of such a disaster was pointed out by many commentators in the 1970s, most notably Conor Cruise O'Brien. The fear was of an 'Irish Bosnia', with tribal warfare engulfing all of Ireland. The crucial difference is, however, that Britain's military might can be seen as holding all of Ireland together; only a precipitate British withdrawal from the North could conceivably destabilise both Irish polities. If that were to happen, the Protestants, heavily armed as they are, and with the allegiance of the Ulster police, the British-organised militia and many British Army veterans, might conceivably try to set up their own state in eastern Ulster, drive Catholics west of the river Bann, and take in Protestant refugees from western Northern Ireland. The Republic's Army might likewise conceivably be drawn in to come to the aid of their Catholic fellow-countrymen.

The Republic might then be forced into behaving like Serbia, and the Protestants like Slovenia, or worse, Croatia. This was the scenario, incidentally, that the PIRA – fascistic and romantic in its deepest and often unadmitted instincts – has long dreamed of, but would never quite admit to: the wrecking of democratic Ireland. The result would be, as O'Brien (*op. cit.*) argued forcefully twenty years ago, a new and more malign partition between a smaller, deeply Orange (i.e. Protestant) state in the northeast, and a larger, 'Greener', mainly Catholic, militarised and post-democratic Republic on the rest of the island.

This scenario is a fantasy. It is unlikely ever to materialise, partly because it is tolerably understood by populations who live in democratic and quasi-democratic cultures in both parts of Ireland. The Republic has a tiny army, and that army is there to ensure that no IRA coup ever occurs in the Republic; in 1922-23, after all, it destroyed the old IRA in eight months, with the quiet approval of the general population. The Republic has no stomach for war, and is one of the most demilitarised societies in Europe. This is partly in reaction to the exaggerated militarism of its founding fathers and partly a reflection of the popular revulsion to the brutality of the PIRA. This brutality has done more to render the partition of Ireland actually popular in the Republic than has anything else. Ironically, the PIRA, by alienating so many southern Irish, may end up in the history books as the force that made Irish partition permanent. This would be a true monument to that organisation's brutality and stupidity.

A far more likely alternative to this scenario is the evolution of a series of pragmatic agreements between London and Dublin, between Northern nationalist elected representatives and both governments, between unionist representatives and both governments and, more covertly, between the paramilitaries and the legal authorities. This alternative came to fruition in the peace agreement of April 10, 1998. It may be that a Basque rather than a Bosnian scenario prefigures the Irish future. Since 1976, Madrid has given up trying to repress Basque identity. Instead it has given extensive devolution to the Basque provinces, recognised

Basque culture officially, and subsidised the area. The armed paramilitary police, the *Guardia Civil*, has assumed a low profile, and a set of civilianised police forces directs traffic and investigates ordinary crime. As a consequence of this increased autonomy and demilitarisation, Basque guerrillas have suffered a substantial erosion of support.

In Ireland, as elsewhere in modern Europe, the model of the sovereign, 'stand-alone' nation-state has lost much of its attractiveness as something to be aspired to. Multinational companies and equally multinational governments have had the effect of making the classic sovereign state appear inadequate if not irrelevant. In Ireland, economies, popular cultures, state services and transport systems are increasingly trans-frontier and transcend the British-Irish state system created two generations ago. A sort of reunification by osmosis is going on, and a potent agent in this process is the European Union, disproportionately important in both of the tiny states of Ireland.

Nationalist and unionist violence appear increasingly pointless, partly because politics has stepped in to the vacuum of Ulster in the form of understandings between elected politicians. A key factor accounting for the change in public attitudes is the development of a Catholic and post-nationalist middle class in both parts of Ireland but particularly, perhaps, in the North. It is not clear that the Ulster Catholic middle class is all that keen on an abrupt reunification of the island. The Republic is, after all, relatively poor, and Northern Catholics have done well out of the artificial and heavily subsidised economy that London has created in Northern Ireland. It could be that British money has created a form of Green unionism.

Northern middle-class Catholics, although appreciative of the moral support provided by the very existence of the Republic, do not necessarily see their short-term future as being inextricably bound up with the South. Their political influence in Northern Ireland has grown considerably, and a certain guarded acceptance of some aspects of the Northern state has evolved among them. In particular, lower taxation and better social services have a powerful appeal. Certainly, a wholesale dismemberment of Northern Ireland, as traditionally dreamed of by the IRA, is not on their agenda. To some extent, Northern Irish nationalists see the possibility of gaining some political clout through the British institutions of the Republic, Europe and the United States: Ireland goes global.

Ulster Protestant unionism seems to feel that it has lost the psychological upper hand that it enjoyed a generation ago. Parenthetically, Protestants in the Republic, few in numbers, have given their allegiance to the Dublin regime, and have a cultural influence in the Republic wildly out of proportion to their numbers. They tend to have little real political sympathy with their Northern co-religionists. Irish nationalists are natural politicians, rather than natural soldiers, and the Republic has played its hand slowly and rather cleverly over the past two decades, lining up domestic and foreign forces on its side. British leaders seem nowadays to get on better with Dublin leaders than with whatever leadership might be generated by Protestant Belfast. Interestingly, the leaders of unionist Ulster are now trying to mend their own hand.

In the final analysis, the London-enforced experiment of anti-Catholic Protestant rule in Northern Ireland simply did not work. The bigotry, incompetence and overconfidence of Protestant rulers in the North after 1920 had much to do with this failure, although it must be admitted that Catholic bigotry permitted itself to be used as an alibi for their behaviour. The kind of politics suited to an imperial dependency just would no longer do in a post-imperial era where the ex-colonies sat at the same tables as their masters, sometimes with ever more clout. Unionist leaders, or more accurately, their followers, have been slow to grasp the fact that they stand among equals, and are certainly in no position of unassailable political or cultural superiority.

Furthermore, they find it difficult to internalise the proposition that they actually have no real enemies. A bargain cut now in the late 1990s will probably be better for them than one in ten years' time; the bargain would be a good one and give them most of what they want: formal recognition by the Republic of the North's 'otherness'. Irish Prime Minister Albert Reynolds (*Taoiseach* 1992-94), leader of Fianna Fail, the most nationalistic of the Republic's political parties, displayed great political courage in declaring unequivocally that Ireland cannot be reunited without the consent of a Northern majority. The realisation that the nationalist siege, always partly imaginary, is over is only now dawning on the democratic representatives of Orange Ireland and their followers.

The historical experience of the Irish, Orange and Green alike, underlines a proposition put forward by a Protestant Dubliner, George Bernard Shaw, three-quarters of a century ago. In effect he argued that if a people do not achieve a means of national and/or cultural self-expression, it will find it difficult to think of anything else until that urge is satisfied in a tolerable, even if imperfect, way.[14] The recognition of sub-state nationalisms, the granting of authority to local institutions, and the recognition of national differences can help satisfy that urge. Above all, the demotion of physical force in favour of political negotiation as a means of settling relationships between those ill-fitting modern entities called nations and states does offer a palliative that can, surprisingly, also become a solution.

There has been a slow triumph of politics over insurrectionism. The nationalist Irish are very willing to settle with the unionist Irish. It remains to be seen whether the unionist Irish have yet come to the conclusion that a settlement is necessary. The votes in both parts of Ireland on 22 May 1998 demonstrate that the people of Ireland passionately want such a settlement. It also remains to be seen whether British, Irish and European political institutions have sufficiently transcended the old nation-state formula to permit them to do so.

Notes

1. On the South Tyrol problem, see Marion Toscano, *Alto Adige/South Tyrol* (Baltimore and London: Johns Hopkins University Press, 1975), *passim*. South Tyrol, formerly part of the Austro-Hungarian Empire, was annexed by Italy after World War I and the claims of the majority German-speaking population were denied. In a series of negotiations in the 1960s and 70s, the Italian government recognised German as a local official language and made general arrangements for the recognition of Austrian identity in the area.

   For an excellent overview of the history, or histories, of the geographical entity the Irish sometimes refer to diplomatically as 'these islands' and which I refer occasionally to as 'the Isles', avoiding that dreadful B...... word deliberately, see Hugh Kearney, *The British Isles: A History of Four Nations* (Cambridge: Cambridge University Press, 1990). The limitation of the numbers of nations in the Isles to four is intriguing and would easily keep a four-day academic conference busy. An interesting, if deeply flawed, attempt at a comparative politics of the nations of the British Isles is Michael Hechter's *Internal Colonialism* (London: Routledge and Kegan Paul, 1975).

2. On the 'Britishness' and 'Irishness' of the Irish, see John A. Murphy, 'Ireland: Identity and relationships', in Bernard Crick (ed.), *National Identities* (Oxford: Blackwell, 1991), 79-89.

3. Paul Bew, *Land and the National Question in Ireland*, (Dublin: Gill and Macmillan, 1979); Samuel Clark, *The Social Origins of the Irish Land War* (Princeton: Princeton University Press, 1979).

4. Kieran Kennedy, Thomas Giblin and Deirdre McHugh, *The Economic Development of Ireland in the Twentieth Century* (London: Routledge, 1988), 3-12.

5. On cultural shift in the Republic on nationalist issues, see Mairin ni Dhonnachadha and Theo Dorgan (eds), *Revising the Rising* (Derry: Field Day, 1991). On secularism in the Republic, see Niamh Hardiman and Christopher T. Whelan, 'Politics and Democratic Values' and 'Values and Political Participation', in C.T. Whelan (ed.), *Values and Social Change in Ireland* (Dublin: Gill and Macmillan, 1994), 100-35 and 136-86.

6. Tom Garvin, 'Wealth, Poverty and Development: Reflections on our Current Discontents', *Studies* 78/311 (1979), 312-25.

7. Charles Townshend, *The British Campaign in Ireland 1919-21* (Oxford: Oxford University Press, 1975), *passim*.

8. Joseph Curran, *The Birth of the Irish Free State* (Birmingham, Alabama University Press, 1982).

9. Conor Cruise O'Brien, *States of Ireland* (London: Panther, 1974), 263-83 and *passim*.

10. Hugh MacLennan, *Two Solitudes* (New York: Duell, Sloan and Pearce, 1945), *passim*.

11. For a fascinating informal portrait of cultural shift in Catholic Northern Ireland, see Fionula O'Connor, *In Search of a State* (Belfast: Blackstaff, 1993).

12. O'Brien, *op. cit.*

13. On the PIRA in general see Patrick Bishop and Eamonn Mallie, *The Provisional IRA* (London: Heinemann, 1987).

14. George Bernard Shaw, *The Matter With Ireland* (London: Hart-Davis, 1962), 32-58, at 55-56.

New Ways to Kill Your Father: Historical Revisionism

Colm Tóibín

In 1969, two years after my father died, my mother, my sisters and I went to Wexford for the launch of a new history of the 1798 Rising called *The Year of Liberty* by Thomas Pakenham.[1] The Rising was important for us: from our housing estate we could see Vinegar Hill where 'our side', the rebels, had made their last stand. From early childhood I knew certain things (I hesitate to say facts) about the Rising, how the English had muskets whereas we just had pikes, how the English poured boiling tar on the scalps of the Irish and when the tar had dried, they peeled it off. The names of the towns and villages around us were in all the songs about 1798, the places where battles had been fought, or atrocities committed. But there was one place that I did not know had a connection with 1798 until I was in my twenties. It was Scullabogue. Even as I write it now it has a strange resonance. In 1798 it was where 'our side' took a large number of Protestant men, women and children, put them in a barn and burned them to death.

It does not come up in the songs, and I have no memory of my father, who was a local historian, talking or writing about it. The landscape of north Wexford where I was born is dotted with memorials to 1798, but there is nothing, as far as I know, at Scullabogue. Its memory was erased, for good reasons, from what a child could learn about 1798. It was a complication in our glorious past, and our glorious past was essential if our present in what the historian Roy Foster calls 'the disillusioned tranquillity of the Free State' was to have any meaning. This was what our ancestors fought for; we had it now; it had to be good.

At the launch of his book Thomas Pakenham sat on a podium at the top of the room. A few introductory speeches were made, and then a man whom I recognised, who had been a friend of my father's, stood up to speak. 'The history of 1798 has still to be written', I remember that his voice shook with angry conviction as he spoke. This book was not the real history, he said. He pointed accusingly at Pakenham. I did not understand.

I understand now because I have been grappling with Pakenham's book for years. In the early drafts of my novel *The Heather Blazing*,[2] the protagonist is working on a history of the rebellion not from the British side, which is what my father's friend accused Pakenham of doing, but from 'our' side, the Irish side. The following passage from Pakenham's preface interests my protagonist:

> Today sources are embarrassingly rich on the loyalist [British] side ... On the rebel side, lack of sources makes it impossible to do justice to the movement. I have found fewer than a hundred revolutionary documents of 1798. For the most part I have had to make do with second-hand (and sometimes second-rate) material; contemporary spy reports, mid-nineteenth century biographies, folk-songs and hearsay ... With the volume of written sources weighed so heavily to one side, it is impossible to avoid giving offence.

The rebels left no documents, then, only songs and stories, and the victors got to write history, until Irish nationalists like my father and his friend became the victors in their own state, to find that there were no reliable papers written by the rebels, no letters, few memoirs. Second-hand, second-rate things, as Pakenham so starkly (and perhaps tactlessly) put it. And the hollow nature of the native Irish past was the source of the anger that day at the launch of Thomas Pakenham's *The Year of Liberty* in Wexford. We had founded our state, but outsiders were still coming to write our history.

'I have tried to be fair', Pakenham wrote in his introduction. 'For the events of 1798, T. Pakenham's *The Year of Liberty* is unequalled', Roy Foster wrote in his bibliographical essay at the back of his *Modern Ireland 1600-1972*.[3] But sometimes, despite the fact that I am not an Irish nationalist (or at least I hope I am not), when I read Pakenham's book about the central event in the history of the place where I was brought up, I find the tone and the use of language offensive and hurtful. For a few seconds I become the man at the launch hectoring Pakenham.

For example, Pakenham writes:

> The next three days passed in mounting hysteria for both the inhabitants of Wexford and their prisoners. The mob made some sort of attack on the gaol. By good fortune, two of the dozen or so Catholic priests in Wexford at this time happened to reach the jail in time to drive off the people. Crowds again gathered outside Lord Kingsborough's lodgings and tried to break in.

'Mob' suggests a sort of mindlessness and a lack of civility. 'Some sort' is also dismissive. 'By good fortune' for whom? Hardly for 'the mob'. 'Drive off' as opposed to persuade, or convince, or warn even. 'Drive off' suggests they were animals. And yet all over Wexford there are monuments to them, and songs about them, and in 1998 the two hundredth anniversary of their rebellion is being celebrated with great gusto ...

In an essay published in 1986, 'We Are All Revisionists Now', Roy Foster, who is certainly the most brilliant and courageous Irish historian of his generation, wrote that 'the last generation to learn Irish history only from the old nationalist textbooks will soon be middle-aged men and women', and he went on to say, 'it is occasionally tempting to feel that something has been lost as well as gained; to miss the compelling Manichean logic of the old 'Story of Ireland' view, with a beginning, a middle and what appeared (up to about 1968) to be a triumphant end'. Twenty years earlier, in the Republic, there were whole-hearted celebrations of the fiftieth anniversary of the 1916 Rising, which included an exciting drama documentary on television, marches, days off school and, even for this eleven year old, a feeling of national pride.

As the Irish nation wallowed in its 'liberation', a Jesuit priest, Father Francis Shaw, submitted an essay to the Jesuit journal, *Studies*, which contained what Roy Foster calls a 'swingeing exposé of lacunae in [Patrick] Pearse's ideology', but it was not published for six years. The editors felt that Ireland was not ready for a critical examination of Pearse. For those involved in commemorations in Ireland in 1966, as now, history has no complications or ironies or half-truths; one thing leads to another; there are heroes and traitors and villains. This was not simply the history taught at school in Ireland to those of us 'who will soon be middle-aged men and women'; it was everywhere in our culture. But in the universities there had always been dogged individuals working against the national grain, dealing with the complexities rather than the simplicities of Irish history. Now in the 1960s, larger numbers of serious historians (I hesitate to use the words 'trained' or 'professional') with louder voices and more confidence and, in some cases, a political agenda, began to work on Irish history, and by the end of the decade as the North blew up they realised that they had a central role to play in moulding an Irish professional class away from ancient pieties.

They tried it on me. I went to University College Dublin in 1972 to study History and English. If there was a forbidden 'f' word, while we studied there, or a forbidden 'c' word, they were 'Fenian' and 'colonial', because all the Irish history we studied was parliamentary and constitutional. The nineteenth century was made up of the Constitutional nationalists O'Connell and Parnell, and there was much emphasis on their time at Westminster. Young Ireland, the Fenians, even the poor old Land League were presented as non-constitutional headaches for O'Connell and Parnell. Michael Collins was a Treaty negotiator rather than a warlord.

Outside in the world in the early 1970s there were car bombs and hunger strikes, much of it done in the name of our nation, in the name of history. Inside we were cleansing history, concentrating on those aspects of our past which would make us good, worthy citizens who would keep the Irish twenty-six county state safe from the IRA and IRA fellow travellers.

One day in the library I was reading an essay by Joseph Lee in a book called *The Irish Parliamentary Tradition*[4] (this title may seem like an elaborate oxymoron, but it was the sort of book published at that time) about 1782 and Grattan's Parliament, an important moment in Irish history, according to our school books. Parnell, Roy Foster points out, constantly referred to this parliament, believing, as our school-books did, that it offered Ireland Home Rule. Joseph Lee made clear that it offered Ireland no such thing, and that it was not

'Grattan's Parliament', in any real way, since Grattan had no real power in it. It was all myth, all nonsense.

I remember feeling a huge sense of liberation. I photocopied the essay and made everyone else read it. I was in my late teens and I already knew that what they had told me about God and sexuality wasn't true, but being an atheist or being gay in Ireland at that time seemed easier to deal with as transgressions compared to the idea that you could cease believing in the Great Events of Irish nationalist history. No Cromwell, as cruel monster, say; the execution after 1916 as understandable in the circumstances; 1798 as a small outbreak of rural tribalism; partition as inevitable. Imagine if Irish history were pure fiction, how free and happy we could be! It seemed at that time a most subversive idea, a new way of killing your father, starting from scratch, creating a new self.

I became a revisionist, luckily, just as the word was coming into vogue; it was a term of abuse used about historians who were peddling anti-nationalist views of Irish history. The most seriously revisionist text, however, to appear in those years was John Banville's *Birchwood* (1973),[5] the year of Ireland's entry into the EC. Here, Irish history was an enormous joke, a baroque narrative full of crackpot landlords and roaming peasants and an abiding sense of menace and decay. In 1975, in his book of poems *The Snow Party*,[6] Derek Mahon allowed one of his characters to be 'through with history'. I understood that to be the whole point of revisionism.

'In a country that has come of age, history need no longer be a matter of guarding sacred mysteries', Roy Foster wrote in his 1986 essay. One of the sacred mysteries remained the 1916 Rising. When in the early 1970s I had imagined a history in which the executions after the 1916 Rising were 'understandable in the circumstances', I meant it as a flight of fancy, much like imagining a future in which the Pope would marry or fish would fly. Now, in 1988, in Roy Foster's *Modern Ireland 1600-1972*, which would be declared a masterwork by most historians who reviewed it, the section on the aftermath of the rising began: 'The draconian reaction of the authorities to the rebellion should be understood in terms of international war and national security'. When I read the book first I spent some time pondering the 'should' and the 'national'. I wondered, suddenly my father's son once more, what nation Roy Foster could possibly be talking about.

In *Modern Ireland* Lord Mountjoy, who 'successfully commanded the English forces that drove the rebels from the Pale 1601-1603', is described as 'a humane man'. On the other hand the United Irishman Napper Tandy who, in a biographical note, is said to be 'eulogised in national folklore', is described by Foster as 'the ludicrous Napper Tandy'. I do not know how it is possible to apply such adjectives from the twentieth century perspective to any figure in the sixteenth century, especially a figure sent by England to Ireland with an army, nor to any figure in the eighteenth century, even one eulogised in national folklore.

The main problem in making such throwaway and offensive (to Irish nationalists past and present) and wrong (Mountjoy was not humane, at least not in

Ireland) judgements and using such an arch tone is that it gives the game away. It suggests that underneath the brilliant insights and real originality in Foster's *Modern Ireland* there is an ideology perhaps not as crude as that of any nationalist historian writing school texts in the 1920s, but just as clear.

In *Modern Ireland* Foster is concerned to make Irish history dense and complex, something constantly awaiting further study and elucidation. He removes the Whig view entirely from Irish history, refusing to see the events which led up to 1916 from the perspective of 1916. The style is, by necessity, nervous and jerky; his judgements are qualified by local studies or detailed work. For anyone who wanted to 'use' history, who wanted to claim eight hundred years of misunderstanding between Ireland and England, as Garret FitzGerald did to Mrs Thatcher, according to her memoirs, Foster's would be puzzling and not very helpful. There are continuities in Foster's *Modern Ireland*, but they are difficult to trace. His book, because of his command of detail, and his ability to construct a narrative, is deeply convincing and valuable.

The problem, perhaps, is not his, but ours. The underlying message in Foster's book, his revisionism, is best defined in an attack on revisionism by Desmond Fennell, an Irish anti-revisionist commentator:

> A retelling of Irish history which seeks to show that British rule of Ireland was not, as we have believed, a bad thing, but a mixture of necessity, good intentions and bungling; and that Irish resistance to it was not, as we have believed, a good thing, but a mixture of wrong-headed idealism and unnecessary, often cruel violence.

This is precisely what our state needed to establish once the North blew up and we joined the EC, in order to isolate Northern Ireland from us and our history, in order to improve relations with Britain, in order to make us concentrate on a European future. Foster and his fellow historians' work became useful, not for its purity, or its truth, but its politics. It can be argued that many of these historians did not 'seek to show' anything, they merely and dispassionately showed it, and the implications of what they showed happen to coincide with public policy. But it cannot be argued with much conviction. In 1971, in that same book, *The Irish Parliamentary Tradition*, F.S.L. Lyons, the most senior and respected Irish historian at that time, wrote: 'The theories of revolution, the theories of nationality, the theories of history which have brought Ireland to its present pass cry out for re-examination'. As the historians set out to re-examine Irish history, they did so not in an ivory tower of disinterest, but in a country of car bombs and warring factions.

Every night during Easter Week 1966 our family watched the drama-documentary about Easter 1916 on state television. A friend of the family who had been in the Rising and had known the leaders came to watch it with us. The executions were drawn out, each moment dramatised, with the grieving family, the gaunt prison and the lone leader in his cell, writing his last poem or letter. Sometimes the emotion in the room in our house was unbearable, and when it came to James

Connolly's turn to be executed my mother ran out of the room crying. We had never seen her cry before.

In less than ten years we moved from the state sponsoring such emotions to a time when the songs we learned at school were banned on the state radio. Such sudden shifts cannot occur without consequences, and these were best described in a pamphlet by the poet Michael O'Loughlin written from his exile in Amsterdam in 1988:

> For my generation the events of Easter 1966 were crucial, so much so that I think it is almost possible to speak of a generation of '66. People from that generation tend to share a number of characteristics. An almost total alienation from the state, a cynicism with regard to national institutions and political life ... an unspoken assumption that everything emanating from official sources is a total lie ... In my school, and in other schools and in the media, republican emotions, if not republican principles, were openly encouraged ... What [later came] from Northern Ireland was republicanism with a vengeance. The South's political lies were finally catching up with it. One of these was that 1916 was the culmination of the 700 year struggle for an 'Irish Republic'. This lie ... eventually became too embarrassing. In an act of astonishing political opportunism, 1916 was revised.

One can hardly blame the historians, however; most of them believed they were going against the grain in the service of truth, believing themselves under attack from republicans (and they still do), never realizing that they were justifying the new state, an Ireland cleansed of its history, which politicians had planned. The received wisdom about the 1916 executions was that they stirred the Irish population into instant and then constant anger. I had always been suspicious of this, especially the constant part. Foster's analysis of this in *Modern Ireland* remains judicious, and he makes a case for viewing the aftermath of the Rebellion in the light of the First World War as much as the Rebellion itself. If this is revisionism, it is something we badly need to help us think straight about the recent past. But the sudden shift in the state view of the Rising hung heavily on those of us who were watching television in 1966.

Thus we waited for the seventy-fifth anniversary of the Rising with considerable interest. This time state television did not re-show the drama documentary and there were no days off school. State television, instead, interviewed various historians and public figures about the Rising: did they think it was right or wrong? Did they think it should be commemorated? Roy Foster said: 'Celebrating 1916, or commemorating it, I think there's a big difficulty there. To celebrate something is, presumably, to say it was wonderful and to, in a sense, re-enact it as a communal ritual. I would think that is undesirable'. If, this time, anyone ran out of the room crying, they were in tears of rage, but most people in Ireland remained reasonably indifferent.

In a brilliantly detailed and lucid essay in his book *Paddy & Mr Punch*[7] about the uses to which Irish history has been put, Roy Foster alludes to 1991:

When the seventy-fifth anniversary of 1916 arrived in 1991, it was treated by the Irish government as a sensitive issue, to be approached in a deliberately restrained way – very different from the unequivocal celebrations of 1966. This caused a small-scale but vociferous old-Republican reaction – featuring not historians but out-of-office politicians, freelance journalists, ex-1960s activists (including, quaintly, a Pop Art painter) and the members of the Short Strand Martyrs Memorial Flute Band.

There is a sense here that Foster really enjoyed writing the word 'quaintly' and, since this book appeared, there have been earnest letters to the Irish newspapers to point out, among other things, that no one can remember 'the members of the Short Strand Martyrs Memorial Flute Band' being in Dublin for the 1991 commemoration. Even for this over-sensitive, former nationalist reader, the inclusion of the Flute Band in Foster's list is extremely funny. It must have been even funnier in Oxford, where Foster is Carroll Professor of Irish History.

Things were not as simple in Dublin, however. I had planned to be in Seville for Easter 1991, mainly because I get very depressed in Ireland on Good Friday when the pubs close all day and the sky is low and the churches are full. In the middle of February I received a letter from an organisation called The Flaming Door which, using state money and with state encouragement, sought to commemorate the seventy-fifth anniversary of the 1916 Rising by asking Irish writers to join in a marathon reading at the General Post Office in Dublin where the Rising took place. I thought of attending to read from Beckett's *First Love*:

> What constitutes the charm of our country, apart of course from its scant population, and this without the help of the meanest contraceptive, is that all is derelict, with the sole exception of history's ancient faeces. These are ardently sought after, stuffed and carried in procession. Wherever nauseated time has dropped a nice fat turd you will find our patriots, sniffing it up on all fours, their faces on fire.[8]

But I decided it would be easier to decline. I did not want any work of mine (or any work of anybody else's) being used by the state to replace its own half-heartedness about the past and insecurity about the present. As far as I know, the novelist Anne Anright and I were the only writers to turn down the invitation.

But others were planning commemorations elsewhere. I met a local politician in Wexford whom I knew and liked. He asked me to join other descendants, mostly grandchildren, of the men who had fought in the Easter Rebellion in the town of Enniscorthy, where I was born and where my grandfather had fought, in a march through the town on Easter Sunday to celebrate the seventy-fifth anniversary of the Rising. This one was closer to home; there would be no quoting Beckett in Enniscorthy. No one at any of the meetings to plan the march, I was assured, had expressed the slightest doubt about the Rising; no one knew anything about revisionism; it had filtered from the universities to the middle classes in the cities, but not beyond. People in Enniscorthy were simply proud that the town and their forebears had been involved in the Rising. I would have loved to march with them. I wandered around Seville that Easter wishing things were simpler, wishing that I was not in two minds about everything.

Roy Foster loves two minds, the dual inheritance. Although the essays in *Paddy & Mr Punch* were written for different occasions and contexts, there is a single concern running through the book – the way in which the intersection between Ireland and England affects individuals and institutions. He is always deeply aware that this intersection can be dangerous and dark, but, in a few essays, he shows that it has also been enriching, and these essays are important and original.

This is a better and more relaxed book than *Modern Ireland* because Foster can choose his ground, write about things which fascinate him, notably individuals such as Parnell and Lord Randolph Churchill, about whom he has already written books, and Yeats (he has written the authorised biography). Others to appear are Trollope and Elizabeth Bowen and Maud Gonne. It is clear that Foster is more interested in posh Protestants than in the members of the Short Strand Martyrs Memorial Flute Band or their like. It is also clear that he does not favour Irish commemorations, even ones which occurred in the past: 'The great Anglophobic outburst of the 1798 centenary celebrations should be seen as therapeutic Anglophobia as much as an endorsement of separatism', he writes.

My grandfather and my grand-uncle took part in those celebrations, as my father and uncle did fifty years later in 1948. They were complex men who had read a great deal of English literature, and they were not much given to Anglophobic outbursts, nor Anglophobia, however therapeutic. It is a pity that Foster is not prepared to offer the same level of nuanced study to the contradictions and complexities in the Irish revolutionary tradition, or to the individuals who took part in it, as is to, say, Elizabeth Bowen. Thomas Pakenham's 'mob' awaits its historian.

But the descendants of the 'mob' rule Ireland now, on both sides of the border, and do so with the happy conviction that the island is somehow naturally theirs, that history has offered them this birthright, and that outsiders (or indeed minorities) have no natural place on the island. The tone of openness in John Hume's rhetoric, for example, implies that this is his home, and he is ready to make the Unionists welcome here under certain conditions.

Roy Foster has tried to establish what he calls in the final sentence of *Modern Ireland* 'a more relaxed and inclusive definition of Irishness', which has obvious political implications. Elizabeth Bowen, he tells us, 'felt most at home in mid-Irish sea'. That journey back and forth, the political and spiritual dislocation involved, and how crucial it has been in the Irish experience, concern Foster in most of these essays.

He is respectful about Elizabeth Bowen, as he is generally about people who did not support Irish nationalism. In an essay called 'Protestant Magic' he defines and finds a context for a tradition in Irish fiction – nineteenth century Irish supernatural fiction – which includes Sheridan Le Fanu and Bram Stoker and leads to Yeats's interest in the occult.

In his study of Bowen's Irishness Foster is perhaps at his best, prepared to sift through every nuance, examine every shade and never overstate his case, because his case is delicate, as delicate and complex as he wants the strands between the varieties of Irishness to remain. Bowen's Irishness is not of mere academic interest to him; there is always the implication that Ireland must take Bowen and her tradition on board if Ireland is to survive.

What, then, asks the ghost of my father's friend who rose in anger to tackle Thomas Pakenham in 1969, are we to do about Elizabeth Bowen's activities in Ireland during the war years when she posed as a journalist or a woman-about-town when she was, in fact, spying for the British Ministry for Information? Where was her Irishness then? In any other country, would this not be treachery? 'She was now a kind of spy', Foster writes, referring to 'the ambiguity of her stance'.

I know that ambiguity is what is needed in Ireland now. No-one wants territory, merely a formula of words ambiguous enough to make them feel at home. If we cannot understand Elizabeth Bowen's Irishness, and her British allegiances, then there are other forms of Irishness, and other allegiances, more insistent and closer to us, that we will fail to understand as well. Foster's position is clear, he wants Ireland to become a pluralist, post-nationalist, all-inclusive, non-sectarian place. So do I. But there are other (I hesitate to use the word atavistic) forces operating within me too that I must be conscious of. Maybe it comes out in odd moments when I read a book like this, or Thomas Pakenham's *The Year of Liberty*, and know that I am not part of the consensus of which they are part. Maybe it would be good if they looked again at Catholic Ireland. We, in turn, are learning to talk in whispers. It will take time.

Notes

1. Thomas Pakenham, *The Year of Liberty* (London: Weidenfeld, 1969).
2. Colm Tóibín, *The Heather Blazing* (London: Picador, 1992).
3. Roy Foster, *Modern Ireland 1600-1972* (London: Allen Lane, 1988).
4. Brian Farrell (ed.), *The Irish Parliamentary Tradition* (Dublin: Gill & Macmillan, 1973).
5. John Banville, *Birchwood* (London: Minerva, 1992).
6. Derek Mahon, *The Snow-Party* (Dublin: Gallery Books, 1975).
7. Roy F. Foster, *Paddy & Mr Punch: Connections in Irish and English History* (London: Allen Lane, 1993).
8. Samuel Beckett, *First Love* (London: Calder & Boyars, 1973), 30-31.

The Uses of the National Anthem

Ruth Sherry

The use of national anthems, now almost universal, is in general a nineteenth century invention. Although there is a widespread impression that there must be some standard and appropriate procedure for designating an anthem, individual countries have in fact arrived at their choices of anthem in a wide variety of ways, and the actual legal status of anthems is often unclear.

In some cases, national anthems such as 'God Save the King' and 'La Marseillaise' seem to have acquired their positions spontaneously, perhaps achieving formal status only much later; 'The Star Spangled Banner' was not formally adopted as the American national anthem until as late as 1931, a few years after 'The Soldier's Song' (see pp. 54-55) was designated as the Irish national anthem.

The *Grove Dictionary of Music and Musicians* summarizes five broad categories for the musical characteristics of anthems: hymns, marches, operatic anthems, anthems derived from folk pieces, and fanfares. It notes that many of the oldest anthems, including those of Britain, France and the United States, have their origins in a time of national crisis, although others have more often been adopted in peaceful circumstances, especially in the 19th century when anthems proliferated in South America and in Central Europe.[1]

National anthems also have a variety of origins. Some of those adopted have been familiar songs or pieces of music by known composers, often having a traditional popularity and familiarity among the people. A very few, including the German anthem with music by Haydn, are by internationally recognized composers, and a very few have texts by recognized writers, such as the Indian and Bangladeshi anthems (which are the same) with words by Rabindranath Tagore.

Music and words are not necessarily composed together or at the same time; the Mexican anthem, for example, was first performed in 1854 but got a new tune later as the result of a competition. Furthermore, changes can occur, sometimes as a result of a changed political situation. The Chinese anthem, to take only one example, was approved in 1949, but new words were adopted in 1971; the original words were restored in 1982. For British dominions, 'God Save the King/Queen' generally served as the anthem until the countries concerned designated another, as Canada, Australia and New Zealand all have; New Zealand now gives equal status to both 'God Save the Queen' and its own anthem. South Africa, since its reform in the 1990s, has used two anthems, adding 'N'Kosi Sikelele Afrika' to the previously existing anthem, 'The Call of South Africa'. A few countries, especially in the Middle East, have anthems with music but no words, and a few countries have no anthem at all. In some other cases, as mentioned above, the same anthem (or the same music) is used by more than one country.

Competitions for words and/or music are a fairly common way of arriving at an anthem, but are by no means universal. Where some kind of competition is used, it may involve either an invitation to write new words or new music, or it may take the form of a vote to choose between possible existing songs. Sometimes decisions about anthems have been made by a government, in other cases by a legislative act, or by a popular vote. Formal designation may simply confirm a long-standing practice.

As this overview suggests, there are no internationally accepted rules for how an anthem should be chosen or what it should be like, although there is a certain accepted protocol about how anthems should be treated.

In the twentieth century, choosing an anthem has been an issue for new sovereign states produced by the process of decolonization. In many such cases the process of becoming independent was relatively well-ordered, with time to plan for constitutions and governmental arrangements and to designate symbols such as flags and anthems which could be in place on the date of formal independence being achieved. But the Republic of Ireland, as one of the first modern nations to emerge from colonial status, found itself, in this matter as in many others, obliged to improvise when it came to establishing the institutions of statehood.

During the nineteenth century the government established the practice of playing the air 'St. Patrick's Day' (of folk origins) on formal official occasions in Ireland. Although 'St. Patrick's Day' continued to be used, throughout the 19th and early 20th centuries a large number of other tunes and songs emerged as bearers of nationalist sentiment. The most familiar of these were the rallying songs, Thomas Davis' 'A Nation Once Again', which is still widely used at Republican gatherings, 'God Save Ireland', which was particularly associated with the Fenians, and 'The Wearing of the Green'. The songs of Thomas Moore's *Irish Melodies*, in many cases written to traditional airs, did not lend themselves to being used as battle hymns in the same way, but were very popular across a wide social spectrum, and certainly reinforced a sense of national identity and loss, even among those who were not politically activist.

In general, one can say that there was (and continues to be) a particularly close association between music and national (including nationalist) feeling in Ireland. Unionist sentiment is also closely tied to music, although Unionists have rather tended to preserve and play old tunes while new songs with a nationalist burden, such as Tommy Makem's 'The Four Green Fields', continue to appear.

Sometime in the first decade of the 20th century, an IRB member, Peadar Kearney, the author of a number of popular political verses, produced the text of

'The Soldier's Song', working in collaboration with Patrick Heeney, who was mainly responsible for the melody.[2] The exact date for the writing of the words and music has never been established, but may have been as early as 1907.[3]

The text was certainly first published in Bulmer Hobson's *Irish Freedom* in September 1912, with, however, no attribution of author.[4] The song became increasingly popular as a marching and rallying song among the Volunteers as that movement strengthened between 1912 and 1916. Some of its popularity came, no doubt, from its affirmation that the Volunteers were 'soldiers' rather than 'rebels'. On the belts of their uniforms, the Volunteers wore the words *Óglaigh na hEireann*, in English, 'Soldiers of Ireland'. 'The Soldier's Song' appears to have been first sung in public by Seamus Hughes at a fund-raising event for the Volunteers in Clontarf in March 1915.

By general account, however, it was in the internment camps after the Easter Rising that 'The Soldier's Song' came to be so widely used that it was felt to mark the identity and cause of those committed to armed resistance.

After the establishment of the Free State, when the Army was organized, it was composed chiefly of pro-Treaty men who had served in the Volunteers and its later manifestation, the IRA. In keeping with the idea that the Free State Army was a natural continuation of the resistance army, 'The Soldier's Song' continued to be strongly associated with the military. It was played routinely as a ceremonial closing at Army meetings and festivities, in a manner parallel to that in which 'God Save the King' was used by the British.

The text of 'The Soldier's Song' by Peadar Kearney, consisting of three stanzas and a chorus, was written in English, and phrases from it were frequently used in public discourse in the early years of the State, as for example in Frank O'Connor's short story, 'Soldier's Are We', (1930) which derives its title from the first line of Kearney's chorus: 'Soldiers are we, whose lives are pledged to Ireland'. The English text of the song was, for a long period, the one in general use.

Perhaps not surprisingly, however, in the years after 1916, a number of writers, including Pádraig Mac Cárthaigh, Seán Dubhthaigh, Séamus Mac Grianna and Earnán de Blaghd (Ernest Blythe) produced Irish language translations of 'The Soldier's Song'.[5] The translation which in time became generally known and used was however that written by Liam O Rinn – later the official translator to the Oireachtas – perhaps as early as 1917. This translation was, notably, published in the Army's fortnightly magazine *An tÓglach* (*The Soldier*) on 3 November 1923.

The Army's *An tÓglach*, a successor of the Volunteers' journal of the same name, was bi-lingual. While reporting extensively on internal Army matters, it also reflected a concern for Gaelicizing the Army and for promoting cultural awareness generally, in accordance with the policies of the Army's first general and Minister for Defence, Richard Mulcahy. At the same time, the Army's resolutely non-political stance was being established.

Although the Army was using 'The Soldier's Song' in ways reminiscent of the British use of 'God Save the King', there was no officially adopted national anthem in the first years after the establishment of the Free State, and no mention of an anthem was to be found in the Free State Constitution.

Other melodies than 'The Soldier's Song' were still being used in various contexts. Thomas Moore's 'Let Erin Remember', based on a traditional air, was often played on formal occasions abroad, and was felt by some to have musical qualities superior to those of other potential anthems, although the words were not thought appropriate to the situation of the new State. 'God Save Ireland' and 'A Nation Once Again' also continued to be played at some gatherings. While all of these pieces of music had widespread popularity and long traditions, what they also had in common was that they derived from and had associations with the period of the struggle for independence; if they represented the national identity, it was implicitly being defined by opposition to Britain and by a tradition of rebellion and resistance. Of these melodies, 'Let Erin Remember', with a text referring to legend, had the fewest direct martial or militant associations.

As the new state took its place internationally, the government and other bodies came to feel the need to designate an anthem formally, not least to underline that the Free State was not part of the United Kingdom. Some members of the unionist population continued to use 'God Save the King' in the same way as before the establishment of the Free State. The approach of the Olympic Games in Paris in 1924 prompted the Department of External Affairs to ask the office of the President of the Executive Council, on 1 February 1924, to take steps to establish an anthem. Various suggestions as to how this might be done were made, including that of instituting a public competition or, alternatively, asking 'a number of Irish poets and writers' to submit verses which might be used together with the music of 'Let Erin Remember'. The need for the text to be in the Irish language was assumed.[6]

However, the only action the government took at this time was to make an informal decision on 27 May 1924 to use 'The Soldier's Song' as the anthem *within* the state while preferring to use 'Let Erin Remember' abroad,[7] and it was the latter which was played at the Olympic Games.

This confused situation reflects the fact that 'The Soldier's Song' was somewhat controversial in the early years of the State, and in varying degrees it has continued to be so. On the one hand some felt that the military sentiments expressed, in an assumed context of guerrilla warfare, were inappropriate to a country now independent and expressing a dedication to peace and international cooperation. The circumstances of the Civil War also made the use of the song sensitive, as the anti-Treaty forces felt as much entitlement to it as the Free Staters did, and its symbolic force was strong. From an official viewpoint the Army's use of 'The Soldier's Song' would seem designed to defuse any anti-Treaty associations that might be attached to it. On a different level, there was and is a feeling, frequently expressed, that neither the words nor the music are of a calibre consistent with a formal and dignified expression of national identity. In defence of Peadar Kearney and Patrick Heeney it should be noted that they were not trying to write a national anthem.

Whatever public dissatisfaction may have been felt in this situation was given expression when on 12 June 1924 the *Dublin Evening Mail* announced a competition for a set of verses for 'A National Hymn to the Glory of Ireland', occasioned by the lack of any 'national hymn or anthem for use on ceremonial or convivial occasions' – a formulation that implied that none of the existing pieces was adequate. A prize of 50 guineas was offered for a text; interestingly, the assumption was that music could later be written to suit the text – perhaps a convenience for a newspaper, which could publish words more readily than a musical score. A very distinguished committee was appointed to evaluate the results: W.B. Yeats, Lennox Robinson, and James Stephens.

On 22 October, *The Dublin Evening Mail* was forced to publish its committee's conclusion that having 'read the poems ... we are all agreed that there is not one amongst them worth fifty guineas or any portion of it ... Most of the verses submitted to us were imitations of "God Save the Queen"' (3). It is tempting to speculate that the members of the committee may well have thought privately that any of them could have produced a superior text if only someone, like the government, would ask – as the Department of Foreign Affairs had indeed suggested. The committee expressed the view that 'National Anthems have always in the past been one man's thought, written out for that man's pleasure, and taken up by a nation afterwards'.[8] This statement bears little relation to historical fact, and indeed could perfectly well have been applied to 'The Soldier's Song', but Yeats, for example, was probably aware of the Norwegian adoption of 'Ja, vi elsker', a poem by another Nobel prize winning poet, Bjørnstjerne Bjørnson, for its national anthem.

The entries in the *Mail*'s competition were not made public, but if the committee's assessment that they were imitations of 'God Save the King' was accurate, it is another piece of evidence reinforcing the impression that in the early years of the Free State, the problem of establishing a sense of public, national identity was that of coming up with something that was sufficiently like what the British did to mark equality of status, while at the same time sufficiently different to mark the separateness of the new state.

In accordance with the committee's recommendation, the *Mail*'s competition was opened once again, but on this occasion no evaluating committee was appointed. Rather, the editors themselves selected six entries and asked readers to vote for their favourite. The entries were anonymous.

On 10 March 1925, the newspaper reported that the winner was Mrs. Mary Farren Thomas of Clontarf, whose 'God of Our Ireland' was awarded the 50 guinea prize. Mary Farren Thomas's text looks, to a later observer, neither significantly better nor significantly worse than that of many another national anthem, and one is left to wonder how many of the entries were by women, and to what extent this fact influenced either the original committee or the newspaper's editors – who presumably paid Mrs. Thomas her 50 guineas but otherwise dropped the matter completely at this point.

The government does not seem to have interested itself officially in the *Mail*'s activities, but *An tÓglach* commented on the *débâcle* of the competition,

'The Soldiers' Song' is good enough for the present ... The note of defeat or sorrow is absent from it. In the songs of the past, sadness, disappointment and failure had too much prominence. The new spirit was caught by the writer of 'The Soldiers' Song'. ...There is no crying need for a new National Anthem for Ireland.[9]

In the event, a simple decision was made by the Executive Council on 12 July 1926 that 'The Soldier's Song' should be used alone as the national anthem. 'It was considered desirable that there should be a uniform practice in regard to this matter, and it was decided that the "Soldier's Song" alone should be used'.[10] Although William T. Cosgrave was on record in 1924[11] as favouring retention of 'The Soldier's Song', the Executive Council's reasons for finally choosing this rather than another air are not recorded, nor is it clear how enthusiastically the decision was made. It seems likely that by this point 'The Soldier's Song' had become so firmly established by custom that replacing it would prove difficult.[12]

The decision was not gazetted at the time nor accompanied by any publicity, and it was made known to the public only by means of a brief answer to a question asked in the Dáil on 20 July 1926. On the background of the problem that more than one tune was being played at official functions, O. Grattan Esmonde (Cumann na nGaedheal, Wexford) asked if the Minister of Defence would state, so far as the army was concerned, what was considered to be the National Anthem. The leader of the Labour party, Thomas Johnston, followed up: 'What is the name of the National Anthem?' The Minister for Defence, Peter Hughes, replied 'The Soldier's Song' – to laughter, according to *The Irish Times* (21 July 1926, 7).

Formally speaking, the announcement was thus made in response to a question by a back-bencher from the government's own party. It is not clear whether Grattan himself initiated the query which led to the Executive Council's making a decision on the matter, or whether the question was engineered by the party so that the announcement could be made. But while the timing of the decision may not have had any particular object, it was in one way convenient, as it came shortly before that year's Dublin Horse Show.

The annual Dublin Horse Show was a main item on the social calendar, but it was a domestic rather than an international event before 1926. That the playing of 'God Save the King' had formerly been an important feature of the ceremonies seems indicated in a negative way by the fact that W.B. Yeats's sisters, attending the climactic last day of the show for the first time in 1921, noted that 'there was *no* National Anthem – it was significant of the changed public opinion in Ireland – as regards England'.[13]

In 1926, however, invitations were issued to foreign teams, including one from England, and the event was bigger and more festive than ever before. When the various teams arrived at Kingstown, they were met by bands playing their own national anthems. *The Irish Times* reported 'For the first time the tricolour flag of the Free State floated over the Governor General's box on the grand stand' (4 August 1926, 7). The newspaper also reported that when the Governor General, Tim Healy, visited the show on the second day (and enjoyed himself so much that he returned, impulsively, on the succeeding days), 'The Soldier's Song' was played. Similarly, national anthems were played as teams were led onto the field for the culminating international competition on Friday, August 6. The attendance of the visitors, and the accompanying ceremonies, were seen as marking a stage in the international recognition of the new State. The participants from the new Army show-jumping team were particularly struck by the significance of the occasion. 'It was as though the nation itself had now come of age and it was in a sense a manifestation of its taking its place among the nations of Europe'.[14]

The Irish Times, in a leader, also saw the ceremonies of the 1926 Horse Show as a sign of reconciliation between Unionist and Nationalist in the Irish Free State.

> Foreign visitors cannot have realised how electrical was the atmosphere when the Band of the Free State Army heralded the teams with the strains of their national anthems. They cannot have known how thousands of Irish hearts throbbed to a dear and unfamiliar music, and greeted with a new respect music which till then had the most painful associations for them. Nor could foreigners have guessed that ceremonies which, to them, were ordinary exchanges of courtesy represented for thirty thousand Irishmen and Irishwomen a whole precious catalogue of hardly-won concessions and tolerances, or that on Friday evening the Free State Army became suddenly a national army in a sense hitherto unconceived? There was history made yesterday in the jumping enclosure at Ballsbridge. (7 August 1926, 6)

In view of the previously pro-unionist stance of *The Irish Times*, one can perhaps assume that the music of 'The Soldier's Song' was not necessarily as unfamiliar to everyone as it evidently was to the leader writer. The pattern established in 1926 is, however, the one still familiar today, when the arrival of the President and the playing of anthems by the Army No. 1 Band in conjunction with the Nations' Cup competition on the Friday of Horse Show Week are high points of the event. Together with GAA finals in Croke Park and some international events at Lansdowne Road, the Nations' Cup competition provides one of the very few recurrent occasions on which thousands of Irish people together stand for, and perhaps sing, the anthem.

These practices are of course well in accord with the international tendency to use national anthems in connection with sporting events in particular; in the United States, for example, the anthem has not been played in connection with theatrical performances, but is traditionally played or sung at the beginning of sporting events such as baseball games. Most visible are award ceremonies at international competitions, particularly the Olympic Games, where having one's anthem played for the world to hear seems to be part of the prize, along with the gold medal. The tension between what may seem like nationalist triumphalism and the proclaimed aims of friendship in sporting competition are regularly the subject of rather acid comment.

In the 1920s Trinity College continued to be generally pro-Union. When Governor General James McNeill (who succeeded Healy) attended a Trinity garden party in June 1928 at the invitation of the Provost, he was met by a British Legion band playing 'God Save the King'. Such practice was in fact not out of accord with that in other Dominions, but in Ireland it was of course emotionally and politically loaded. McNeill later asked the advice of the Executive Council on the matter, and was advised that the government considered that only 'The Soldier's Song' should be played for the Governor General.

Accordingly, in the following year, McNeill declined to attend the college races during Trinity Week when he was unable to obtain a guarantee that 'The Soldier's Song', not 'God Save the King', would be played on his arrival. The matter attracted press attention and led to a prolonged, but diplomatically-worded, exchange among several individuals representing the Free State government, the Dominions Office in London, and the King. Those on the Crown side emphasized the possibility that refusing to play 'God Save the King' could be interpreted as a slight to the King; those on the Free State side emphasized that within the Commonwealth, there was national diversity, and that in the Free State the use of 'God Save the King' was still potentially inflammatory. Neither side seems to have wanted a show-down on the matter, which ended with an exchange of courtesies but the Free State practice unchanged.

James McNeill worked harmoniously with the Cosgrave government but soon fell out with Eamon de Valera, whose Fianna Fáil party succeeded to power in March 1932. De Valera's express aim was to abolish the office of Governor General. As one means of reducing the dignity of the office, de Valera adopted the device of refusing to allow Army bands to play the national anthem in the presence of the Governor General, a situation which caused repeated problems for McNeill and contributed to his giving up his office in October 1932. De Valera's appointee, Domhnall O Buachalla, went along with reducing the office to virtually nothing, paving the way for its final elimination in the 1937 constitution.[15]

Nor was establishing the anthem internationally without its snags. Particularly in early years, foreign bands did not always have the music of 'The Soldier's Song' available and played something else – at worst, 'God Save the King'. As late as 1932, the officer in charge of the Irish show-jumping team had to listen to the head of the Olympia Show in London tell him that 'God Save the King' was the only real national anthem – although he made a formal protest about the matter (Toomey, 106, 140).

As we have seen, although Irish language translations of the text of 'The Soldier's Song' existed from as early as 1917, the song appears to have been sung – to the extent that it was sung, rather than played, at all – almost exclusively in English during the 1920s. Indeed, the relationship between the text of Peadar Kearney's 'The Soldier's Song' and the Irish National Anthem is still complex and problematic.

Kearney's song consisted of three verses and a chorus. Not long after the song was adopted as the national anthem, however, the Executive Council embarked upon the practice of regarding only the chorus of 'The Soldier's Song' as constituting the anthem. In March 1929, the Executive Council authorized Colonel Fritz Brasé, the director of the Army Band, to make an arrangement of the anthem for use by the Band; in July the Executive Council approved the arrangement for use and publication.[16] This move was made partly because of the felt need for some uniformity in the playing of the anthem, as well as the need to provide a score of the anthem for bands abroad.

Col. Brasé produced an arrangement of the chorus only, and by implication therefore from this point on only the chorus of 'The Soldier's Song' constituted the National Anthem. In the absence of any legislation, one may say that a national anthem is whatever a legitimate government orders its obedient army to play.

It was also at this point, with the publication of scores for the use of bands, that the question of the title of the anthem was settled. The many earlier publications had given a variety of versions of the title: 'A Soldier's Song', 'The Soldiers' Song', and even an American publication under the title 'Soldiers of Erin'. It was however determined to use the title 'The Soldier's Song', although variants of this title are still seen in non-official publications.

That only the chorus of 'The Soldier's Song' constitutes the anthem remains the official position, confirmed by successive governments in their correspondence, despite the fact that the other verses are frequently printed by non-official sources. For example, *National Anthems of the World*, a widely distributed reference work, which has been published in a number of continually revised editions, for some years printed the words and music of all three stanzas, in addition to the chorus, in both English and Irish. More recent editions have corrected this practice to indicate the existence of the three verses in the original version, but to print only the chorus and to specify that the chorus alone is the National Anthem.[17]

Given the manner in which the anthem was adopted in 1926, with a minimum of publicity and a paucity of details announced, it is probably not surprising that so much public confusion persists. Today, relatively few people can ever have heard the music of the verses of 'The Soldier's Song' played or sung in public in Ireland, although a popular, currently available cassette to accompany a poster version of the text purports to provide 'the *complete* version of the National Anthem'. It seems aimed mainly at the tourist market.

The American bands which played for the football World Cup matches in the United States in 1994 in fact also played, once through, the music of the verses, creating some evident confusion among the players on the field,[18] and the same happened when Michelle Smith won gold medals at the 1996 Olympics in Atlanta. Aertel reported at the time that the Embassy in Washington was making another arrangement available to the officials in Atlanta, but in the absence of any more gold medal winners, it was not required.

One motivation for the Executive Council's action in 1932 in wanting an approved arrangement of the anthem may have been objections which were voiced to the arrangement of the anthem which was being used by the Irish broadcasting station. Radio Éireann (initially known as 2RN) had adopted the practice of closing its broadcasts with 'The Soldier's Song' from its inception on New Year's Day in 1926. This practice, presumably initiated in emulation of the BBC, it continued until New Year's Day 1996, when Radio One went over to twenty-four hour broadcasting.

For practical reasons it made use of a commercial recording, but in the early years of the station the only one available was an American one which many listeners felt was too 'jazzy'. Radio Éireann (and later, Radio Telefis Éireann) in time commissioned their own arrangements, nevertheless continuing to use the American recording for closedown for many years.

The increasing use of the anthem in other contexts led to another set of difficulties. From 27 March 1932, Dublin theatres and cinemas publicly confirmed the practice which had been informally adopted of playing the anthem at the close of performances. Again, there was a British model, but the theatres may have been partly responding to the injunctions of a Republican group called Clann na nGaedael.[19] The theatres too used an arrangement which was officially felt to be undesirable, and this was the situation which precipitated Col. Brasé's producing arrangements which could be used by orchestras and other instruments.

Although the government had adopted 'The Soldier's Song' as the anthem in 1926, it had paid no compensation to Peadar Kearney or the heirs of Patrick Heeney for its use. In 1932, Kearney threatened a lawsuit against the Irish broadcasting station and the owners of Dublin theatres for using his material without paying him a royalty. This situation led to a legal squabble in which the government at one stage claimed that it had adopted only the music, and not the words, of 'The Soldier's Song', as the anthem. In the event, it bought the copyright of both words and music from Kearney and from Heeney's heirs on 10 October 1933, and made the anthem publicly available for general use.[20]

Whatever their formal status, there seems never to have been any official encouragement for citizens to sing the words of 'The Soldier's Song'. Today, most people, if asked, will probably say that they learned the anthem at school, but at no time has the anthem – words or music, in either English or Irish – been part of the official, *prescribed* curriculum of the schools.

This situation was the subject of questions in the Dáil in the 1930s, with TD Eamonn O'Neill (Cumann na nGaedheal) of West Cork asking questions of the Fianna Fáil Minister for Education, Thomas Derrig, in both 1933 and 1934. O'Neill evidently believed children were not learning the anthem, and wanted the words of it to be taught in both English and Irish. The Minister however gave only brief replies; he did not agree that the situation was as O'Neill presented it, and felt that no action on the matter was called for.[21]

The 1930s was however a period in which definition and consolidation of national feeling was high on many agendas, and the function of symbols of national identity was taken seriously by many, as was the role of various institutions in promoting a sense of national identity. Joseph Hanley, for example, produced an entire book on the subject, *The National Ideal*, in 1931. In it he expressed dissatisfaction with 'The Soldier's Song' but nevertheless advocated that 'when an appropriate anthem is approved, it and its meaning should be taught in every school in the country without distinction'.[22]

Another advocate of the use of the anthem in schools was D. O Céilleachair, whose 1933 article 'Nationality in Our Schools' includes (amongst other, more risible, advice):

> On a solemn national occasion, facing the flag with bared heads let the national anthem, taught in the school in Irish, be sung. You may also seize the chance at the end or beginning of a school term or at the close of a school concert or at a game. In residential schools it should be sung by the massed pupils once a week, say, on Sunday nights, last thing before prayers and bed.[23]

These exhortations, whatever else one may think of them, imply that the teaching of the anthem in schools was not as widespread as the Minister's complacency in 1933 and 1934 suggests.

Indeed, successive Ministers of Education, of whatever parties, have evidently felt reluctant to instil an explicit nationalism through education. One interesting exchange, which involves not the anthem but the flag (with which it is often coupled as a national symbol), occurred in the Dáil on 17 July 1951. Sean MacBride (Clann na Poblachta) asked the Minister for Education about the possibility, *inter alia,* of flying the flag each day in the schools, ceremoniously raising and lowering it. Minister Sean Moylan replied:

> A sound knowledge of the national and cultural heritage that has come down to us is, to my mind, the surest foundation for a spirit of patriotism ... I do not consider that symbols of national significance should be made a matter of such every-day familiarity that reverence for them would become superficial, mechanical and meaningless ... .
>
> That method is very much in vogue in America, but the American problem is completely different in so far as school children in America come from homes of so many different nationalities ... and in America the government, apparently, do consider that the main problem is trying to make Americans of children of a number of varying nationalities. We have not that problem here and I do not think we should adopt the method the Deputy suggests.[24]

Very possibly the implicit sense of governments was that the weight of the nationalist program was being carried by compulsory Irish in the schools and civil service, and that this itself was being found more than sufficiently hard to implement.

Certainly civics textbooks which were in use in the schools do not assume that pupils already knew the anthem. In the 1960s and 1970s, learning the words or music of the anthem were 'suggested activities' for post-primary students – with the obvious implication that they could not be expected to know them already.[25]

In spite of uncertainties about official policy, the evidence does suggest that during the 1930s, the public use of the anthem became increasingly common. It is also during this period that one first finds significant reference to use of an Irish-language text.

Perhaps the largest and most influential non-official body to encourage the use of the anthem and the use of the Irish language (if not necessarily together) in the 1930s was the Gaelic Athletic Association. There is evidence of the anthem being sung in Irish at GAA events as early as 1931[26] and also in 1932.[27] In 1933, a celebration of St Patrick's Day was held in Croke Park. Speakers, including Eamon de Valera, stressed the importance of the use of Gaelic (as the language was still commonly called) on all possible occasions. The GAA's periodical, *An Camán*, reported:

> When spectators, youth and players, stood to attention and joined in the National Anthem in the Gaelic tongue, we had an environment appropriate to the Young Ireland there assembled. (1 April 1933, 1)

Shortly afterwards, at the 39th Annual GAA Congress on April 16, 'it was urged that Irish should be used to the fullest possible extent in the work of the Association'.[28] On the same occasion, 'it was decided that the National Flag should be displayed at all matches, and the proceedings ... were brought to a close with the singing of the National Anthem'.[29]

At the end of 1933, *An Camán* printed the text of Liam O Rinn's translation of 'The Soldier's Song', titled 'Amhran na b'Fiann',[30] perhaps as a ceremonial close to the year, comparable to the close of a concert or theatrical performance.

Throughout the 1930s, GAA publications continue to record the frequent use of the anthem, often to bring an occasion to a ceremonial end, but both English and Irish versions seem to have been current.

The GAA's organ *An Camán* joined with that of the Gaelic League (*Conradh na Gaeilge*) in the new publication *An nGaedheal* in 1934. In 1935, a columnist for *An nGaedheal* commented on the changing status of the anthem. He observed that, at a ceilidhe, young people's attention during the playing of the anthem was perfunctory, and he contrasted their response with that of a group of men in their thirties at a GAA match:

> For them the rousing, martial air was finished all too soon. It took them some seconds to find their normal senses again, to talk and laugh as if nothing had happened to take their thoughts above the commonplace. [The younger people] can have no recollections of the stirring days before, during and after 1916, when every word in 'The Soldier's Song' was pregnant with meaning.[31]

And in 1938, Peadar O'Dubhda, in 'A Rallying Song for Croke Park', recommends that the GAA promote the singing of songs in Irish at matches, indicating that he had frequently heard 'The Soldier's Song' being sung in English at GAA matches in Croke Park.[32] In the light of the encouragements to use Irish, and the promotion of the Irish language version of the anthem, it is an oddity that, throughout the 1930s, *An Gaedhael* published a number of poems, in English, by Peadar Kearney, at the same time that the organizations sponsoring the periodical were in effect promoting a policy of supplanting his text with the Irish text of Liam O Rinn.

Eamon de Valera's 1937 constitution makes no mention of the anthem, although the flag is designated as the tricolour in Article 7. However, it was probably the 1937 constitution which precipitated some new action on the part of Peadar Kearney: he wrote an additional verse to 'The Soldier's Song' for use by Republicans in Northern Ireland, printed as follows:

Extra Verse added to:

THE SOLDIER'S SONG

in answer to a request that the Irish of the Six North-Eastern Counties could register a protest against the British-planned partition of Ulster.

And here where Eire's glories bide
    Clann London fain would flourish
But Ulster-wide what e'er betide
    No pirate blood shall nourish;
While flames the faith of Con and Owen
    While Cave Hill guards the fame of Tone
From Gullion's Slopes to Inishowen
    We'll chant a Soldier's Song.

Peadar O Cearnaigh
(Summer, 1937)[33]

The rather bewildering reference, at this date, to the 'British-planned partition of Ulster' possibly refers to Article 3 of the new Constitution as a British-inspired move to confirm partition; if so, it gives a good sense of Kearney's persistent political convictions. It has been difficult to find any evidence that this new verse is used or even known in Republican circles in Northern Ireland, although the symbolic force of 'The Soldier's Song' may be felt more strongly there than elsewhere.

It is not entirely clear what the process was by which Liam O Rinn's Irish language text of 'The Soldier's Song' eventually took over completely from the English. Today the original English language text, although sometimes printed, is virtually never heard. It is in fact not uncommon to encounter references to 'the English translation' of 'Amhrán na bhFíann'.[34]

Yet, although the issue has been raised from time to time, no definitive action has ever been taken by any government on the question of an official Irish text

– indeed, from 1932 there remains the somewhat ambiguous question of whether there is even an official English text.[35] Certainly the State has never acquired the copyright of O Rinn's translation of Kearney's text or paid anyone for its use. This situation comes as a surprise to almost all citizens, who now, if they sing any words at all when the anthem is played, are almost certain to sing in Irish.

Heads of State do not generally sing when national anthems are played, and Irish Presidents observe this protocol, but taoisigh have followed a much more uncertain practice and sometimes seem visibly uncomfortable about singing. Indeed, the fact that the commonly used words are in Irish may contribute to the evident diffidence of the public about joining in singing on occasions such as the Horse Show; perhaps the Irish language words are not as well mastered by many people as an English text would be.[36]

Certainly it is notable that on many occasions any singing associated with the anthem is very hushed and quiet, and the mood created is almost sacral, an effect very remote from the militant feeling which many object to finding in the text. A notable exception is, however, to be heard in the lusty singing at the annual GAA finals at Croke Park.

The text of even the English chorus of 'The Soldier's Song' has long been a source of controversy. As indicated earlier, objections, made over many decades, to its use as the national anthem have often related to the idea that it is a song written for war purposes, and is therefore ill-suited to be the anthem of a deliberately neutral, non-belligerent nation which no longer is at war with the ancient enemy and has no plan ever to be at war with anyone else.

Such objections were made to using 'The Soldier's Song' as the anthem before it was adopted, and they have surfaced at very regular intervals ever since. A letter to an editor on the subject of the suitability of the anthem has always been guaranteed to produce a flurry of correspondence and possibly some suggestions for finding an alternative anthem.

In the last three decades comment has become politically more explicit. It has been objected that retaining 'The Soldier's Song', with its emphasis on war against a traditional enemy, presents a continuing obstacle to peace and to Unionist acceptance of the Republic. It is sometimes seen as reinforcing the fears roused by articles 2 and 3 of the Constitution.

In the context of events since the late 1960s, one might note that by 1972, the Dublin theatres had abandoned the practice of concluding each evening's performance with the national anthem. The reason given was that this ceremony was not in accord with international custom, and tended to bring the anthem into disrespect (as will be remembered, one could no longer guarantee that the audience would stand quietly at attention). Some citizens complained, however, and in the climate of the time it was at least possible to impute to those in authority a willingness to placate unionist opinion by de-emphasizing symbolic expressions of nationality.[37]

In more recent times, politicians, including the leaders of both Fianna Fáil and Fine Gael, have expressed a willingness to reconsider the anthem if doing so would assist the peace process. Startlingly, Bertie Ahern (not at that point Taoiseach) suggested to the Forum for Peace and Reconciliation that 'A Nation Once Again' would be an acceptable alternative to him personally. Given the continuing associations of 'A Nation Once Again' with the IRA, it is not surprising that the remark was quickly taken up by John Lowry of the Workers Party, who questioned whether Ahern was being flippant.[38] Perhaps correspondingly, the anthem is popular and quite widely used in Republican circles, not least in Northern Ireland.

In the light of the controversial nature of the text, it is interesting to observe how Radio Telefis Éireann, the national broadcasting company, has treated the anthem, which it has used as the closedown for one of its television channels, at least until the end of 1997, when RTÉ One began to move to all-night broadcasting. From the first television broadcast on New Year's Eve 1961/62, RTÉ – again probably in emulation of the BBC – used an orchestral version of the anthem, as arranged by Brian Boydell, accompanied by a film, for closedown. The musical arrangement stayed the same throughout the years, but the film changed at intervals.

The inception of the television service was (like that of the radio service in 1926) seen as evidence that Ireland was a modern nation keeping up with the times. Perhaps accordingly, although the first close-down film included a shot of Cobh cathedral and one of the GPO, it mostly emphasized recent, technological developments in Irish life. Motifs included a hydroelectric scheme, a tractor in a field, a plane taking off from Dublin airport and the RTE Television Centre at Montrose. Although the flag was also shown, the message in general was not heavily political.[39]

By the mid-1970s, this film had been replaced by one consisting entirely of nature scenes – flowers, leaves, insects, running water – none of which could be clearly localized. It culminated in a view of the sun either going down or coming up over a mountain. This film was used for many years and replaced sometime in the 1980s with another which was different but nevertheless used entirely similar elements; perhaps the motivation for the new film was the spread of colour television. No human activity or presence of any kind was indicated in either of these two closedowns.

This approach effectively emptied the anthem of any residual political content. The message in the 1970s and 1980s seemed to be that Irish identity was associated with Ireland as a natural site, and a charming one at that, entirely devoid of any human significance beyond, perhaps, the inspiration to a vague romanticism on the part of the viewer.[40]

On 1 June 1994 RTÉ's close-down film was replaced by another, no longer devoid of any human reference. This film emphasized the distant past, beginning with sunrise seen at the stone-age burial site at Newgrange, and including Celtic artifacts as well as readily identifiable features of the landscape such as the Cliffs of Moher and Slea Head. The conclusion was still devoted to nature, water and the sun.

It will be noted that none of these films in any way refers to or invites contemplation of the text of 'The Soldier's Song'.

The content of the most recent close-down film, whatever it has to say about the significance of the national anthem, seems to reflect an increasing tendency, now at the end of the century, to identify Ireland in terms of the Celtic, and indeed to a very large extent, the pre-Christian (or at any rate the non-Christian) heritage. This strategy – conscious or otherwise – might be seen as a means of de-emphasizing the political conflicts and events of the past two hundred years, and also as a means of divorcing Irish identity from any specific or confessional religious identity. Neutralizing a potentially embarrassing anthem is part of that process.

Notes

1. Malcolm Boyd, 'National Anthems', in Stanley Sadie (ed.), *The New Grove Dictionary of Music and Musicians*, vol. 13 (London: Macmillan, 1980). See pp. 46-75 for a more detailed discussion of individual countries and anthems, from which much of the following discussion of national anthems in general is taken.
2. The names of both these men can be found in a variety of spellings.
3. Seamus de Burca, *The Soldier's Song: The Story of Peadar Kearney* (Dublin: P. J. Bourke, 1957) gives an account of the origins of 'The Soldier's Song' from a family perspective. A manuscript, believed to be the original, is in the possession of John J. McDonnell of Vancouver.
4. *Irish Freedom*, September 1912, no. 23, 7.
5. National Archives S/8607 (hereafter N/A).
6. N/A S/3767A.
7. Minutes of the Executive Council, 27 May 1924, N/A S/3767A.
8. The statement is signed by all members of the committee, but the wording is very much in the style of Yeats.
9. 22 November 1924 (vol. 2 N.S., no. 2), 18.
10. Minutes of Executive Council meeting, item no. 2. N/A G2/5 C2/278, also S/3767A.
11. N/A S/3767A, letter to Secretary of the Executive Council, 28 April 1924.
12. However, an anonymous commentator stated some time later that the 'The Soldier's Song' 'was obviously adopted by the government not because of its inherent qualities but because otherwise it would have been appropriated by Mr. de Valera'. 'Ireland: Events in the Free State', *The Round Table: A Quarterly Review of Politics in the British Commonwealth*, no. 76, September 1929, 828.
13. Letter from Elizabeth Yeats to John Butler Yeats, [12 August 1921], quoted in Gifford Lewis, *The Yeats Sisters and the Cuala* (Dublin: Irish Academic Press, 1994), 157-58.
14. Thomas Toomey, *Forgotten Dreams: The Life and Times of Major J.G. 'Ged' O'Dwyer* (Limerick: O'Brien-Toomey, 1995), 91.
15. For a more detailed account of these events, see Brendan Sexton, *Ireland and the Crown, 1922-1936: The Governor-Generalship and the Free State* (Dublin: Irish Academic Press, 1989), 118-21.
16. Letter of 26 March 1958 from the Department of the Taoiseach to the Department of Defence, N/A S/3767B.

17. *National Anthems of the World* was initially published by Blandford, London, later by Cassell, London. The most recent edition is the 8th, 1993.
18. J.M. Doyle, Letter to the Editor, *The Irish Times*, 9 July 1994, 11. J.M. Doyle, Colonel Retired, is former Director of the Army School of Music.
19. N/A S/7395A.
20. For more details of these and other legal and political issues, see my article 'The Story of the National Anthem', *History Ireland* 4/1 (Spring 1996), 41-45. Some of the other material in this present article also appeared in a different form in the *History Ireland* article.
21. *Dáil Debates*, 25 July 1933 and 26 April 1934.
22. Joseph Hanly, *The National Ideal: A Practical Exposition of True Nationality Pertaining to Ireland* (Dublin: Dollard, Printinghouse, 1931), 201.
23. *An Camán*, 15 April 1933, 6.
24. *Dáil Debates*, 17 July 1951.
25. See, for example, John Waldron, *The Young Citizen and his Environment T2: Workbook for Senior Standards* (Dublin: Fallon, 1971), 43-44 and Sean de Bhaldraithe, *An Saoranach Óg agus a Thimpeallacht T2: Leabhar Saothair le hAgaidh Ranganna Sinsearacha* (Indreabhán, Co. na Gaillimh: Comharchumann chois Fharraige Teoranta, 1974), 43-44.
26. [Report of football final], *An Camán* 1/2, July 1931, 1.
27. 'Boyle Roche's Bird', *An Camán* 1/12, Bealtaine (May) 1, 1932, 11.
28. Pádraig Puirséal, *The GAA in its Time* (Dublin: Ward River Press, 1982; rpt. 1984), 222.
29. *An Camán*, 22 April 1933, 6.
30. *An Camán* 2/52, 30 December 1933, 11.
31. 'An Fear Faire', 'Responding to Our National Anthem: Does "The Soldier's Song" Still Thrill?', *An nGaedheal* 2/25, September 1935, 3.
32. *An nGaedheal* 4/2, Feabhra (February) 1938, 5.
33. de Burca, *The Soldier's Song*, 246.
34. See, for example, a World Wide Web information page on Ireland: http://sunsite. unc.edu/ gaelic/ Eire/eire.html. This source is, needless to say, not an official one.
35. The Department of Foreign Affairs has published a number of editions of a book entitled *Facts About Ireland*. The music of the chorus of 'The Soldier's Song', together with the words of the chorus in English and in Irish, are printed in this book. This publication seems to be as close as one can come to an official sanction of any texts for the anthem. The Stationery Office also prints scores of the chorus for bands, but with no text.
36. The Belfast *Andersonstown News* has, however, published a phonic transcription of O Rinn's Irish text, ostensibly intended for the benefit of non-Irish speakers in New York but perhaps felt, tongue in cheek, to be of some potential use to others. *Andersonstown News*, 23 July 1994, 16.
37. See *Dáil Debates*, 27 January 1972, and report in the *Irish Independent*, 10 January 1972, 18, as well as letters to the same newspaper, 11 January 1972, 8 and 14 January 1972, 8. See also letters to *The Irish Times*, 25 January 1972, 9 and 28 January 1972, 11.
38. *Report of Proceedings of the Forum for Peace and Reconciliation*, 24 February 1995, vol. 7, 84.
39. 'Adapting "A Soldier's Song" for Television', *RTV Guide*, 9 March 1962, 6.
40. Belinda Loftus does however observe that there is a long-standing nationalist tendency to identify Ireland as *the land*, especially as a wild, green, probably Western image. *Mirrors: Orange and Green* (Dundrum, Co. Down: Picture Press, 1994) 108-10 and plate VIII.

IRISH REPUBLIC
Amhrán na bhFiann
(The Soldier's Song)

Words by
PEADAR KEARNEY (1883-1942)

Music by
PATRICK HEENEY (1881-1911)
Arr. by T.M. CARTLEDGE

Tempo di marcia

Sin - ne Fian - na Fáil, a - tá faoi gheall ag Éi - rinn,
Sol - diers are we, whose lives are pledged to Ire - land;

Buíon dár slua thar—toinn do rái - nig chughainn, Faoi— mhóid bheith
Some have come from a land be-yond the wave, Sworn— to be

saor, Sean - tir ár sin - sear feas - ta, Ní fhág - far faoin
free, no more our an - cient sire - land, Shall shel - ter the

There were originally three verses and a chorus.
The latter was adopted as the National Anthem in July 1926.

54

tior - án ná faoin tráill. A - nocht a thé - am sa____
des - pot or the slave. To - night we man__ the__

bhear - na baoil, Le gean ar Ghaeil chun báis nó saoil, Le
bear - na baoil,* In Er - in's cause, come woe or weal, 'Mid

gun - na - scréach, faoi lámhach__ na____ bpiléar, Seo libh
can - non's__ roar and ri - fles__ peal, We'll__

can - aig amh - rán na bhFiann.
chant__ a sol dier's song.

* Pronounced 'Barna Bwail'. It means 'gap of danger'.

55

Sean O'Faolain as Biographer and Commentator

Marie Arndt

Sean O'Faolain's biographies have largely been neglected by critics, despite the fact that they provide significant clues to an understanding of Sean O'Faolain in the Irish cultural context. O'Faolain himself, when responding to the question of what he regarded as the most significant influences in his thinking and writing, enumerated 'the Catholic Religion (God damn and blast it) and Ireland (Ditto); add England, i.e the Empire'.[1] This revealing statement encapsulates O'Faolain's agenda as an Irish writer living in Ireland. It also discloses the love-hate relationship to his native country that he constantly battled to come to terms with, which is also demonstrated in his biographies.

Before proceeding any further, it is relevant to explore the meaning of biography. The Oxford English Dictionary gives the following definition, from 1661: 'The history of the lives of individual men, as a branch of literature'. Another definition, from 1791, refers to biography as 'A written record of the life of an individual'.[2] These definitions are not satisfactory. Biography must be seen in a wider literary perspective and must not disregard the author. A more recent argument about biography by Robert Gittings expands the previously quoted definitions. He declares that writing about another person gives the author a chance to hide behind an alter-ego that can be used as a mouthpiece for the writer. Gittings also remarks that the biographed subject's life and activities can be interpreted by the author to reflect his or her inclinations and opinions as much as – or maybe even more than – those of the subject of the book.[3] My argument in this article will be based on the assumption that Sean O'Faolain as biographer is closer to Gittings' definition than the traditional ones in the *OED*.

1. O'Faolain's Understanding of History

My argument will partly be linked to some ideas on the writing of history, on historicism and of liberalism proposed by the Italian philosopher Benedetto Croce, who was influential in the intellectual debate in the first part of this century. In my discussion I aim to explore elements in O'Faolain's biographies in order to build an argument for a conclusion based on the questions of O'Faolain's aim as biographer and how he chose his subjects for these works.

O'Faolain's biographies are written in a popular style, demonstrated by a flowing narrative free of jargon, including both personal and public aspects of the biographed subjects, often as anecdotes – in other words, a 'good read'. An added aspect of interest concerning O'Faolain's biographies is that they deal with individuals who in different, often turbulent, ways have played their part in Irish history: Constance Markievicz, Eamon De Valera, Daniel O'Connell, Hugh O'Neill, and Cardinal Newman.

An investigation of O'Faolain's biographies shows that they are good indicators of his general political outlook over time in Ireland. This has been observed by previous critics, in particular by Maurice Harmon.[4] However, what I believe is often missing in those critical arguments is a recognition of O'Faolain's inability to reconcile his critique of certain elements in Irish history with aspects of current Ireland of which he approves. For instance, Harmon acknowledges that

> although [O'Faolain] is deliberately trying to evade the romantic tradition of late nineteenth- and twentieth-century historians ... he succumbs to his own instinctive romanticism by searching in history for heroes with whom he can identify, whose actions give proof of an outlook similar to his own, and from whose behaviour he can draw satisfying support for his own opinions about the new Ireland.[5]

I agree with Harmon's deduction, but it is, nevertheless, incomplete, as there are additional reasons why O'Faolain wrote biographies. To explore this matter further I want to turn to Benedetto Croce.

There are several reasons for including Croce as an aid in this essay. Firstly, O'Faolain has referred to Croce in his writing in a way which suggests familiarity with Croce's work. Secondly, O'Faolain's liberal, idealist anti-Marxist discourse echoes that of Croce.[6] Thirdly, Croce's writings on history and historicism are also highly relevant in this context.

Croce's prime interest in liberalism is what he calls its rejection of the 'nationalization of the soul'.[7] Liberalism guarantees individual freedom of thought. However, Croce's form of liberalism has its limitations. For instance, in his concept of liberty, equality does not signify the right for everybody to claim their space; rather, it takes on a utilitarian meaning, where everybody has their particular station in life.[8] He further argues that liberalism does not seek to overthrow the past but aims to build on its traditions (*History*, 244). As Croce sees liberalism as an evolutionary process, he believes it can help avoiding conformity and loss of historical awareness.

Croce juxtaposes liberalism and history in the writing of history by his emphasis on morality. Croce believes that politics and economics should be left to the politicians, while the true liberal should concentrate 'on moral history, where is unrolled the drama which also goes on in himself' (*Philosophy*, 239-40).

Croce argues that history is never far away in life, as there is an interdependence between individuals and their past. The only way for them to be relieved from this burden is through rational linkage and assessment of past and present (*History*, 43-44). His conclusion is that 'life and reality are history' (*ibid.*, 65). This consequently enables the author to convey his or her own idea of reality and life through writing history. Croce points out that imagination is important for an historian to avoid becoming a 'chronicler' of events.[9] This, in Croce's argument, results in the writer's practical assessment of history and constitutes 'the pleasures of imagination'. A lasting sense of pleasure, however, can only be achieved through creating images. When pleasure cannot be fulfilled in real life, this human need is compensated by 'imagining things'.[10] So to Croce, there is room for imagination within history as well as within art, for example in writing.[11] These ideas are clearly applied by O'Faolain in his writing of biographies.

Croce and O'Faolain are also on common ground in their opinion of the Catholic Church. Croce states that this institution is a power that believes it cannot rule without 'mortifying the intellects and oppressing the wills of men' (*History*, 236). However, Croce sums up the Church as 'human', without defining this term (*ibid.*, 255). Croce distinguishes intellectual and liberal Catholics from the Renaissance onwards. He claims that the clerical legacy of the Renaissance even during his own time – in the early 20th century – makes it possible to call Christianity a liberal ideology (*Philosophy*, 234-35).

2. O'Faolain's Biographies

Let us now turn our attention to O'Faolain's biographies. Sean O'Faolain's first biography deals with Constance Markievicz, who had done a U-turn in life in leaving her privileged Anglo-Irish Ascendancy environment for an uncomfortable life among the people at the lower levels of society in revolutionary Ireland.

2.1. Constance Markievicz

On the first publication of *Constance Markievicz*, a reviewer in *The Irish Times*[12] wrote that O'Faolain 'put[s] forward a brilliant artist's conception of what the Countess was, and how she became what she was', rather than presenting an historically fully accurate picture of her. The reviewer hereby touches on a significant problem for a writer of fiction writing biography, namely to balance fact and fiction. O'Faolain himself recognises this issue in the later edition of the book when he states that until the time of the 1916 Rising, Markievicz 'had the interest that any personality might have for a novelist', but after that event she takes on a more public role and therefore does not leave the novelist much space for 'manipulation with facts'.[13] In this statement O'Faolain confirms that aiming for historical accuracy is secondary to him as a biographer. The freedom of the fiction writer takes precedence.

In some sections of the book Markievicz drifts into the background of the narrative, significantly, when her activities do not coincide with major political events of the time. This brings us to the question of the primary aim of this biography. Is it primarily meant to portray Constance Markievicz herself, or to focus on a string of historical events during her lifetime? This question is particularly justified when considering the middle section of the book. When the narrative reaches the events of the 1916 Rising, O'Faolain temporarily drops Markievicz, and his focus is switched to the principal male participants in Irish affairs at the time, on which O'Faolain keenly offers his opinions. It is only after a lengthy appraisal of James Connolly that O'Faolain brings Markievicz back into the narrative. O'Faolain is not primarily concerned with Constance Markievicz but with political developments during her time. This is clearly indicated in the foreword to the revised edition of 1967, in which O'Faolain states that he has corrected 'factual errors' from the first edition. He continues:

just because it was so contemporary it cannot but reflect some of the impatience, even of the disillusionment, the weariness of soul with all patriotic emotion that, as we now see, looking about us at other newly-risen peoples, seem to be part of the inevitable aftermath of every nationalist upheaval. But times change and opinions with them. (*Ibid.*, 10)

For O'Faolain, Markievicz represents the average emotional revolutionary, often lacking in ideological substance. However, we cannot ignore the fact that O'Faolain is eager to be more conciliatory to Markievicz thirty years on, which is highlighted in the following passage: 'Whatever we may decide to think about her as a political leader is, to a lesser or greater extent, equally applicable to all her associates. She is, toutes proportions *gardées*, a representative figure' (*ibid.*, 171-2). Many years have passed since the time of the action of the book – events in which O'Faolain himself played a marginal role – and also since the time of the initial writing of the biography. O'Faolain can now stand back from the period as well as from Constance Markievicz and his own assessment of her in the light of a greater historical awareness. But, as Gary Davenport has remarked, the fact remains that O'Faolain makes Markievicz into a representative of those revolutionary Irishmen who shared an 'obsessive devotion to causes and lack of critical intelligence'.[14] For O'Faolain Markievicz represents the 'emotional average revolutionary', often lacking in ideological substance.

In *Constance Markievicz*, O'Faolain demonstrates his regret at the decline of the Anglo-Irish in Irish society with the emergence of nationalism, and sees a connection between these two processes. He reflects that 'Dublin society did not realize that it was attenuated, even as Dublin democracy to-day does not realize that its city at the end of all is but a parlour full of bailiffs'.[15] As Maurice Harmon has pointed out, O'Faolain 'idealized Dublin society in the years preceding 1916'.[16] But Harmon does not acknowledge fully the implication that O'Faolain, by so doing, aims to stress the folly of the fact that the cultural contribution to Irish society offered by the Anglo-Irish – Markievicz's social class – had been rejected in favour of unsophisticated and heavy-handed nationalism, and that the Irish, particularly O'Faolain himself, were suffering from this unwise choice.

2.2. de Valera

Eamon de Valera personified partially the detrimental nationalist option. O'Faolain's ambivalent attitude to de Valera is reflected in his two biographies of this key politician in twentieth-century Ireland. The subject is approached in different ways in the two texts. The first book (1933) takes a positive stance towards de Valera, and focuses on his dedication and hard work for Ireland. The book is a general description by an admirer of de Valera's political involvement; the historian F.S.L. Lyons has aptly referred to it as 'hagiographical rather than historical'.[17] Only at the very end of the book is there a hint of criticism of de Valera, mainly about his character and personality, which are described as unsociable, aloof and ascetic.[18] O'Faolain foreshadows what would later be established in the 1937 Constitution, as he pictures de Valera's hope for Ireland to develop into a 'Christian State with an individual culture based on the old traditional Gaelic State, yet modern in so far as it takes everything acceptable to the Christian, i.e. Catholic ideal' (*ibid.*, 106). However, at this stage O'Faolain interprets this as a positive urge for Irish 'self-reliance', and liberty for the Irish. Strangely enough Maurice Harmon does not pursue the trace of ambivalence in his account of the biography; instead Harmon simplifies the issue by fleetingly proposing the possibility that O'Faolain's devotion to de Valera at this stage was not honest.[19] Harmon's evasion of the matter allows him to escape the dilemma of O'Faolain's revised biography of de Valera six years later.

O'Faolain's revision of Eamon de Valera is central in his second biography (1939). For example, O'Faolain remarks on de Valera's narrow-mindedness and his anti-intellectual pursuits. He labels de Valera's patriotic involvement as provincial, and a sign of 'lack of humanity, if by that word one is willing to understand an intelligent and indulgent interest in all classes of people and ideas'.[20] In other words, O'Faolain is proclaiming his own concept of humanity and implies that he himself subscribes to this way of thinking. O'Faolain's criticism is based on his own disillusionment with the result of de Valera's polities; instead of having increased liberty, de Valera's Ireland had developed into a 'Dreary Eden', steeped in provincialism and puritanism, confirmed in the 1937 Constitution.

O'Faolain links the restrictions of intellectual life in Ireland to the anti-intellectualism of the Catholic clergy, which became increasingly influential in Irish society under de Valera. However, O'Faolain simultaneously insists that the Church of Ireland – the Protestants – is equally 'puritanical and narrow-minded' (*ibid.*, 167-69). His fear of intellectual decline in Ireland is also blamed on de Valera's insistence on linking Catholicism to the Gaelic Revival, which

O'Faolain regards as yet another form of provincialism, an issue that would have to wait decades before being widely discussed in Ireland.

To O'Faolain, de Valera stands as a symbol of the new Irish State, and in that capacity he puts himself beyond reach of the common people, by, for instance, not showing ordinary human sentiments and concerns; he is seen as standing abstractly aloof, as a symbol, living up to the generally accepted perception of a leader – a perception also accepted by O'Faolain. This is O'Faolain's problem; he wants the symbol but not the aloofness. But at the same time the convincing leader must stand above the crowd. The heroicism explicated by O'Faolain in 1933 has in 1939 given way to a picture of de Valera as a kind of theologian of the nation (*ibid.*, 53-54). O'Faolain's lasting and final remark about de Valera is that he imposed and institutionalised provincialism on the Irish people, and restricted the individual right to express thoughts freely and inspire intellectual debate.

2.3. King of the Beggars

O'Faolain's biography of Daniel O'Connell, *King of the Beggars*, was to some extent a reaction against de Valera's leadership, and the way in which the ideals of the Liberator, O'Connell, had been betrayed when political independence was finally achieved in Ireland. *King of the Beggars* is by many considered O'Faolain's best work in this genre. In 1938 one reviewer praised it for 'precision in judgement of major aspects of O'Connell's political career'.[21]

In *King of the Beggars* O'Faolain takes the opportunity to proclaim his view of Ireland in the 1930s by way of an appreciation of O'Connell. O'Faolain considered O'Connell the first modern Irish politician, and more broad-minded than de Valera and other political leaders of his own time. An additional reason for O'Faolain's admiration for this 19th century leader was O'Connell's international reputation as an inspiration in the struggle for liberty.

O'Faolain links the past to the present in several ways in the book. This was also recognised by critics at the time of publication. In a series of short articles in the Catholic journal *Studies*, *King of the Beggars* is called 'a masterpiece of biography ... and a masterpiece of ... concrete criticism of the present'.[22] The book clearly demonstrates that O'Faolain adopts Croce's ideas of the influence of history and, to allude to Gittings, how the writing of history gives the author the opportunity to promote his own views on different matters. Despite the fact that his romantic idea of a wise leader of the people still remains, O'Faolain takes a firm stance against romantic nationalism in *King of the Beggars*. This is evident in, for example, his criticism of the republican movement for ostracising O'Connell, mainly because of his desire for a peaceful Ireland, where all religious denominations and classes could live in harmony. Instead, the young nationalists had preferred to capitalise on the Gaelic past. O'Faolain detested this notion, which he also saw clearly in his own time. According to O'Faolain, the nationalist movement developed after O'Connell into a non-democratic and narrow-minded institution. O'Faolain implies – and echoes his criticism in his biography on de Valera – that the Irish people had, as part of this movement, been deceived by undemocratic and patriarchal leaders such as de Valera and the Irish Catholic Church. O'Faolain's firm belief is that O'Connell – unlike current leading Irish politicians – was able to combine Catholicism with liberalism.

In the introductory 'Proem' of *King of the Beggars*, O'Faolain expresses disagreement with the idea that O'Connell's struggle for Emancipation had been a fight not only against English supremacy, but also against the Irish people's own insistence on clinging to the Gaelic past – 'the outer trappings of Gaeldom' – which O'Faolain thought had never served them well.[23] He takes the opportunity to develop his criticism by discussing Daniel Corkery's ideas in *The Hidden Ireland*. To O'Faolain, Corkery was caught in the Gaelic mist, preventing him from seeing that the Gaelic poets he praised as ideal men of literature were on the same level as the rest of the miserable people, and that there was no reason to glorify their situation (*ibid.*, 37). However, it must be stressed that O'Faolain does not oppose the Gaelic heritage *per se*, but its constant theme of 'weaving ... endless classical myths into hare-brained visions about the return of James Stuart' (*ibid.*, 153). To O'Faolain, O'Connell had been the vanguard of a realist force, and had understood that it was crucial to look forward and unload the burden of the Celtic cross from the Irish people's backs. O'Faolain confirmed his own rapture by underlining how '[w]armly [O'Connell had] received the future' (*ibid.*, 213).

In the end, O'Faolain presents a very sweeping and inconsistent conclusion about O'Connell's achievement. On the one hand he sees O'Connell as the leader of the masses, but, on the other hand, O'Faolain admits that O'Connell at times pursued policies that were not in the interest of the majority of those he was supposed to represent. O'Faolain's idealistic and intellectual perspective is underlined by his argument concerning the difficult social conditions in O'Connell's time. Significantly, O'Faolain does not react against poverty itself but deplores the degradation it brings in its train. 'The horror ... is the mental horror – the murder of the mind, the spiritual chloroform, the creeping paralysis of the soul' (*ibid.*, 153). The conclusion reveals that intellectual liberty is O'Faolain's primary concern.

O'Faolain condones O'Connell's acceptance of a hierarchical society, not as derived from the Catholic Church, but from the feudal tradition from which O'Connell originated, or from his own sheer common-sensical view of the crude Irish life in his time. O'Faolain's firm belief was that a society like that 'absolutely necessitated leadership and an intellectual' ethos. In other words, those who were less fortunate socially had to be guided but by the Catholic Church or any other authority with a similarly restrictive mind (*ibid.*, 301-7). This argument actually reveals more about the biographer himself than about his subject.

O'Faolain echoes his own criticism of de Valera's development in his conclusion in *King of the Beggars* about O'Connell's relationship with the Irish people. From having been a 'Man of the People' O'Connell later in life turned into 'The Sphinx', gradually alienated from the people he originally set out to serve. But in his general appreciation, O'Faolain regards O'Connell as personifying the watershed between the old and the modern kind of broad-minded political leadership, with connections to the outside world. However, O'Faolain does not fully confront the flaws of O'Connell's supposed broad-mindedness, for example that he sometimes did political deals which did not favour the interests of the general population but the more privileged and politically and economically more important layers of society, the classes with which both O'Connell and O'Faolain – hand on heart – sympathised.

2.4. The Great O'Neill

Sean O'Faolain valued Hugh O'Neill, the Earl of Tyrone, as O'Connell's forerunner in Ireland. In *The Great O'Neill* O'Faolain portrays O'Neill as a character standing above and aloof from his own people; partly because of his intellectual pursuits, drawing him away from the Gaelic tradition towards Europe, and partly due to his ability in dealing with the colonial power, for personal rather than social ends. O'Faolain highlights the patriarchal society of O'Neill's day and sees an opening up towards Europe as an escape to intellectual freedom and away from patriarchy.

O'Faolain saw O'Neill as the bridge between the unsophisticated Gaelic culture and the more polished outside intellectual world, particularly with England and later with Europe. In a review in *The Dublin Magazine*, Francis MacManus claims that, 'O'Faolain rightly attempts to restore O'Neill to the European scene to which he rightly belonged by virtue of his stature as a soldier, by his international affiliation and by contemporary esteem'.[24] O'Faolain regarded O'Neill as essentially a broad-minded and intelligent man, greatly improved by his English education, and by his contacts with part of the English literati of the time.[25] However, it has in recent years been argued by historians that O'Neill spent much less time in England than the number of years claimed by, among others, O'Faolain. O'Faolain's distortion of history is not challenged in Harmon's more recent biography of O'Faolain.

O'Faolain supports his image of Hugh O'Neill as an early O'Connell by arguing that 'O'Neill was the first modern man who gave [the Gaelic people] a form, by giving it a speech that it could understand and which made it understand itself intelligently'.[26] But he implies that the people did not take this opportunity, and still have not done so. O'Faolain takes the opportunity to criticise Gaelic society, thereby bringing his critique in *King of the Beggars* backwards in time. He claims that during O'Neill's time Gaelic Ireland suffered from the backwardness caused by the fact that for centuries it had been a victim of intellectual undernourishment. O'Faolain assures the reader that O'Neill – had he been given the opportunity – would have rectified the situation (*ibid.*, 32). Strangely enough, Harmon firmly states that O'Faolain claims the opposite.[27] O'Faolain sees O'Neill's pursuits as a valid reason for his association with the English to acquire power,[28] as this provided the link to broader intellectual life and Renaissance culture, of which O'Faolain wants to make O'Neill a part. He further emphasises this picture by claiming O'Neill's connection with Europe and how he reached out to the Counter-Reformation (*ibid.*, 278-79). O'Faolain saw the Catholic Church in O'Neill's time as an intellectual force (*ibid.*, 65), which parallels Croce's idea of the liberal Catholic clergy during the Renaissance.

O'Faolain records how O'Neill demanded some kind of home rule for the North of Ireland, combining this with demands that Catholicism should be allowed to prosper in Ireland. O'Faolain gives the impression that liberty of thought would have been guaranteed by the Catholic clergy, which O'Faolain saw as an intellectual and a liberal force in that era (*ibid.*, 222). He is in this instance blinded by the idea of sweeping away the assumed parochialism of Gaelicism with the help of the Catholic Church to achieve the freedom of thought so long denied the Irish (*ibid.*, 65). But what O'Faolain is really arguing here is that intellectuals are not generally accepted in Ireland, and particularly not in current Ireland, which is confirmed by his own recurring question that he plants in O'Neill's mind: 'Must we Irish always be weaving fancy, living always in the fantastic world of a dream?'(*ibid.*, 281). For O'Faolain this still keeps the Irish from realism and intellectualism.

2.5. Newman's Way

The ability to combine intellectualism and Catholicism was one of Sean O'Faolain's goals for the Ireland of his day. He thought O'Connell had succeeded in this aim, whereas de Valera was a great disappointment in this respect. Another man who, in O'Faolain's view, had parallelled O'Connell's achievement on this matter was Cardinal Newman; it was a great incentive for O'Faolain to write a biography about this famous convert. Another fact to remember is that O'Faolain wrote *Newman's Way* when he was contending with his own idea of Catholicism. The emphasis on Newman's road – as well as O'Faolain's own – to come to terms with his religious beliefs is underlined by the fact that the biography only deals with Newman's life up until his official conversion to Roman Catholicism in 1845. In a review in *The Bell*, Patrick Lynch also draws this parallel, but without exploring the case.[29]

O'Faolain stresses that all Newman's religious thinking was based on 'intellectual accuracy', and that he never allowed emotions to interfere with the final discourse, as his emotions were ruled by fervid Puritanism.[30] O'Faolain believes this often makes men who 'live too much in the mind ... mightily obtuse about other people's feelings in their preoccupation with their own'(*ibid.*, 52), echoing his evaluation of de Valera. Later on O'Faolain makes allowances for Newman's puritan streak without fully accepting it; he objects to its narrow scope and feels it does not fit a 'sensitive', 'civilised' and 'generous' person like Newman.

Newman's conversion to Catholicism, O'Faolain states, came during his trip to Italy, Sicily to be exact. The reason for the occurrence in this particular place O'Faolain claims to be the effect on Newman of the classical location. Newman had found his 'symbol' – O'Faolain is convinced that we all need one – and 'the image of his heart's desire [and] the evocation of a nobility of soul ... a form of classic grace' (*ibid.*, 183). This also refers to O'Faolain's own ideal state of mind as revealed in his travel books about Italy. The references to the Classical epoch also allude to Croce's concept of the Renaissance as the period when the Catholic clergy were a liberal force. In addition, O'Faolain's portrayal of Newman also implies a connection to Croce's idea of liberalism as an individual assessment of a situation based on free, intellectual thought.

Due to Cardinal Newman's involvement as a founder of the Oxford Movement, O'Faolain sees him as the leader of a mass movement of everlasting influence, and as a saviour of lost and lonely people (*ibid.*, 204-5). He points out that Newman attacked the symbol of Infallibility in the Roman Catholic Church because it did not leave any issues to be argued. The 'infallible teacher' is a form of patriarchy which O'Faolain probably had more problems with than Newman, as individual freedom is central in O'Faolain's concern for his own trade: 'We become engrossed in the System and forget the Author' (*ibid.*, 210). He is not solely referring to the Celestial Author but also to the Author of the World; in other words, he wants writers, most of all writers like himself, to receive as much reverence as Yeats ever wished for the bards. O'Faolain extends this theme in his evaluation of Newman as a man of imagination – an artist – rather than, primarily, as a theologian. However, his artistic side gave way to the intellectual, and is therefore flawed in O'Faolain's ideal world. But to O'Faolain, the ideal is really not desirable, because it may cause chaos and disintegration in society. Consequently, O'Faolain wants change to be strictly intellectual and to take place within the established framework of society (*ibid.*, 227-30).

To O'Faolain, John Henry Newman exemplified a person who by his own individual strength of mind and character revised his attitude to spiritual existence through the intellect, and thereby avoided irrational and hasty solutions. Through this amalgamation of the artistic aspect of Newman's character and his intellect, O'Faolain highlights his own cause, as an intellectual writer with religious values.

To conclude, in his biographies O'Faolain wrote the history that allowed him to emphasise characteristics of personalities and certain events to build an argument resulting in a condemnation of Ireland's lost political and intellectual opportunities. He used his imagination to draw the picture he had created in his mind. After all, he regarded himself primarily as a fiction writer who happened to be writing biographies.[31]

O'Faolain saw or wanted to see facets of his own personality in all the biographed individuals. He saw his own shared allegiance to Ireland and the outside world in Hugh O'Neill and Daniel O'Connell. He saw himself as combining religion with intellectualism, like Newman; as standing apart from the people, like the unemotional de Valera; and as refusing to conform to a single ideology and desiring to go against the grain, like the 'overage revolutionary' Markievicz. All these biographed subjects formed links between the establishment and the people – as O'Faolain himself wanted to do – guiding the people towards a certain way of thinking. Finally, O'Faolain used history as a way to create an imagined picture of the past to suit his purpose for writing history, namely to comment on the present, thereby allowing him to take on the dual role of biographer and commentator.

There is no doubt that the efforts of Sean O'Faolain in Ireland helped to pave the way for the Ireland of today. The introduction of new Irish writing in *The Bell*, his own numerous articles on current Irish affairs, and the way O'Faolain included critical comments about the Ireland of his own time in publications as diverse as travel books and fiction are all evidence of this. He was the first writer to attempt to provide intellectual evaluations of important figures in Irish history in his biographies. Despite the fact that he did not manage to refrain from emotional and inaccurate statements, it is still fair to say that Sean O'Faolain's intellectual achievement on the whole largely provided Irish society with the embryo of the revisionist frame of reference needed in order for Ireland to enter the twentieth century, both socially and intellectually. O'Faolain offered the bridge between de Valera's insular Ireland and Europe, as well as the United States, two allies which have proved indispensable for Ireland's development during the last few decades. The concept of the Celtic Tiger – the symbiosis between Microsoft and Riverdance – alludes to Sean O'Faolain's ideal Ireland: a modern state resting safely on its Celtic cultural past.

Notes

1. Letter from Sean O'Faolain to John Kelleher, July 1943, quoted in Maurice Harmon, *Sean O'Faolain* (London: Constable, 1994), 159.
2. *Shorter Oxford English Dictionary, 1933* (Oxford: Clarendon Press, 1973).
3. Robert Gittings, *The Nature of Biography* (London: Heinemann, 1978), 85-86.
4. See for example Maurice Harmon, 'Literary Biography in Twentieth Century Ireland', in Augustine Martin (ed.), *The Genius of Irish Prose* (Dublin, Cork: Mercier Press, 1985), 159-61.
5. Maurice Harmon, *Sean O'Faolain; A Critical Introduction* (1967; Dublin: Wolfhound Press, 1984), 11-12.
6. Sean O'Faolain, letter to Richard Ellmann, Aug. 21, 1954, Richard Ellmann Papers, University of Tulsa. O'Faolain agrees with Croce that reality is always based on individual conception.

7. Benedetto Croce, *History as the Story of Liberty,* trans. Sylvia Spriggs (London: George Allen and Unwin Limited, 1949), 233-34. Further references are given in the text.
8. Benedetto Croce, *My Philosophy,* trans. E.F. Carritt (London: George Allen & Unwin Ltd, 1949), 101, 236-37. Further references are given in the text.
9. Benedetto Croce, *Theory & History of Historiography,* trans. Douglas Ainslie (London: Harrap, 1921), 38-39.
10. Benedetto Croce, *The Conduct of Life,* trans. Arthur Livingstone (London, Calcutta, Sydney: George G. Harrap & Co. Ltd., nd.), 115-22.
11. Benedetto Croce, *Aesthetics,* trans. Douglas Ainslie (London: Macmillan and Co, Limited, 1909), 53-55.
12. 'The Psycho-analysis of Countess Markievicz', rev. of *Countess Markievicz,* by Sean O'Faolain, *The Irish Times* 13 Oct. 1934, 7.
13. O'Faolain, *Constance Markievicz* (1934; Cresset Women's Voices, 1987), 171.
14. Gary Tolleson Davenport, *Four Irish Writers in Time of Civil War: Liam O'Flaherty, Frank O'Conner, Sean O'Faolain and Elizabeth Bowen* (unpublished dissertation, University of South Carolina, 1971), 191.
15. O'Faolain, *Constance Markievicz* (1934), 58.
16. Maurice Harmon, Sean O'Faolain, 107.
17. F.S.L. Lyons, 'Sean O'Faolain as Biographer', *Irish University Review* 6/1 (1976), 95.
18. Sean O'Faolain, *The Life Story of Eamon de Valera* (Dublin: Talbot Press Limited, 1933), 107-9.
19. Harmon, *Sean O'Faolain,* 104.
20. Sean O'Faolain, *de Valera* (Harmondsworth: Penguin, 1939), 25.
21. Review of *King of the Beggars* by Sean O'Faolain, *Irish Book Lover,* Nov.-Dec. 1938, 72.
22. Gerard Murphy, 'Daniel O'Connell and the Gaelic Past', *Studies* 27/2 (1938), 372.
23. Sean O'Faolain, *King of the Beggars* (London: Thomas Nelson & Sons, 1938), 29.
24. Review of *The Great O'Neill* by Sean O'Faolain, *Dublin Magazine,* April-June 1943, 66.
25. Sean O'Faolain, *The Great O'Neill* (London: Longman, 1942), 38-39.
26. O'Faolain, *The Great O'Neill,* 15.
27. Harmon, Sean O'Faolain, 152.
28. O'Faolain, *The Great O'Neill,* 59.
29. Patrick Lynch, 'O'Faolain's Way', Review of *Newman's Way* by Sean O'Faolain, *The Bell,* March, 1953, 628-31.
30. O'Faolain, *Newman's Way,* 36-40.
31. See for example Sean O'Faolain, *The Life of Eamon de Valera,* 181, and Sean O'Faolain, *King of the Beggars,* 227.

With Skill, Endurance, and Generosity of Heart: Frank McCourt's *Angela's Ashes*

Darlene Erickson

Faulkner once said, 'the past is not the past, it hasn't even passed. It is with us always because we are not what we were'.[1] Faulkner points up an interesting reality; the human animal is a continuing project bred of experience and even of cultural ancestry. One function of reconstructing the past in the autobiography or the memoir is to find, perhaps to create, some meaning in one's present life. Tennyson articulates the idea simply but emphatically in *Ulysses* when he says: 'I am a part of all that I have met'.

In 1996-97 one of the most talked about examples of the genre is Frank McCourt's Pulitzer Prize winning *Angela's Ashes*. As Pete Hamill, editor of the *New York Daily News* and writer in his own right points out, 'When practised by politicians and generals, the memoir is an advertisement for the self, a blathering exercise in publicity. But in the hands of an artist [like Frank McCourt] equipped with a ruthless memory, the remembering is meaning, a defiant blow against the general amnesia of modern life' (Hamill, 46). McCourt's kind of art ... and ruthless memory ... are well worth consideration. *Angela's Ashes* is a powerful work – perhaps even in spite of its 'best-seller' status. For by reading McCourt's reconstruction, audiences have the opportunity to share in that fascinating genre which results in what might be called 'fictions of the self'. I would argue that McCourt's version of the memoir is ultimately a skilful literary creation which works with material very close to the bone, not only for himself, but for all of us, subjects such as family, parents, siblings, death, religion, childhood, adolescence, and humiliation. Drawing the fine line between personal pain and artistic objectivity has always been difficult to achieve, but a select number of skilled artists have been able to achieve that goal, and McCourt is one of them. Is the story true, is it in fact non-fiction? Of course not, but that is true of most autobiographies, biographies, or memoirs. They are always to some degree

68

artistic fictions of the self, works designed to teach and to heal both writer and reader, to help people deal with the pains and complexities of human experience, Hamlet's 'slings and arrows of outrageous fortune'. The skilful writer selects from his arsenal of recollections and weaves a tale that makes life seem more real and logical than it ever is. His very words bring control over chaos.

Frank McCourt begins his memoir with:

> When I look back on my childhood I wonder how I survived at all. It was, of course, a miserable childhood: the happy childhood is hardly worth your while. Worse than the ordinary miserable childhood is the miserable Irish childhood, and worse yet is the miserable Irish Catholic childhood.[2]

With this opening he deftly establishes the tone and the themes of his memoir in the Irish fashion: with wit, music, and overstatement. The tone is ironical, as Pete Hamill points out, but it is irony as practised by the Jews and the Irish. It can be wielded as a weapon, but above all serves as a kind of armor. 'It is adapted as a protection against all manner of psychic injury from enemies, from friendly fire, from self-inflicted wounds. Irony creates distance, a certain knowing detachment, while acknowledging membership in the club of human weakness and folly' (Hamill, 42). Looking back, examining the past, is his intent as he undertakes another in the long line of *bildungsroman* that have formed the backbone of Western Literature. But unlike most such novels, McCourt's *Angela's Ashes* is a tough read, tougher than one might even imagine ... especially if the reader is Irish ... or merely human. Nonetheless, it is not an entirely sad book; it is certainly not a sentimental tale. It is filled with irony, dry wit, and even sparks of humor – all stamped with an unmistakable seal of endurance. McCourt is a survivor. Yeats must have been thinking of a person like McCourt when he said of someone else, 'Being Irish, he had an abiding sense of tragedy which sustained him through temporary periods of joy'.[3]

McCourt says of his work, presumably with his usual cynicism, 'People everywhere brag and whimper about the woes of their early years, but nothing can compare with the Irish version: the poverty; the shiftless loquacious, alcoholic father; the pious defeated mother moaning by the fire; pompous priests, bullying schoolmasters; the English and the terrible things they did to us for eight hundred long years' (11). The story describes the first nineteen years of Frank McCourt's life, from his birth in Brooklyn, New York, through the family's emigration four years later to his mother's roots in the slums of Limerick, and ends with his return migration to America, a young man on his own.

The book opens in New York during the Great Depression. The McCourt family, the father Malachy, the mother, Angela, Frankie, his brother Malachy, and baby sister Margaret are eking out an existence on Classon Street in Brooklyn, living, like thousands of Irish and other immigrants, in the tenements of the big American city. There is little or no work, and when there is, Malachy drinks his wages away anyway and the family is in dire straits despite the kindness of friends and neighbors, especially a Jewish neighbor, Mrs. Leibowitz. Eventually, things get so bad, especially after the baby, Margaret, dies that the family decides to return to Angela's family home in the slums of Limerick, Ireland where she hopes they will be greeted by a welcoming family. But sadness persists after the return as first one twin (Oliver) and then the other (Eugene) dies. McCourt reports in an interview, 'When one child dies it's devastating, when you have three go, [Margaret, then the twins, one died in May, the other one died the following November,] you never really recover'.[4] The family staggers through incredible loss, deprivation, and depression. Only four of their seven children survive. Told from the perspective and voice of a four-year-old boy, the memories unwind with the out-of-context *reportage* that only a child could make. He doesn't judge or edit, he merely reports the world he finds around him. 'Children don't lie', McCourt says in an interview; 'they don't know enough to. They learn to lie eventually, but at first they don't know how. I wanted to achieve that quality. Also children are not bitter ... a child lives in a very immediate world which he merely accepts as the only world there is' (Tentler, 3). McCourt tells his story in a kind of continuous present tense which changes only slightly as his namesake and main character, 'Frankie' matures. The voice is one McCourt feels sure he invented for himself. 'I felt very, very comfortable with it', he says (Saah, 4-5).

The voice in the text is, however, only a persona. McCourt is actually 66 years old and *Angela's Ashes* is his first book. He claims to have mastered his craft as a teacher in the exclusive Peter Stuyvesant School in New York City where he served for thirty years teaching English literature and creative writing until his recent retirement. He conjectures that his former students must be gloriously surprised at the success of *Angela's Ashes*, a book that has been in process for more than four decades. As McCourt says, 'I've been writing in notebooks for forty years or so. I have notebooks filled with stuff about Limerick, about growing up there, catalogues, lists, snatches of conversation, things about my mother and father ... and finally I had to write it'.[5] 'I couldn't have written the book 15 years ago because I was carrying a lot of baggage ... I had to become, as it says in the Bible, as a child, and the child started to speak in this book. And that became the only way to do it, without judging' (McNamara, 13). As McCourt describes it, on a day in October 1994, 'I just sat down and started to write. Then I found a voice that said, "I'm on the playground in Brooklyn" and with that child's point of view I was off and running. I found the voice and that was it ... remember what Red Smith the sports writer [for the *New York Times*] said when asked about writing and what you do? Well, said Red Smith, you just sit at your desk and open a vein' (Tentler, 19).

McCourt's is, after all, a very old story. Suffering and survival are nothing new to Irishmen or to the human animal of any nationality. And the Limerick of the late 1930s and early 1940s even bears an uncanny resemblance to the Dublin Dean Swift described in *A Modest Proposal*. Little has changed; poverty and suffering are an old tale in Ireland. But even Swift left us with generalities and the distance of satire. McCourt does not; we are with little Frankie and his family as they descend into a hell even Dante couldn't or wouldn't have imagined. McCourt is visceral in his details. Consider the following passage, which becomes a *leitmotif* for the entire book:

> Above all – we were wet.
> Out of the Atlantic Ocean great sheets of rain gathered to drift slowly up the River Shannon and settle forever in Limerick. The rain dampened the city from the Feast of the Circumcision to New Year's Eve. It created a cacophony of hacking coughs, bronchial rattles, asthmatic wheezes, consumptive croaks. It turned noses into fountains, lungs into bacterial sponges ... From October to April the walls of Limerick glistened with the damp. Clothes never dried; tweed and woolen coats housed living things, sometimes sprouted mysterious vegetations. In pubs, steam rose from damp bodies and garments to be inhaled with cigarette and pipe smoke. (11)

In spite of such portraits of bleakness and misery, Pete Hamill rightly calls *Angela's Ashes* a triumphant book. McCourt's memoir of Irish childhood is in turn hilarious, heart-scalding and bitterly angry. Make no mistake, McCourt is an angry man but he is also a man who is trying to channel his anger wisely. He says in an interview, 'The way we lived we had to turn everything into humor. If you live in gloom all the time it drains you. It's an energy matter – you have to keep lifting yourself. Humor was a resistance to gravity. We were all like characters out of Beckett, everything was absurd' (Hamill, 45).

His story takes us through a world of daily, repetitive, cyclical horrors in the lanes of Limerick in what Hamill calls 'soul-murdering' detail, specifics that no reader can ever forget. The father, Malachy McCourt, is the clichéd shiftless Irish father who seldom works and who drinks away his dole. He is from County Antrim in the North of Ireland, making the entire family pariahs in the Catholic south. But in this writer's capable hands, Malachy McCourt is anything but a cliché. At one point young Frank says

> I think my father is like the Holy Trinity with three people in him, the one in the morning with the paper, [in the mornings Malachy fried bread and read the paper and talked politics and history with Frank] the one at night with the stories and the prayers, and then the one who does the bad thing and comes home with the smell of whiskey. (210)

Frankie's father tells him tales about the great Irish heroes like Cuchulain and makes up wonderful stories about the neighbors down the street. He tells of the Angel on the Seventh step who leaves babies in the night and he awakens his sons from deep sleep to sing patriotic songs and to remind them to 'die for Ireland'. Malachy loves to sing the old songs and the book is laced with their lyrics. Frank's father was an alcoholic, but he was not an abuser; he loved his children and they knew it. McCourt's ambivalence about his father is explored in detail in the book. But despite Malachy's alcoholism, there exists in this family not only the will to survive but a quiet heartbroken love – a love that ultimately holds them together and sustains them.[6]

Angela McCourt, the mother, may well have what Henry James called in *The American* 'a spark of the sacred fire', but that spark is slowly dampened and destroyed by penury. Angela sings romantic ballads and cleans when there are wages and talks to herself and falls into inertia and indolence when there are none. Her struggles to keep her family alive and fed are heroic. The McCourts are too poor to afford sheets or blankets for their flea-infested bed, too poor to buy shoes for the children, too poor to buy milk or medicine for dying babies, too poor even to keep them clean. Author McCourt reminisces: 'we were the great unwashed ... nobody even knew what a shower was ... We washed maybe from eyebrow to chin, ... Our crotches were innocent of water. You wouldn't want to go back in time yourself and mingle with us' (Saah, 3). Angela is always pregnant and exhausted, sending the older children out to the street with their siblings sucking on bottles of sugared water instead of milk and wrapped in dirtied rags for diapers. She must, of course, do her 'wifely duty' the priests tell her, so the endless supply of babies persists until Malachy leaves to find work in England. The reader follows the child's grief and disappointment as the family waits week after week for telegrams with paychecks that never come, and a father who seldom returns:

> I ask if I can go with him to the railway station. No, he's not going there. He's going to the Dublin road to see if he can get a lift. He pats my head, tells me take care of my mother and brothers and goes out the door. I watch him go up the lane till he turns the corner. I run up the lane to see him go down Barrack Hill and down St Joseph's Street. I run down the hill and follow him as far as I can. He must know I'm following him because he turns and calls to me, Go home, Francis. Go home to your mother ... In a week there's a letter to say he arrived safely, that we are to be good boys, attend to our religious duties and above all obey our mother. In another week there's a telegram money order for three pounds and we're in heaven ... The next Saturday there's no telegram nor the Saturday after nor any Saturday forever. Mam begs again at the St. Vincent de Paul Society and smiles at the Dispensary when Mr. Coffey and Mr. Kane have their bit of a joke about Dad having a tart in Piccadilly. (249)

Pap returns occasionally, but only to produce yet another 'miracle' from the Angel on the Seventh Step. McCourt's prose is powerful in its economy when he describes the day Margaret, the baby for whom 'there was a holiday in heaven the day this child was made' dies:

> My mother begs for another few minutes with her baby but the doctor says he doesn't have all day. When Dad reaches for Margaret, my mother pulls away against the wall. She has the wild look, her black curly hair is damp on her forehead and there is sweat all over her face, her eyes are wide open and her face is shiny with tears, she keeps shaking her head and moaning. (36)

Malachy doesn't return for two days, drowning his grief at a local pub. Through it all Angela's one luxury is an occasional Woodbine cigarette which she puffs guiltily to stave off hunger. (The book's title has many reverberations, but

Angela's cigarette ashes are certainly among them.) Angela haunts the St. Vincent de Paul Society and grovels for credit at Kathleen O'Connell's shop. She allows herself to be demeaned by hardened social workers in endless lines at the dole, and covers her head to beg for scraps. Frank and his brothers shrivel in humiliation when they watch their mother begging at the door of the Redemptorist priests.

But there is no work for Frankie's Pap, no decent place to live. When Malachy does get work, he drinks his wages away at the local pubs, reminding his wife that she must not send the boys after him to humiliate him: 'A man has his pride'. After a series of downward moves, including almost total rejection by relatives, the family ends up in a ramshackle apartment that reeks from the stench of the adjacent public privy. (The apartment is not too dear for them largely because it stands beside the repository for every chamber pot in the neighborhood). The downstairs, which Pap calls *Ireland*, is largely uninhabitable because it is flooded in the winter and overrun with flies and rats in the summer; the upstairs, which they call *Italy*, is where the family spends most of its time, enjoying their picture of the Pope, burning wood from the walls when it gets cold, and sleeping in stacks on the only bed, covering themselves with overcoats and rags, sleeping on a flea-infested mattress: 'When Dad leaped from the bed and turned on the gaslight we saw the fleas, leaping, jumping, fastened to our flesh. We slapped at them and slapped but they hopped from body to body, hopping, biting. We tore at the bites till they bled' (60). But Frank gets lucky; he contracts typhoid fever and is sent to a hospital by a charity physician. It is the turning point in the boy's life. Three months in the hospital with clean sheets and regular meals are like a vacation. Frankie is given baths with hot water and most wonderful of all, books to read and a friend with whom to share poetry. Most of all he discovers Shakespeare and 'the jewels in my mouth when I say the words'. 'It's lovely to know the world can't interfere with the inside of your head', he reports (196).

Frank McCourt relishes words and uses them to delight his readers with anecdotes so filled with humor, albeit bittersweet humor (the man is Irish after all) that the reader is charmed by the experience. There are characters to rival any created by Dickens. Mr. Timoney, 'who's a little off in the head after years in the sun in the English army in India' engages Frankie to read to him when his own vision fails, beginning with *Gulliver's Travels* and Shakespeare, giving him a private course in English literature and in thinking for himself. There is Aunt Aggie, as bleak and unhappy a woman as you could ever want to meet:

> She was big like the MacNamara sisters, and she had flaming red hair. She wheeled a large bicycle into the little room behind the kitchen and came out to her supper. She was living in Grandma's because she had a fight with her husband, Pa Keating, who told her, when he had drink taken, You're a great fat cow, go home to your mother ... In the morning Aunt Aggie came for her bicycle telling us, 'Will ye mind yeerselves, will ye. Will ye get out of my way? (58-59)

We meet Nora and Peter Molloy. Peter is a great champion. He wins bets in the pubs by drinking more pints than anyone.

> All he has to do is go out to the jakes, stick his finger down his throat and bring it all up so that he can start another round. Peter is such a champion that he can stand in the jakes and throw up without using his finger. He's such a champion they could chop off his fingers and he'd carry on regardless. (114-15)

He wins all that money but he doesn't bring it home. His wife Nora Molloy is often carted off to the lunatic asylum, demented with worry over her famishing family. Frankie points out that 'It's well known that all the lunatics have to be dragged in, but she's the only one that has to be dragged out, back to her five children and champion of all pint drinkers' (115).

There are wonderful stories of priests and schoolmasters, all generally inept and some downright cruel. Even in a literature filled with examples of the breed, McCourt's schoolmasters hang in the mind. There is Mr. Thomas L. O'Halloran who teaches three classes in one room. He has a head like President Roosevelt and he wears gold glasses. He carries a long stick, a pointer, and if you don't pay attention or give a stupid answer, he gives you three slaps on each hand or whacks you across the backs of your legs. He makes you learn everything by heart (207). And consider Mr. O'Neill:

> we call him Dotty because he's small like a dot. He teaches on a platform so he can stand above us and threaten us with his ash plant and peels his apple for all to see, a cruel gesture when the room is filled with starving boys. The first day of school in September he writes on the blackboard three words which are to stay there the rest of the year, Euclid, geometry, idiot. He says if he catches any boy interfering with these words that boy will go through the rest of his life with one hand. He says anyone who doesn't understand the theorems of Euclid is an idiot. (151)

So much for pedagogical sensitivity. Chapter VI, which details a day in geometry class with a student named Question Quigley, is unparalleled. The reader is swept into the moment; he or she is there with Question Quigley and lost in the maze of geometrical idiocy.

The episodes around First Confession and First Communion are painfully funny. Like many a little Catholic, poor Frank gets it all wrong ... or maybe he has it entirely right. 'The master says it's a glorious thing to die for the Faith and Dad says it's a glorious thing to die for Ireland and I wonder if there's anyone in the world who would like us to live' (113). First Communion, according to the adult Catholics, is the happiest day of your life. Frank concurs, 'First Communion day is the happiest of your life because of The Collection [little boys can go from door to door begging for First Communion gifts and donations] and [they can go to the pictures to see] James Cagney at the Lyric Cinema'. Somehow matters spiritual are pretty much lost on the six-year-old. He does find guilt, however, and the confession scenes are among the funniest in the book ... and also the saddest. Only twice does little Frankie find a loving confessor who reaches out

74

to heal the hapless and guilt-ridden child. Later there are stories of star-crossed loves and sexual guilt which hang in the mind like beautiful melodies.

Sometimes McCourt uses black humor to encapsulate troubles that ruin lives and destroy possibilities. For example, little Frankie tells the story of his own conception in the deliriously unhinging language of his own milieu, a language McCourt handles superbly.

> With Angela drawn to [Malachy's] hangdog look and Malachy lonely after three months in jail, there was bound to be a knee-trembler.
> A knee-trembler is the act itself done up against a wall, a man and woman on their toes, straining so hard their knees tremble with the excitement that's in it (15).

So Frankie becomes the near-occasion of his parents' hapless marriage.

By the time he is seven, Frankie is sent to Catherine Street to Mrs. O'Connor's Irish dancing classes, which cost sixpence every Saturday. The fourth Saturday morning Billy Campbell knocks at the door. 'Mrs. McCourt, can Frankie come out to play?' Mam tells him 'No, Billy, Frankie is going to his dancing lesson'.

> [Billy] waits for me at the bottom of Barrack Hill. He wants to know why I'm dancing, that everyone knows dancing is a sissy thing and I'll wind up like Cyril Benson wearing a kilt and medals and dancing all over with girls. I tell him I'm finished with the dancing, that I have sixpence in my pocket ... and we have a great time [at the cinema] looking at *Riders of the Purple Sage*. (143)

Then there is the off-hand story of a friend:

> I'm nine years old and I have a pal, Mickey Spellacy, whose relations are dropping one by one of the galloping consumption. I envy Mickey because every time someone dies in his family he gets a week off from school and his mother stitches a black diamond patch on his sleeve so he can wander from lane to lane ... and people will know he has grief and pat his head, and give him money and sweets for his sorrow. (171-72)

But when the boys don't get invited to Mickey's sister Brenda's wake, they begin another prayer campaign 'that everyone in Mickey Spellacy's family will die in the middle of the summer and he'll never get another day off for the rest of his life'. Frankie reports: 'One of our prayers is surely powerful because next Mickey himself is carried off by the galloping consumption. And he doesn't get a day off from school and that will surely teach him a lesson' (172).

There is no shortage of blarney in McCourt's memories. But there are serious issues as well, where laughter doesn't cover the pain. There is the day Frankie has his first pint; he is sixteen years old.

> The barman at South's remembers me from the time I sat with Mr. Hannon, Bill Galvin, and Uncle Pa Keating. He remembers my father, how he spent his wages and his dole while singing patriotic songs and making speeches from the dock like a condemned rebel.

Uncle Pa lifts his glass, tells the men in the pub, This is my nephew, Frankie McCourt, son of Angela Sheehan, the sister of my wife, having his first pint, here's to your health and long life, Frankie, may you live to enjoy the pint but not too much.

The men lift their pints, nod, drink, and there are creamy lines on their lips and mustaches. I take a great gulp of my pint and Uncle Pa tells me, Slow down for the love o'Jasus, don't drink it all, there's more where that came from as long as the Guinness family stays strong and healthy. (340)

Along with a deep awareness of the strangle-hold alcohol has had over the Irish, *Angela's Ashes* is also an anti-Catholic text. McCourt, like many Irish writers, blames the Catholic Church for a good share of his country's miseries. Speaking of Ireland's major problems he says

It wasn't the English, it was the Catholic Church. It has a lot to answer for ... Roy Foster's history about Ireland is a fine book, but it misses Ireland's major tragedy: The coming of the Catholic Church and the incredible power it was to enjoy for such a long time. All the lives it ruined with its bullying. It left a legacy of retarded sexuality. You can't forgive damage like that.[7]

Speaking of his mother, McCourt says, 'Giving birth to six children, including twins, within five-and-a half years, Angela merely existed ... It was monstrous. Continuous pregnancy. As soon as one had been born, it was a case of "here we go again"' (3). Like many 'recovering Catholics', Frank felt tormented. Fear and trembling. And a sense of doom. A literal belief in hell. That if you, as they say,

interfered with yourself, self-abuse, self-pollution, and you died that night, that's it. Hell for eternity ... I couldn't go to sleep for fear I might die and wake up in hell. I was in agony. I had to divest myself that there's any idea of a ... I had to get rid of any idea of hell. That's what kept me down. So now I just have nothing but contempt for the institution of the church. And the priests who should have known better, who were ... not just of no use to us, they ignored us. Except to threaten us. They were always looking for money. And they lived well. They were nice and fat, glowing. They had cars, they had crates of whiskey and wine delivered to their houses, and they preached poverty. (Saah, 6)

Pete Hamill says that Frank McCourt struggles against what he has called 'the *Green Ceiling*, that repulsive self-limiting strain in Irish life that discourages all dreamers, all those attempting excellence, with the question: *Who do you think you are?*' (Hamill, 45).

There were some positive things about the church, Frank remembers, 'the architecture, the liturgy, the music, the art, such as it was. The atmosphere of miracle, one of mainly mystery, that's what fascinates me, that you can intellectually and theologically, reach a certain point in argument and discourse, but after that, it's a mystery, you have to have faith' (Saah, 6-7). But McCourt values education over faith: 'One of the reasons [Limerick] was such a grim town ... was that it was the only large town in Ireland that didn't have a university. So they put in a university about twenty years ago ... so you see a university booming and the church begins to recede' (9).

76

McCourt's struggle – and actually much of his memoir – will inevitably remind the reader of Joyce's *Portrait of the Artist as a Young Man*. Joyce had his Dublin, McCourt has his Limerick. Comparisons are inescapable, although McCourt argues repeatedly that he was not influenced by Joyce stylistically and that he is 'not one of those James Joyce intellectuals who can stand back and look at the whole edifice [the Church] and say, "I reject that"' (6). After I finished *Angela's Ashes*, I re-read *Portrait of the Artist as a Young Man* to find those places where McCourt was indebted to the master in spite of himself. Certainly the stream-of-consciousness technique bears some resemblance to Joyce, as does the out-of-time nature of the discourse. The voice of the little child is present in Joyce's first pages. Even the lyrics to songs and snatches of Irish poetry, although very different selections, function similarly. The struggle with politics, and more especially Catholicism, also has some parallels to Joyce, although McCourt's work is less cerebral and more emotional in its appeal. And Stephen Dedalus's worst day of misery scarcely reflects Frankie McCourt's best ones. Poverty is, it seems, relative. And Frankie McCourt never plays the intellectual, although there are parallels to Dedalus in his experiences as a young scholar. One clear point of divergence is humor; Joyce's wit is far more restrained than McCourt's. There is a self-consciousness, perhaps more accurately a self-absorption in Joyce that one does not find in McCourt. Frankie hopes only to survive, not to change intellectual and literary history.

McCourt is often asked which authors did influence him and his list is predictable. Shakespeare, of course, and Jonathan Swift. [McCourt set Dean Swift's birthday, November 30, 1995, as his deadline for completing the manuscript of *Angela's Ashes*.] He is especially indebted to Rabelais for style and tone. He likes Thoreau and Emerson; he was influenced by Dickens, Edgar Wallace, Barbara Cartland. He loved Faulkner, Steinbeck, Hemingway ... anybody who was banned in Ireland. He is indebted to Gore Vidal for many things, including the notion that an autobiography is an account of your life whereas a memoir is an 'impression of your life'. He is fond of Irish writers in America: Eugene O'Neill, William Kennedy, Pete Hamill, Jimmy Breslin. McCourt is very careful to steer around any discussion of Joyce and *The Portrait* (Battersby, 2), although any serious reader will notice the parallels. I am interested in the fact that McCourt sees himself as merely a survivor, while Joyce exhibits real expectations of greatness.

To McCourt the project was less about literature then it was about coming to terms with his own origins and forgiving his parents, his country, his religion, and himself for who he is. He asserts that writing the book was a little like 'cleaning out sewers; dredging up stuff. There were parts I wanted to leave out but Malachy [his brother] urged me to leave them in' (Hamill, 44). The book is, after all, entitled *Angela's Ashes*. McCourt says he held the title in the recesses of his mind since he carried his mother's ashes back to Limerick to spread on the family plot in 1981. (Angela came for a visit to the States with baby brother Alfie in 1959 and stayed for 21 years.) McCourt knew that day in Ireland that he had his title. With her ashes he carried his bitterness, his anger, the feeling that life had cheated him. But somehow he realized that the painful process of releasing that anger, and the memories they carried, had to be completed. The book served to disperse Angela's ashes, and his own. And then there was the matter of his father, who had all but deserted the family. Forgiving him would be difficult for everyone. In 1963, Malachy McCourt sent Angela a letter with a view towards a reconciliation. But the miseries persisted. He came to New York on the *Queen Mary* claiming he hadn't had a drink in three years, but he made up for that in Brooklyn. He was probably in every bar in Brooklyn, and then he decided to get amorous with Angela. She started screaming, called the cops and the next morning he was gone on the Queen Mary. Frank McCourt visited him in Belfast in 1971 and saw him one last time in his coffin in the Royal Victoria hospital.

Forgiving his parents for their poverty and neglect was a monumental task for McCourt. Forgiving himself for his own misery and for his marital entanglements [there were two failed marriages before his current marriage to Ellen Fry] was a project of its own. But the book helped him work his way through his own bitterness. In true Irish fashion, McCourt uses laughter to cover lingering deserts of pain, but the residual of suffering and grief is never far from the surface. He often jokes about some of the very impediments to his success, but the attentive reader senses always the irony lingering just below the surface:

> I had menial jobs until I was rescued by the Chinese. They attacked Korea, and I was drafted and sent to Germany for two years. When I came back I applied to New York University, and they let me in because I convinced them I was somewhat literate, which I was compared to most high school graduates at that time. I got my degree and teaching became my life. (45)

And so with the luck of the Irish – and skill, endurance, and ultimately generosity of heart – Frank McCourt has been able to offer *Angela's Ashes* to a large reading public. And the book has been very successful. As critic Linnea Lannon writes, 'Every once in a while, a lucky reader comes across a book that makes an indelible impression, a book you immediately want to share with everyone around you'.[8] *Angela's Ashes* is such a book. Is it great literature? Perhaps only time will tell. But it will certainly hang in the minds of countless readers. It is literate, beguiling, and unforgettable. And it is a reminder to all displaced and oppressed persons that they are not alone. McCourt's years of teaching have made him keenly aware that young people, particularly young American blacks, need to understand that. Humanity is a condition to be shared by all humans. But resolution and affirmation are not only possible, they are mandatory in his version of the universe. No one else will do the healing for us; it is always our own work. McCourt ends his memoir with a tone of forgiveness to family, country, and himself, while at the same time expressing an optimism for the future. He stands on the deck of the *Irish Oak*, bypassing New York City on his return to the States at nineteen:

> A Wireless Officer looks at the lights of America twinkling. He says, 'My God, that was a lovely night, Frank, Isn't this a great country altogether?'
> 'Tis'. (363-64)

Notes

1. Quoted in Pete Hamill, 'Memoir of An Irish Childhood', *Irish America Magazine*, Sept./Oct. 1996, 46.
2. *Angela's Ashes* (New York, NY, Scribner 1996), 11. Hereafter cited in the text.
3. Jim Saah, 'There Once Was A Man From Limerick ... an interview with author Frank McCourt', *Uno MAS Magazine*, 11 June 1997, Info@dualtone.com, 4-5.
4. Kate Tentler, 'Chat With Frank McCourt', *Simon Says*, 2. http://www.simaessays.com/fresh.../chats/uncourt.html.
5. Devon McNamara, 'Son of Ireland Tells His Bittersweet Story', *Christian Science Monitor*, 4 Dec. 1996, 13.
6. Katherine Harrison, 'Angela's Ashes', *Book Page*, http://www.bookpage.com/9609bp/nonfiction/angelasashes.html, 1.
7. Eileen Battersby, 'The Great Anger', *Irish Times on the Web*, 31 Oct 1996, 4.
8. Kate Lannon, 'Growing Up Wretched and Irish and Wise', *The News-Times*, 11 Sept. 1996, 1.

Nationalism and Unionism in Northern Irish Identities in the 1990s: The Interplay of Politics, History, and Culture

Lissi Daber

For non-Irish scholars, the situation in Northern Ireland is not particularly easy to understand. News media usually present a picture of two groups of inhabitants of the territory who have appeared in the recent past to hate one another so intensely that peaceful coexistence was impossible. The current peace seems fragile, uncertain. This essay, completed in June 1998 and based in part on research conducted by the author in Northern Ireland during 1993 and '94, represents her interpretation of the interplay of politics, history and culture in contemporary Northern Irish identities.

Since the mid 1980s, and especially since the election of Mary Robinson as President, the Republic of Ireland has undergone fundamental social and cultural changes. These are mirrored in new Irish writing, in new Irish attitudes and concepts of self and nation, and, not least, in friendly and confident relations with the close neighbour and 'other', the United Kingdom.

What is of special significance here is that political and emotional ties to Northern Ireland have diminished dramatically, while neither the Republic nor the UK any longer has any economic or territorial interest in claiming Northern Ireland for itself; both state this openly, to the dismay of traditional loyalism and republicanism in the North.

Although their attitudes to Northern Ireland are not based on parallel causes and experiences, British and Irish interests have never been so close this century as they are today. Both states are simultaneously willing to co-operate to reach a disinterested settlement, showing a rare common readiness to create long-term stability in Northern Ireland by locking the Northern Irish parties into a peace settlement of their own choice, and not one dictated by special British or Irish interests.

So if the old interpretation of the Northern Irish conflict as the final battlefield between unsolved Irish and British animosities held good, might we not now expect a speedy end to the conflict as a result of the changed perceptions by the two external actors? Similarly, might not Northern Ireland be expected to benefit from its geographical position as mediator, or 'cultural corridor'[1] between Ireland and Great Britain? Yet neither of these things seems to be the case.

1. The Reality of Northern Ireland

The reality of Northern Ireland, in spite of considerable improvements as regards old Catholic grievances about discrimination and second rate citizenship, is an increase in polarisation of attitudes and residential segregation, and a strengthening of political fundamentalist positions, as seen for example at the Forum elections in 1996 and the general election in May 1997. Nationalists and unionists share feelings of mistrust and uncertainty about Britain's motivations and intentions today.

At times of increased tension, for example during the marching seasons of the summers of 1996 and 1997, claims and accusations tend to take on distinctly sectarian overtones, while the Royal Ulster Constabulary often appears to operate on sectarian principles, and not as a neutral police body. This is a situation that is difficult to begin to change. But the Peace Agreement of April 10th, 1998, and the strong 71 per cent 'yes' vote for the agreement on May 22nd, may be just such a beginning: the agreement constitutes a framework for political co-operation between the parties in the North and between Northern Ireland and the Irish Republic which may, in the long term, put the relationship between people in the North on a different footing, and bring about a sense of shared identity and place.

Police records show that there has been a steady increase in loyalist marches in the past ten years, so that they now number well over 3,000 annually. The figures also show a vast imbalance between the number of marches and parades held by the two communities. Loyalist marches outnumber republican ones by 9 to 1.[2] The marching season now spans the period from Easter to early autumn. The right to march has become a highly contentious issue; as Barry White wrote on July 19, 1996, in *The Belfast Telegraph*, it is a manifestation of division and power:

> We have no common nationality to rediscover, and the two mother countries we look to regard us as aliens. The lesson of last week was that if we can't learn to tolerate our differences, and find some way of accommodating our conflicting aspirations, we'll destroy ourselves, either in an all-out conflagration or a slow death.[3]

The past 30 years have seen the establishment and perpetuation of a culture of violence, where violence has altered social norms and behaviour. Solutions to social problems are not necessarily reached through negotiation and compromise, as is clear from the continuation of 'policing' and punishment beatings by paramilitaries, even in times of cease-fire, and the more or less overt acceptance of the use of violence to achieve political ends. This affects everybody, not just active participants in or supporters of violence.

The culture of violence is also manifested passively. Those who oppose it, even by the act of opposition, are also subject to it. Hence many people react to the culture of violence by seeking either to deny or escape it – through emigration, or internal migration (as, for example, the middle-classes' gravitation to suburbs when inner cities become too violent), or mentally turning off. In Northern Ireland, for example, there was a measurable decline in the willingness of people to watch the local television during the height of the Troubles. These denials are also part of the culture of violence.[4]

For a culture of violence to begin to move towards a culture of sharing or of co-existence and mutual acceptance, not to speak of a common culture, entails much more than just the absence of violence. A shared project, feelings of there being sufficient common ground, and agreed changes and common goals are all necessary prerequisites for a shift away from established sectarian attitudes, and from strong and frequently reinforced feelings of mistrust and fear. Until now, there has been a resistance to change: a resistance based on sectarianism, partiality, and pervasive distrust.

Martyn Turner, *The Irish Times*, 1995

The cultural divide in Northern Ireland is very real, and has it own dynamic. On the whole, community relations in the 1990s appear to have worsened, in spite of an enormous amount of good intentions and hard work on the part of individuals and organisations.

This worsening ... is because when the bombings and shootings were common, the majority on 'both sides' transferred all culpability to the paramilitaries: if only they would stop, this would be a great wee place. And then they did stop. And the silent majority became vocal. And the voices were discordant.[5]

In Northern Ireland there was considerable distrust of the political process itself, partly because of wasted opportunities following the first IRA cease-fire in 1994 and earlier, and partly because of the very different priorities and solutions of the two communities for a lasting settlement. According to the 1997 Queen's University/Rowntree Survey Report, it would appear that the British and Irish governments, who set up the Stormont talks, 'and the politicians elected to take part, were not focusing on the issues that are of the greatest importance to their respective communities'.[6]

So much divides the people of Northern Ireland that as confidence-building or trust-building measures, talks ought perhaps to have concentrated at first on issues that receive high priorities on both sides, such as a Bill of Rights that guarantees equality for all and protects each community's culture, and a right to choose integrated education. It would seem that much preliminary ground-work had to be in place before the big issues as regards constitutional belonging (to Britain or Ireland) and political structure could really be tackled. There were, after all, mutually exclusive aspirations at stake here; there exists very little middle ground in Northern Irish politics, just as there is no floating vote on the constitutional question. So the revision of the Irish constitution from staking 'a claim' on Northern Ireland to one of 'future aspiration of unity in the event of consent' significantly changed the question and most contentious issue.

The Northern Irish parties taking part in the recent very difficult but success-fully concluded talks were in a curious double bind. On the one hand, they could not afford to be seen to be unwilling to negotiate; on the other hand there was a fear of the political peace process itself, a fear that negotiation might lead to unacceptable compromise. For nationalists, being forced to accept partition might be such an unacceptable compromise, just as some hard-core unionists would find unacceptable any Dublin role in a future settlement. Sinn Fein was constitution-ally restricted from taking their seats in any partitionist body[7] till the Dublin Ard fheis voted overwhelmingly to end abstentionism, and thus paved the way for the inclusion of Sinn Fein in a future government of Northern Ireland. This is not so much a matter of allowing terrorists to participate in politics, as some commenta-tors have feared, but rather one of removing 'the cause' from the terrorists, or of redefining that cause.

It is, of course, admirable that Tony Blair and Mo Mowlam have acknowledged Britain's responsibility and involved themselves personally in Northern Ireland. However, there are mindsets to be reckoned with, and old attitudes may defeat the best-intentioned solutions. In the events leading up to the Northern Ireland Agreement, the various parties had a veto of sorts over the outcome. The Democratic Unionist Party attempted to exercise such a veto by boycotting the talks and mounting a massive 'no' campaign. Sinn Fein could have been forced to refuse to take their seats in a newly elected Northern Irish Assembly; after all, abstentionism is an old republican tradition. If mainstream republicanism and loyalism are not active parties to any future agreement or settlement, it will endanger lasting peace.

2. Identity as Difference

The mutually exclusive political and constitutional aspirations for the future on the part of different groups in Northern Ireland and their very different interpretations of the past help to explain why national identity there is formed just as much on the basis of what *it is not* as on what *it is*; identity in Northern Ireland *is* difference, and must always be formed in close contact with what is considered 'the other'. The social categorization process in Northern Ireland is a division of people into groups which is made for historical and economic reasons. It has taken on strong cultural and ethnic overtones, because it offers a definition of 'us' and a characterization of 'them' as mutually exclusive categories, with strong group demands and loyalties being passed down through the generations. Thus, Ken Maginnis of the Ulster Unionist Party in a recent Ulster Television interview criticized young unionists for being bigoted extremists with attitudes like 'only people who hate Taigs (i.e. Catholics) should represent unionists'.[8]

The two groups in Northern Ireland are today sometimes euphemistically referred to as 'two traditions' (the new politically correct expression); though much more than tradition is at stake, tradition is frequently invoked as justification for action, and both sides stress and celebrate different myths, symbols, and values, sometimes to the point of cultivating or inventing difference. They are also very much aware of which myths, symbols, and values to ascribe to the out-group/the other side. A sophisticated system of 'telling' has evolved in Northern Ireland, whereby – through cues like first name, address, family background, accent, and school attended – people can easily be placed in their respective groups, and a whole set of values and attitudes automatically ascribed to them. John O'Farrell, the editor of *Fortnight*, calls this 'the partition no amount of talking can unite'; he says that 'Politically, the partition of Ireland has been a dismal failure; culturally it has succeeded beyond the wildest dreams of its instigators'.[9]

If we consider nationalism to be a cultural construct, then national identity must ultimately be defined in cultural terms. However, in a Northern Irish context, the terms *nationalist* and *nationalism* denote Catholics and Irish Catholicism. The Irish use of the term *nationalist* goes back to the mid- and late-19th century fight for home rule, and of course entailed anti-British and, ultimately, anti-Protestant attitudes, particularly in Ulster after the Ulster Unionists at the time of partition got worried about their future position and managed to secure for themselves a large slice of Ireland, and were allowed to do so by the British.

In the ensuing Orange State the majority community ruled: the law was theirs, the Stormont Parliament and most political institutions were theirs, the minority could be effectively ignored, and to begin with chose to be ignored politically, as they did not accept partition. So whereas a century and a half earlier, Ulster Protestants had been among the loudest campaigners against British rule, and had seen themselves as Ulster Irish liberal nationalists, they now disassociated themselves from everything Irish and nationalist, and stressed their British and Protestant identity. As a result, a polarized sectarian society emerged in the North, where the state played the key role in structuring sectarian relations, and made no secret of this. From the beginning, the *raison d'être* of Northern Ireland was sectarian. Several Northern Irish sociologists and historians have questioned whether – given its nature and structure – Northern Ireland can be reformed at all.

The weakening of the links between the state and Orangeism/Unionism since direct rule from Westminster was introduced in 1972 has caused substantial changes in cultural and political identity within the Protestant/Unionist/Loyalist community, just as the increased opportunity to work with and for the state has encouraged changes on the Catholic/Nationalist/Republican side, particularly within the newly emerging Catholic middle-class and within the Catholic Church. But:

> sectarianism continues to structure almost every aspect of life within the six counties – if anything it has intensified since Direct Rule ...The state has intervened to reform some of the more blatant instances of sectarian discrimination. But it has simultaneously vastly increased the capacity of the repressive state apparatus and done nothing to change the sectarian nature of this apparatus.[10]

From the beginning, the uncertainties of the constitutional position of Northern Ireland forced the Protestants to stay firmly and exclusively united, especially in view of the Irish Free State's (later the Irish Republic's) claims and threats questioning the legitimacy of the Northern Irish state.

To a considerable extent the system was to blame: it was fatal to rely on a political system that could easily be manipulated into something resembling apartheid, rather than on civil rights. Northern Ireland has recently been called 'the graveyard of Britain's unwritten constitution'.[11]

Two institutions provided cultural and political identities for the two groups: the Orange Order and the Catholic Church. Both institutions were very conservative in outlook, and both contributed to the exclusive mythologies of both sides. The Catholic view of history stressed exploitation, sacrifice, emigration, and the nationalist fight for self-determination, with Planter and Gael as oppressor and oppressed. Orangeism and unionism stressed the importance of the British connection, and proclaimed their loyalty to crown and country – a loyalty built on myth, since there never was any great attraction to Britain, or similarity of cultures, or love of British life-styles and values; rather, the union was and is important as a protection against inclusion in an all-Irish Catholic state, and one may therefore ask, 'loyalism? loyal to whom and to what?'.

3. Specific Dimensions of Northern Irish 'Culture'

Culture can be defined as the whole set of norms, values, attitudes, mores, behaviours, interpretations of the past, and political ambitions for the future.

In Northern Ireland, *cultural group* and *national group* are often used interchangeably, just as there is a close connection between religion and culture, since religion constitutes part of and gives access to cultural and to political groups. We can say that religion is a badge of cultural and political identity. This is seen, for example, from the fact that religious symbols are typically read and understood politically, which is particularly striking when we look at the murals and graffiti of the ghettoes, e.g. the unionist use of the symbols of the crown and the Bible; and Northern Irish Protestants clearly associate Catholic religious symbols with the wish for a united Ireland.

In my research in Northern Ireland in 1993 and '94, I chose to look at four parameters in order to get an idea of the degree of cultural separation or integration that existed. These parameters were *education, employment, cross-community marriages,* and *territoriality/demography*, and I examined them by comparing data from *observations (field work), interviews,* and *documentary material*. The four parameters of course mutually influence and reinforce each other. Marriage and education are clearly controversial issues. Only one per cent of the children in Northern Ireland attend integrated schools in spite of more than ten years' hard work on the part of the Integrated Schools Movement. Mixed marriage figures vary slightly according to source, being given as 2.3 per cent in the 1991 Census and 6 per cent in the 1989, 1991, 1993, and 1994 Northern Irish Social Attitudes Surveys;[12] this difference may be attributable to differences in whether religion is taken as religion at birth or religion at the time of marriage. It appears from interviews that couples in mixed marriages may face problems of safety, and consequently may have to move away from areas in which they have networks of relationships and family, if those networks are in segregated areas, resulting in the social isolation of the couple. The very fact that organisations exist to support and advise couples contemplating marriage 'across the boundary' indicates that it is problematic.

However, the territorial aspect proved most significant for identities and attitudes in Northern Ireland. This underlines the importance of using field work in order to gain an idea of popular sentiments and reactions; bottom-up dialogue in Northern Ireland has been very limited, and attitudes 'from below' tend to be disregarded, which, on the one hand, is a sign of arrogance, and, on the other, may be detrimental to any solutions or change.

It is important to distinguish between *the Northern Irish problem* on the one hand and *the Northern Irish conflict* on the other. *The Northern Irish problem* has existed since the partition of Ireland and the establishment of Northern Ireland in 1922, and it concerns the state's constitution, its political structure and government, and civil rights. *The Northern Irish conflict* broke out in 1968 as a result of discrimination against Catholics, and quickly led to armed conflict, with paramilitary groups being formed on both sides. Reading journalistic accounts from recent years, especially continental ones, one occasionally gets the impression that if only peace were declared, the British army withdrawn, and paramilitary arms decommissioned, then the conflict would be resolved. This is, of course, only partly true. What remains is the difficult unfinished business of Northern Ireland's political structure and constitutional belonging, where, as already mentioned, attitudes can be very confrontational and with very little middle ground. This is where the inheritance from a rather hasty partition of Ireland enters the picture, a partition with very little in the way of hearings, with no plebiscite, which resulted in a polarization of the population from the very beginning. This polarization has been strongly reinforced by the built-in discrimination against the Catholic minority group during the first fifty years of Northern Ireland's existence, and also by the constant, and slightly neurotic, focusing on 'head counts', that is 'how many are we', 'how many are they'. This has resulted in attitudes and mentalities which emphasise differences without respecting them, which confuse myth with history, and which endow members with group identities and strong group loyalties.

This became obvious during the 17 months of cease-fire 1994-96. The cease-fire changed very little, as none of the underlying political problems were tackled, there was no working towards political goals (nor even attempts at defining political goals), and the cease-fire was not tied in with negotiations. Consequently, when the IRA took up arms again in February 1996, everything was quickly back to square one.

In a paper entitled 'Decommissioning the potential for conflict' published by the Mitchell Commission in January 1996, Harri Holkeri, the Finnish member of the Commission, stressed that 'what is really needed is the decommissioning of mind-sets and mentalities in Northern Ireland'. The Commission recommended immediate negotiations with all groups present, in an acknowledgement of all aspirations, however contradictory these might be.

Events from recent marching seasons also show that deep-rooted attitudes of fear and distrust still characterize large sections of Northern Irish society, and that polarization and majority dominance are still central issues. This is perhaps understandable: little has happened to change or challenge people's thought-processes, and the rhetoric of many of the politicians has been confrontational and traditional, showing up the so-called 'peace process' as so much hot air. The very fact that the Orange Order and the Apprentice Boys and their loyalist supporters want to march and insist on marching, even when this is seen as confrontational and as triumphalist, indicates a fear of accommodation, a fear that listening to the other side might involve some kind of compromise or sell-out. There is a rationale or a logic of the old 'zero-sum game' or double minority situation here: a Protestant majority acting and behaving as if they were a threatened minority.

Parading is often claimed to be a specific feature of Orange or loyalist culture, and a parade an expression of Orange culture. The implication of this statement is that parading is not a feature of nationalist culture. But the discrepancy between the number of loyalist and nationalist parades can also be related to the broader political history of Ireland. The imbalance of power in the north has historically been used to constrain nationalist and republican parades, while loyalists have come to regard parading as a key element of their culture and an expression of their inalienable civil rights and liberties. Loyalists expect to be able to march where and when they will in their country; but they regard nationalist parades as a threat to public order. Loyalist parades are inevitably presented as cultural and traditional rather than political, while nationalist, and in particular republican, parades are seen as political and therefore provocative and confrontational. Traditional parades are presented as unproblematic and uncontentious, whereas political parades need to be carefully policed and constrained. The opportunity to demand and to exercise the right to march is thus a symbol of the distribution of political power in Northern Ireland. Tradition is invoked wherever possible, while the language of politics is avoided.[13]

So culture has become a significant element in the continuance of the conflict in Northern Ireland, just as culture was a significant element in last century's long campaign for home rule and independence. As Dominic Murray claims,

it is not difference itself that causes problems, but rather people's inability – for various reasons – to handle difference. Nor is it the existence of differing cultures that sustains violence, but rather the associations and appendages which accompany their manifestations. An Orange parade provides a good example of this. To the people involved it may be seen as a natural and enjoyable demonstration and celebration of Protestant culture and tradition. However, in a divided society, the enactment of such ritual is less important than how it is perceived. Nationalists may (and do) see such events as examples of Protestant ascendancy, cultural dominance, and as coat-trailing exercises.[14]

A Protestant march will be seen as an exercise in 'staking out their territory', and 'showing who is boss' by nationalists. So symbols, as manifestations of cultural identity, are very important in Northern Ireland, and divisions are highlighted by marches, which can sometimes take on distinct tribal overtones.

As it is the group that is important, the Northern Irish conflict is a *group* conflict and not an *individual* conflict and it is the groups' mutually exclusive interpretations and aspirations that are problematic – we find parallel sets of cultural symbols, of myths, heroes, martyrs, songs, marching rituals, banners, and institutions to cement the group identities and uphold group prejudices. Group identity (Protestant or Catholic) is salient in Northern Ireland.

The issue of territorial segregation in Northern Ireland, the very nature of the separated areas or ghettoes, the way they function and perceive themselves, came as a surprise to me, because what matters in Northern Ireland is the reality of perception rather than the actual reality of events. So although you either live with 'the other', or are surrounded by 'the other', there are very fixed ideas concerning what this 'other' consists of, what characterizes it and its actions. Representation of 'the other' tends to be stereotypical.

In the Protestant areas of Donegall Pass, Tiger's Bay, and the Shankill Road of Belfast, the attitude prevails that the Catholics are getting favourable treatment everywhere, that they are taking over houses, jobs, educational places, etc., in short, that they are taking over or 'winning', however many statistics on higher Catholic unemployment rates one may quote.

There is considerable mistrust of the work of the Community Relations Council and the Fair Employment Agency. The population figures of these areas are falling, but this is mainly due to slum clearance and the fact that more well-to-do Protestants move out to the new housing estates on the outskirts of the city. The 'greening' of Queen's University (55 per cent Catholic students today) is not a result of special treatment, but of the fact that young Protestants tend to study at British universities on the mainland. There is a strong feeling among the Protestants that their state, Ulster, for whose survival they have worked and fought hard and loyally, and in relation to which the Catholic population was regarded as disloyal, is getting 'greener', that is more Irish. What used to be understood as being their proud and Protestant state and their proud and Protestant industrial city no longer feels this way for the Protestant working class. They interpret their situation as one of loss, and see themselves as surrounded and threatened, or at best disregarded. Many fear change and are uncertain about the future. This is again the problem of 'head counts' and the thinking that one side's gain must entail the other side's loss, because there is felt to be so little common ground, and because regarding 'the other' as the enemy is such a well-internalized response.

It is sometimes said jokingly that in Northern Ireland the Catholics have culture and the Protestants have politics, except that Protestants do not really have politics any more; direct rule and successful activities by the many local community groups have seen to that.

On the Catholic side, in spite of some success stories and a much less homogeneous population group today,[15] there is still strong distrust of the state and a sense of minority status, especially in the Catholic areas of North and West Belfast and some border regions, and a sense of not having benefitted much from the changes of recent years. Fear of a Stormont revival in any form is latent, and is perhaps even strengthened by unionist conservatism and Protestant uncertainty about the future. It is interesting that in recent years a spate of books has been published analysing and redefining Unionism, so-called New Unionism, Liberal Unionism, and Unionist/Protestant identity.[16]

From my interviews and observations in the ghettoes, the significance of yet a further division became clear, namely the old one of class.[17]

There is a strong sense in the segregated areas that they have been let down by the middle classes, whom they see as opting out and just making money and leading the good life; that it is the people of the ghettoes who are made to bear the brunt of the conflict and who are economically deprived, and that peace money and special aid rarely trickles down to them. They may have a point. Quite a number of people profit considerably from the conflict in various ways and are only slightly inconvenienced by it, though they will of course pay lip-service to the horrors of terrorism and the embarrassment of punishment beatings.

Sectarianism is a 'bad', almost a taboo, word, especially in middle-class and intellectual circles, and a certain amount of denial seems to be taking place, or explaining away of atrocities as examples of individual psychopathic or irrational action. However, sectarianism should not be regarded as a question of isolated evil deeds by paramilitaries, but must rightly be seen in the context of complex social phenomena and old-established structures and mindsets. Perhaps the lessons and messages sent out by the unionist establishment in the old days, when it 'played the Orange card', were learnt too well.

Even if the two old life-lines to Great Britain and the Irish Republic respectively are loosened considerably today – with lack of interest in the North and no wish for a united Ireland on the part of the Republic, with the nationalist project, originating in a pre-modern pious romantic rural Ireland, having proved a complete failure and having been largely abandoned by modern Irish politicians in favour of a 'new Ireland', and with the Downing Street Declaration's statement that the British government has no selfish strategic or economic interest in Northern Ireland – this has not really contributed to an opening up of mentalities or group identities in relation to traditional aspirations and uncertainties.

Harri Holkeri's claim that what needs to be decommissioned is mind-sets is perhaps a little facile and begs the question of how one should set about decommissioning mind-sets anyway. The many well-intentioned initiatives on the part of the Community Relations 'industry' cannot stand alone, and absence of conflict and modification of enemy images and change of attitudes to in-group and out-group are, in themselves, extremely slow processes. It would also involve some understanding by the people of Northern Ireland of how the present creates the past, that is an awareness of how selectively appropriated and selectively remembered – or invented – histories and mythologies form the bases for cultural identities.

But what is needed first and foremost, and needed urgently, is a plausible framework to define the future relationship between the two communities, so that people may begin to feel secure enough to let go of the past and the inflexible positions of that past. At the time of writing, it is a question whether the Good Friday Agreement and the referendum result of Great Friday 1998 can begin to achieve this. It needs strong public support for these to constitute a real break-through and provide the possibilities of long-term peace. It seems that the referendum result of 71 per cent 'yes' and 28 per cent 'no' is a strong indicator of a readiness for change and a willingness to begin to work together.

There is understandable international enthusiasm and optimism about the agreement, and similar reactions among the majority of people in Northern

Ireland. However, it should be remembered that the quite considerable 'no' vote may constitute a risk for the successful operation of a future elected Northern Irish assembly. At the time of writing, there is a debate on the different interpretations of the 'no' vote, with unionists arguing over who speaks for unionism, echoing the old mentalities. So even though there was a strong 'yes'-vote, it is not a clear-cut approval. It would appear that Ian Paisley will not take no for an answer, and he will go down shouting 'no surrender'.

There was a discussion in the early nineties about whether the European project could perhaps constitute a framework for peace in Northern Ireland, or help define one; or whether a shared European dimension within a Europe of the regions could help diffuse the situation in Northern Ireland. The questioning of identity, sovereignty, and loss of independence may put the question of self-determination in a new light for the people of both Ireland and Britain. But, on the other hand, the nature of much present-day political debate in Great Britain about Europe and European membership is not very promising.

All that can be said is that there is certainly considerable Euro-enthusiasm in the North, even if this seems mainly to spring from the economic benefits of EU membership. So far, the EU has not played a significant political role in Northern Ireland, and it is indeed difficult to see any outside actor as Northern Irish problem solver, although increased economic cross-border activity may eventually lead to an erosion of the political significance of the border, and perhaps help redefine it.

4. 'Negative Definitions' of Identity

As yet it has been difficult, if not downright impossible, for many in Northern Ireland to acknowledge that identity is not static, unchangeable, and impervious to outside influence. Identity in Northern Ireland is fossilized: a fixed, well-established, narrow, inclusive construction, shaped around tokenism and symbolism. It is something which people do not question, do not challenge, and rarely joke about, precisely because of the siege mentalities, of perceived threats to culture and identity, and of the cultivation, for political reasons, of difference. So much Northern Irish discourse about culture and identity has been expressed in terms of what you are *not*, just as so much political discourse is expressed in terms of what you do *not* want – what I call the Northern Irish 'negative definitions', such as 'no surrender', 'not an inch', 'Ulster says no' – rather than in terms of what you are and what you *do* want. The mural from the Sandy Row area of central Belfast from 1996 illustrates this attitude of negativity.

It also shows how terms have special meanings in Northern Irish discourse: the concept 'cultural identity' in the mural could be translated as 'political aspiration', and the term 'Irish' is often taken to mean a united, Catholic-dominated Ireland, or as referring to the South.

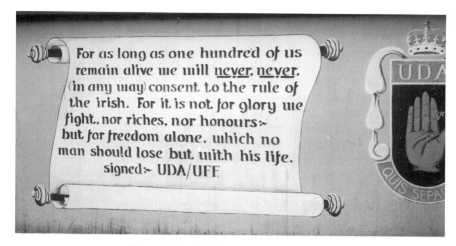

For as long as one hundred of us remain alive we will never, never, (in any way) consent to the rule of the Irish. For it is not for glory we fight, nor riches, nor honours:- but for freedom alone, which no man should lose but with his life.
signed:- UDA/UFF

Photo: Lissi Daber, November 1996

Irish nationalism and unionist nationalism differ in two fundamental respects. It is actually questionable whether they are parallel or comparable movements at all. Where the Irish nationalist or republican demand is for the classic 'freedom' and independence, sovereignty and self-determination, and democratic and civil rights – an internationally understood and a recognized cause to which the world is implicitly sympathetic – unionist nationalism or loyalism is of a different kind and speaks a different language, much less able to command international recognition and sympathy. Unionist nationalism is unique in the sense that it is non-territorial. The last thing the unionists want is independence; instead, they would prefer stronger integration into the UK. This is where the importance of the unity of the crown and Bible comes in. Traditional unionist Orange Order ideology is best understood as an expression of fundamentalist Protestantism: a persecuted, misunderstood, and innocent God-fearing people doing battle against evil, in the shapes of republicanism, Catholicism, or mere secularism. Thus the Free Presbyterian Church of Ulster claimed a few days before the referendum that the April agreement has 'hallmarks of devilish craft', and 'is unscriptural, unethical and immoral'.[18] This kind of discourse, with its tendency to read back the events in Northern Ireland into a mythical reading of the Bible, is incomprehensible or anachronistic to the world at large.

On a much more down-to-earth level it should also be remembered that until recently unionists did not need to justify themselves, to argue their case, or convince the world of their just cause. Northern Ireland was theirs, and they ran it. This inexperience at telling *their* story is perhaps a contributory factor to the 'Ulster says no'-discourse. Irish nationalism, on the other hand, had the world's ear and sympathy, and the famous 'gift of the gab' to put *their* case. If we add to this traditional unionists' fear of a British sell-out, then their mistrust and alienation perhaps become understandable. The frequently used 'God Save

Ulster' took on a different meaning from the time of the Anglo-Irish agreement of 1985, once the old friend began to appear more like an enemy; and loyalists expressed their loyalty to Britain by being disloyal to her wishes.

The new optimistic sense of being Irish, and the openness or healthy indifference about Irish-Irish, British-Irish, Anglo-Irish, or whatever, in the Irish Republic, cannot really penetrate into the North, because of the continued uncertain political climate of Northern Ireland. But now the situation may begin to change. The possibilities for change are there: the nature of the debate leading up to the May referendum, the size of the 'yes' and 'no' vote, and the reactions to the referendum results give an indication of where Northern Ireland is moving, and, hopefully, this will justify the initial optimism and so generate its own momentum.

What is significant is that, for the first time, the referendum result cuts across the old divisions, as the 'yes' group comprises not only almost all nationalists and but also the majority of unionists. It thus reflects an entirely new constellation.

Gerry Adams of Sinn Fein and David Trimble of the Unionist Party have managed to redefine their parties' positions and get popular backing for these changes, even if the Unionists are divided. However, this is perhaps as much a generational change as an attitudinal shift. The old politicians such as William Thompson, Robert McCartney and Ian Paisley, with their unforgiving rhetoric and angry refusals to accept the referendum result, and their bitter pledges to wreck the new assembly, were clearly given the message that they do not any longer speak for the people they claim to represent. The result of the referendum seems to suggest that they should withdraw and let a younger generation of politicians carry out the wishes of the large 'yes' majority, so that politics in Northern Ireland may enter a new stage of a common middle-ground, which could in turn eventually spill over into and contribute to changes in attitudes and identities.

That is why it is vital that people should stick to the 'yes' politicians and make the Assembly workable, so that it may generate a sense of confidence in a new and stable Northern Ireland.

The Northern Irish peace is a fragile peace. It is clear that many people gave a lot of thought to their response to the peace agreement. It was perhaps a choice between an unknown but different future, and a going back into the all too well-known darkness that had begun no longer to make sense. It was certainly striking that many relatives of victims, terrorist prisoners, and ex-paramilitary politicians campaigned very strongly for a 'yes'. Even if there was much understandable rejoicing after the referendum result, there is clearly also apprehension about the future and about what change will bring. Most especially, there is a very realistic sense of all the difficulties still to be faced.

'Protestant' and 'Catholic' will still be salient groups, but difference may become an accepted and unthreatening reality of the North. After all, 'Peace in Northern Ireland has to be built on its divisions, not on a fiction of unity which does not yet exist'.[19]

Notes

1. Edna Longley's metaphor, from *From Cathleen to Anorexia – The Breakdown of Irelands* (Dublin: Attic Press, 1990).
2. Neil Jarman, *Material Conflicts: Parades and Visual Displays in Northern Ireland* (Oxford: Berg Publishers, 1997).
3. Barry White in *The Belfast Telegraph*, 19th July, 1996.
4. John Darby, *Scorpions in a Bottle, Conflicting Cultures in Northern Ireland* (London: Minority Rights Publications, 1997), 117-18.
5. John O'Farrell, 'Reinventing Partition', *Index on Censorship*, 6 (1997), 154.
6. Colin Irwin, *The Search for a Settlement, The People's Choice* (Belfast, The Queen's University/Rowntree Survey Report produced by Fortnight Educational Trust, 1998), 3.
7. Gerry Adams in *The Irish News*, 24th March, 1998.
8. Ken Maginnis in *Hearts and Minds: The Future of Northern Ireland*, BBC2 documentary, 24th October, 1996.
9. O'Farrell, 151.
10. Robbie McVeigh, 'Cherishing the Children of the Nation Unequally: Sectarianism in Ireland', in Patrick Clancy *et al.* (eds), *Irish Society, Sociological Perspectives* (Dublin: Institute of Public Administration, 1995), 631.
11. Kevin Boyle, 'The Irish Question and Human Rights in European Perspectives', in Harald Olav Skar and Bjørn Lydersen (eds), *Northern Ireland: A Crucial Test for a Europe of Peaceful Regions?* (Oslo: Norwegian Institute of International Affairs, 1993), 94.
12. Valerie Morgan, Marie Smyth, Gillian Robinson and Grace Fraser, *Mixed Marriages in Northern Ireland* (Coleraine: Centre for the Study of Conflict at The University of Ulster, 1996), 4.
13. Neil Jarman, *op. cit.*
14. Dominic Murray, 'Culture, Religion and Violence in Northern Ireland', in Seamus Dunn (ed.), *Facets of the Conflict in Northern Ireland* (London: Macmillan, 1995).
15. See for example Fionnuala O Connor, *In Search of a State: Catholics in Northern Ireland* (Belfast: Blackstaff Press, 1993).
16. See for example Richard English and Graham Walker (eds), *Unionism in Modern Ireland: New Perspectives on Politics and Culture* (Dublin: Gill and Macmillan, 1996); Norman Porter, *Rethinking Unionism: An Alternative Vision for Northern Ireland* (Belfast: Blackstaff Press, 1996); John D. Cash, *Identity, Ideology, and Conflict: the Structuration of Politics in Northern Ireland* (Cambridge University Press, 1996); and J. Wilson Foster (ed.), *The Idea of the Union: Statements and Critiques in Support of the Union of Great Britain and Northern Ireland* (Vancouver: 1995).
17. Compared to politics and history, the important questions of social class and territorial segregation in Northern Ireland seem to command relatively little interest in recent academic research.
18. Rev. Alan Smylie in *The Irish News*, Belfast, 18th May, 1998.
19. Neal Ascherson in *The Observer*, London, 24th May, 1998.

Northern Ireland Peace Agreement

DECLARATION OF SUPPORT

1. We, the participants in the multi-party negotiations, believe that the agreement we have negotiated offers a truly historic opportunity for a new beginning.

2. The tragedies of the past have left a deep and profoundly regrettable legacy of suffering. We must never forget those who have died or been injured, and their families. But we can best honour them through a fresh start, in which we firmly dedicate ourselves to the achievement of reconciliation, tolerance, and mutual trust, and to the protection and vindication of the human rights of all.

3. We are committed to partnership, equality and mutual respect as the basis of relationships within Northern Ireland, between North and South, and between these islands.

4. We reaffirm our total and absolute commitment to exclusively democratic and peaceful means of resolving differences on political issues, and our opposition to any use or threat of force by others for any political purpose, whether in regard to this agreement or otherwise.

5. We acknowledge the substantial differences between our continuing, and equally legitimate, political aspirations. However, we will endeavour to strive in every practical way towards reconciliation and rapprochement within the framework of democratic and agreed arrangements. We pledge that we will, in good faith, work to ensure the success of each and every one of the arrangements to be established under this agreement. It is accepted that all of the institutional and constitutional arrangements – an Assembly in Northern Ireland, a North/South Ministerial Council, implementation bodies, a British-Irish Council and a British-Irish Intergovernmental Conference and any amendments to British Acts of Parliament and the Constitution of Ireland – are interlocking and interdependent and that in particular the functioning of the Assembly and the North/South Council are so closely inter-related that the success of each depends on that of the other.

6. Accordingly, in a spirit of concord, we strongly commend this agreement to the people, North and South, for their approval.

CONSTITUTIONAL ISSUES

1. The participants endorse the commitment made by the British and Irish Governments that, in a new British-Irish Agreement replacing the Anglo-Irish Agreement, they will:

(i) recognise the legitimacy of whatever choice is freely exercised by a majority of the people of Northern Ireland with regard to its status, whether they prefer to continue to support the Union with Great Britain or a sovereign united Ireland;

(ii) recognise that it is for the people of the island of Ireland alone, by agreement between the two parts respectively and without external impediment, to exercise their right of self-determination on the basis of consent, freely and concurrently given, North and South, to bring about a united Ireland, if that is their wish, accepting that this right must be achieved and exercised with and subject to the agreement and consent of a majority of the people of Northern Ireland;

(iii) acknowledge that while a substantial section of the people in Northern Ireland share the legitimate wish of a majority of the people of the island of Ireland for a united Ireland, the present wish of a majority of the people of Northern Ireland, freely exercised and legitimate, is to maintain the Union and, accordingly, that Northern Ireland's status as part of the United Kingdom reflects and relies upon that wish; and that it would be wrong to make any change in the status of Northern Ireland save with the consent of a majority of its people;

(iv) affirm that if, in the future, the people of the island of Ireland exercise their right of self-determination on the basis set out in sections (i) and (ii) above to bring about a united Ireland, it will be a binding obligation on both Governments to introduce and support in their respective Parliaments legislation to give effect to that wish;

(v) affirm that whatever choice is freely exercised by a majority of the people of Northern Ireland, the power of the sovereign government with jurisdiction there shall be exercised with rigorous impartiality on behalf of all the people in the diversity of their identities and traditions and shall be founded on the principles of full respect for, and equality of, civil, political, social and cultural rights, of freedom from discrimination for all citizens, and of parity of esteem and of just and equal treatment for the identity, ethos, and aspirations of both communities;

(vi) recognise the birthright of all the people of Northern Ireland to identify themselves and be accepted as Irish or British, or both, as they may so choose, and accordingly confirm that their right to hold both British and Irish citizenship is accepted by both Governments and would not be affected by any future change in the status of Northern Ireland.

2. The participants also note that the two Governments have accordingly undertaken in the context of this comprehensive political agreement, to propose and support changes in, respectively, the Constitution of Ireland and in British legislation relating to the constitutional status of Northern Ireland.

ANNEX A

DRAFT CLAUSES/SCHEDULES FOR INCORPORATION IN BRITISH LEGISLATION

1. (1) It is hereby declared that Northern Ireland in its entirety remains part of the United Kingdom and shall not cease to be so without the consent of a majority of the people of Northern Ireland voting in a poll held for the purposes of this section in accordance with Schedule 1.

(2) But if the wish expressed by a majority in such a poll is that Northern Ireland should cease to be part of the United Kingdom and form part of a united Ireland, the Secretary of State shall lay before Parliament such proposals to give effect to that wish as may be agreed between Her Majesty's Government in the United Kingdom and the Government of Ireland.

2. The Government of Ireland Act 1920 is repealed; and this Act shall have effect notwithstanding any other previous enactment.

SCHEDULE 1

POLLS FOR THE PURPOSE OF SECTION 1

1. The Secretary of State may by order direct the holding of a poll for the purposes of section 1 on a date specified in order.

2. Subject to paragraph 3, the Secretary of State shall exercise the power under paragraph 1 if at any time it appears likely to him that a majority of those voting would express a wish that Northern Ireland should cease to be part of the United Kingdom and form part of a united Ireland.

3. The Secretary of State shall not make an order under paragraph 1 earlier than seven years after the holding of a previous poll under this Schedule.

4. (Remaining paragraphs along the lines of paragraphs 2 and 3 of existing Schedule 1 to 1973 Act.)

ANNEX B

IRISH GOVERNMENT DRAFT LEGISLATION TO AMEND THE CONSTITUTION

Add to Article 29 the following sections:

7.

1. The State may consent to be bound by the British-Irish Agreement done at Belfast on the day of 1998, hereinafter called the Agreement.

1. Any institution established by or under the Agreement may exercise the powers and functions thereby conferred on it in respect of all or any part of the island of Ireland notwithstanding any other provision of this Constitution conferring a like power or function on any person or any organ of State appointed under or created or established by or under this Constitution. Any power or function conferred on such an institution in relation to the settlement or resolution of disputes or controversies may be in addition to or in substitution for any like power or function conferred by this Constitution on any such person or organ of State as aforesaid.

1. If the Government declare that the State has become obliged, pursuant to the Agreement, to give effect to the amendment of this Constitution referred to therein, then, notwithstanding Article 46 hereof, this Constitution shall be amended as follows:

i. the following Articles shall be substituted for Articles 2 and 3 of the Irish text:

"2. [Irish text to be inserted here, yet to be drafted.]

3. [Irish text to be inserted here, yet to be drafted.]"

ii. the following Articles shall be substituted for Articles 2 and 3 of the English text:

"Article 2

It is the entitlement and birthright of every person born in the island of Ireland, which includes its islands and seas, to be part of the Irish nation. That is also the entitlement of all persons otherwise qualified in accordance with law to be citizens of Ireland. Furthermore, the Irish nation cherishes its special affinity with people of Irish ancestry living abroad who share its cultural identity and heritage.

Article 3

1. It is the firm will of the Irish nation, in harmony and friendship, to unite all the people who share the territory of the island of Ireland, in all the diversity of their identities and traditions, recognising that a united Ireland shall be brought about only by peaceful means with the consent of a majority of the people, democratically expressed, in both jurisdictions in the island. Until then, the laws enacted by the Parliament established by this Constitution shall have the like area and extent of application as the laws enacted by the Parliament that existed immediately before the coming into operation of this Constitution.

2. Institutions with executive powers and functions that are shared between those jurisdictions may be established by their respective responsible authorities for stated purposes and may exercise powers and functions in respect of all or any part of the island."

iii. the following section shall be added to the Irish text of this Article:

"8. [Irish text to be inserted here, yet to be drafted]"

and

iv. the following section shall be added to the English text of this Article:

"8. The State may exercise extra-territorial jurisdiction in accordance with the generally recognised principles of international law."

4. If a declaration under this section is made, this subsection and subsection 3, other than the amendment of this Constitution effected thereby, and subsection 5 of this section shall be omitted from every official text of this Constitution published thereafter, but notwithstanding such omission this section shall continue to have the force of law.

5. If such a declaration is not made within twelve months of this section being added to this Constitution or such longer period as may be provided for by law, this section shall cease to have effect and shall be omitted from every official text of this Constitution published thereafter.

Part II

Irish Identities:
Literary Representations

Northern Ireland: Poetry and Peace

Edna Longley

I am going to start with a few appearances of the word 'peace' in Irish poetry, and with some questions about what happens when we put poetry and peace together. Then I will outline my understanding of relations between poetry and recent Irish history. I will also briefly indicate a contrary view of how the Northern Irish conflict should be conceived by literary criticism and literary theory. Finally I will discuss four recent poems to see whether or how they qualify as poetry of the 'peace process'; the poems are: 'Jacta Est Alea' by Ciaran Carson, 'Cease-fire' by Michael Longley, 'Credenza' by Medbh McGuckian and 'Tollund' by Seamus Heaney.

A theoretical term that I find useful in discussing poetry from Northern Ireland is 'intertextuality'. But I apply the term in the older sense, which brings it closer to 'tradition', though tradition as metamorphic rather than monolithic. For me, intertextuality denotes a range of ways in which poems talk to one another, criticise one another, revise one another's perspectives, structures, language and images. With reference to a small country like Ireland, it may be easier for poems to communicate in this way. And I see their intertexuality as operating in terms of time and sequence, not of space. As compared with modernist or post-modernist collage, Irish poets more often seem to be working on forms, on tradition, in close proximity to history. And this especially applies to the raised consciousness of history enforced since 1969 by the Troubles, as we call them. At the same time, poetic intertextuality also works on a longer time scale. It may refer back to Homer or to Irish and English poetry written earlier in this century.

1. Poetry and Recent Irish History

In fact, my preliminary case-study of intertextuality begins in the nineteenth century with the English poet Coventry Patmore (1823-1896), initially as mediated by Arthur Symons in a review (January 1897) of Patmore's *Religio Poetae*. Symons discusses 'that joy which [Patmore] notes as the mark of fine art, that peace, which to him was the sign of great art, themselves the most final of the emotions [and which] interpenetrated for him the whole substance of thought, aspiration, even argument'.[1] Yeats writes in 'Samhain: 1905': 'If we understand our own minds, and the things that are striving to utter themselves through our minds, we move others, not because we have understood or thought about those others, but because all life has the same root. Coventry Patmore has said, "The end of art is peace", and the following of art is little different from the following of religion in the intense preoccupation that it demands'. In this passage Yeats is reflecting on the tension between art and 'opinion': an issue which engaged him throughout the struggles between his literary movement and Irish political ideologies. He sees the artistic enterprise as necessarily quarantining 'all opinion that [a poet] holds to merely because it is right, out of his poetry if it is to be poetry at all', and equates oratory with 'insincerity'.[2] Here peace characterises the inner state of the artist rather than the effects of art in the outer world. In a cognate passage Yeats writes: 'there is only one perfection and only one search for perfection, and it sometimes has the form of the religious life and sometimes of the artistic life; and I do not think these lives differ in their wages, for "The end of art is peace," and out of the one as out of the other comes the cry: *Sero te amavi, Pulchritudo tam antiqua et tam nova! Sero te amavi!*'[3]

Yeats's later poetic use of 'The end of art is peace' (in 'To a Wealthy Man who promised a Second Subscription to the Dublin Municipal Gallery if it were proved the People wanted Pictures') suggests that the reception of his work, and of the Revival more generally, has made it difficult for him to maintain this opposition between the religion of art and the public world, between cloister and agora. What he sees as emanating from the cloister is received politically:

> And when they drove out Cosimo,
> Indifferent how the rancour ran,
> He gave the hours they had set free
> To Michelozzo's latest plan
> For the San Marco Library,
> Whence turbulent Italy should draw
> Delight in Art whose end is peace,
> In logic and in natural law
> By sucking at the dugs of Greece.[4]

'To a Wealthy Man' was written at the end of 1912. The 'rancour' of this volcanic year had included not only the controversy over a gallery for Hugh Lane's impressionist pictures, but also the signing of a massive Covenant by Ulster Protestants opposed to Irish Home Rule. Despite his nationalism, Yeats understood fears of Catholic hegemony in an independent Ireland, and he wrote in December 1912:

> I often see the life of Ireland today (so full it seems to me of prejudices and ignorances in all matters of science, politics and literature) under the image of a stagnant stream where there drifts among the duckweed, pieces of rotting wood, a dead dog or two, various rusty cans, and many old boots. Now, among the old boots drifting along there are a very objectionable pair, Catholic and Protestant bigotry.[5]

104

This may explain why 'To a Wealthy Man' is not itself a very peaceful poem. The speaker's polemic is inflected, even infected, by rancour and turbulence that belongs to Ireland rather than Italy. 'Indifference' seems harder won than 'intense preoccupation' some years earlier. Yet the speaker's effort to subdue his own 'rancour' may tell us something about the public meaning of 'peace'. Yeats's identification with Cosimo di Medici enables him to quarantine opinion in a different way: in the name of a longer-term cultural agenda that sees beyond the tunnel-vision of politics. Here the relation between art and peace is represented not as a religious given but as an educational outcome. And the education of 'ignorances and prejudices' through 'delight' also involves logic and natural law as well as art – the full Renaissance package.

The last stanza of Seamus Heaney's 'The Harvest Bow' picks up on Yeats in a related context of political turbulence sixty-seven years later:

> *The end of art is peace*
> Could be the motto of this frail device
> That I have pinned up on our deal dresser –
> Like a drawn snare
> Slipped lately by the spirit of the corn
> Yet burnished by its passage, and still warm.[6]

'The Harvest Bow' takes 'The end of art is peace' out of libraries and galleries into a poetic environment which allows Heaney to exploit traditional links between peace and pastoral. The image which the poem explores, and which also constitutes its self-image, is an artefact made by the poet's father. A harvest bow is fashioned from the corn of one year's harvest to bring luck to next year's crop. Here art resides in folk-art, and some form of 'spirit' resides in that. The 'spirit of the corn' as captured in the harvest bow ratifies a transaction between humanity and nature. The love between father and son, crystallised by memories of walking 'Into an evening of long grass and midges', adds to the resonances of 'peace'. Heaney implicitly represents the Troubles as violating all the bonds signified by the bow's 'golden loops', and as putting poetry itself under strain. Nonetheless, when he hypothetically pins 'The end of art is peace' on the 'frail device' of his own poem, he insinuates that poetry cannot but harbour a positive spirit that goes into its making. If art points towards peace, it does so by virtue of a human 'warmth' intrinsic to the personal and communal impulses that condition the poetic act.

By the time 'The end of art is peace' reaches Paul Durcan, a decade and a half later, it is obliged to jostle with more disquieting refrains:

> I take pride in my work;
> Delight in art whose end is peace;
> The way I lead out a song;
> The way I hold the reins of a song in my hands ...

I in my red blanket
Under the Cave Hill Mountain
leading out the Grey of the Blues:
The blindness of history in my eyes;
The blindness of history in my hands.[7]

The speaker of this poem, 'The Riding School' after (a painting by) Karel Dujardin, combines the personae of poet and groom. Since Pegasus presumably links these roles, other intertextual vistas connect 'The Riding School' with Yeats's 'The Fascination of What's Difficult' ('There's something ails our colt') and his representation of poet-rebels in 'Easter 1916' ('This man had kept a school/ And rode our wingèd horse'), and Patrick Kavanagh's poem 'Pegasus'. At first the Yeats-Patmore line 'Delight in art whose end is peace' functions as a charmed mantra endorsing the singer's 'pride in his work'. Then the mantra reverses and parodies itself in the outburst: 'My song is nearing the end of its tether;/ Lament in art whose end is war; / Opera glasses; helicopters; TV crews;/ Our slayings are what's news'. Here Durcan may also ironicise Ezra Pound's remark that 'poetry is news that stays news'. The symbiosis between media and violent events, suggested by the images of surveillance and voyeurism, further parodies, displaces and may disprove 'The end of art is peace'. The tonal shift is from pacifism to protest, cloister to agora again. And the line 'My song has reached the end of its tether' seems to stretch back a hundred years to encompass all the poets who had any kind of belief in peace as the condition, object or outcome of art. Like Yeats's, this is an angry poem which implies that poetry itself may need to go to war in the interests of peace. Of course, the protest poets of the Great War had to be there. 'War poets' are usually peace poets.

I would suggest that this intertextual riff presents the relation between poetry and peace in interconnected ways: poetry might tend towards peace by virtue of its religious intensity, its educational thrust, its human warmth, its capacity for protest. The poems do not cumulatively suggest that poetry is *ipso facto* peaceful or that it can transcend conflict at a single bound. Yet they might rule out certain kinds of poetry as ending in peace and therefore, perhaps, as poetry – Serbian war songs, for instance. A forthcoming book on religion and Northern Irish poetry will ask whether a sectarian poem is a contradiction in terms. So we might call poetry a peacemaker insofar as its direction is inclusive and constructive. Yet this need not repress quarrels with others or with oneself. To say that the end of art is peace is not to say that the beginning of art is pacifism: the anger of Yeats and Durcan serves to internalise the roots of war and violence. Similarly, peace itself may not be a process – 'peace process' has become as devalued a phrase in the Northern Irish as in the Middle Eastern context – but a consequence of other processes, some of which might be modelled by poetry. In a forthcoming article on the Northern Irish playwright, the late Stewart Parker, Marylinn Richtarik quotes Parker writing in 1970 against the glib injunction to 'forget the past' and saying: 'it is survival through comprehension that is healthy, not survival through amnesia'. A recent poem by Michael Longley called 'All of These People' begins: 'Who was it who suggested that the opposite of war is not so much peace/ As civilisation?' This could be civilisation in the (complementary) terms of either 'To a Wealthy Man' or 'The Harvest Bow'. Another of Yeats's sources for 'The end of art is peace' was Walter Pater's dictum: 'The perfection of culture is not rebellion but peace.'[8]

2. Irish Poetry and 'Civilization'

I now want to consider in what senses Irish poetry, and especially Northern Irish poetry, has been in the business of building 'civilisation'. This is an issue that implicates Irish history and literary history since 1922. Other critics might see earlier dates as more significant. But for me, mid twentieth-century Ireland is the crucial historical phase that is still being worked out and worked through in literary terms. I view this period (North and South) as a kind of Dark Age, during which it was mainly writers who kept alive the spark of civilisation. Although the tendency at the moment is for the Republic to celebrate its writers, partly as 'heritage', it was not ever thus. We might compare the proposal to build a monument to William Faulkner in the place where his books, to quote one inhabitant, used to make him 'as popular as a dead skunk in a sleeping bag'. Irish writers, too, have been unpopular for letting skunks into or out of bags, and some smells have become sweeter only with distance. Literary intellectuals from all backgrounds were rebuffed and alienated by the 'Catholic' ethos of the Free State, and by an official ideology that stressed Gaelic traditions to the exclusion of other cultural strands. In the early 1930s Eamon de Valera announced that he was 'a Catholic first'. Meanwhile, in a darker mirror-image, the unionist North repressively consolidated 'a Protestant parliament for a Protestant state'.[9] Unionist cultural ideology emphasised links with Britain. Of course, the Northern Catholic-nationalist population was thereby doubly cast into limbo. It still sees itself as having been abandoned by Dublin as well as oppressed by the Northern régime. A new history of education in Ireland from the 1920s to the 1960s confirms that denominational control over education was the major determining force in Irish life during these years.[10] This, of course, served to strengthen the ideologies of history and culture that constituted nationalism and unionism. And forms of censorship applied to sexuality as well as to politics. The Calvinist element in Ulster Protestantism helped unionism to keep the lid on the North. The Irish *Free* State introduced a Censorship of Publications Act in 1929. The last great *cause celèbre*, the banning of a novel by John McGahern, occurred as recently as 1965.[11]

I was once asked by an American student: 'Whatever happened to the Irish Literary Revival?' Perhaps it is not over yet. In some dimensions of some texts, writers are still working on a collective project that can be called 'Ireland'. However, most are certainly not doing so according to the original script of cultural nationalism as laid down by Yeats, and which Yeats himself was continually obliged to revise. Indeed, his later poetry was fuelled more by the failure than the success of this project, by its rejection as not truly 'Irish'. Only a few years ago Seamus Deane described Yeats as exhibiting 'the pathology of literary unionism'.[12] Yeats's real crime, however, may be that his career disturbs the pathology of literary nationalism. When Yeats brought literature within the orbit of Irish nationalism, he simultaneously brought nationalism within the highly unstable orbit of literature. So what we have in the mid-century is Irish literature largely in dissident mode, at odds with the nation. I see this dissidence as having opened up new horizons and possibilities.

The literary repercussions of the Dark Age, like its political repercussions, are not identical in the North and in the South. I have briefly discussed a poem by Paul Durcan. His poetry incorporates a response to the Troubles in Northern Ireland which is shaped by his critique of the Republic's history: how that has contributed to the conflict, and still conditions attitudes. For example, one of his poems is called 'What is a Protestant, Daddy?' Durcan's actual father was a high-court judge; through his mother he is related to Maud Gonne McBride. Thus he can be seen as a dissident from his inheritance: the founding ideology of the nationalist establishment. Durcan was the most prominent literary advocate of Mary Robinson, and the ethos of the Republic, as it becomes more open and liberal, is more in tune with Durcan's poetry than it used to be. The dissidence of Northern poetry has always been complicated by there being two communities, even if the differences are not as absolute as politicians like to pretend. The contrast with Durcan's tactics appears in voice, perspective, genre. The outspokenness, the sudden *j'accuse*, of 'The Riding School' is characteristic. Northern poems are rarely so upfront: not on account of censorship or self-censorship, but owing to their consciousness of multiple angles, codes and audiences. Durcan has only one historical narrative to deconstruct; whereas Northern poetry at its most philosophically complex (e.g. in the work of Paul Muldoon) relativises narrative itself.

One thing that happened to the Literary Revival was that, in the 1940s, the Northern poet John Hewitt tried to redefine cultural nationalism in terms of an Ulster cultural regionalism that would enable writers from both Protestant and Catholic backgrounds to adumbrate healthier politics. Hewitt's own Protestant background and his socialist politics served to keep him at odds with nationalism and unionism. His project failed at the time, and he subsequently rethought regionalism; but his ideas have influenced recent thinking about cultural diversity and the work of the Cultural Traditions Group, which is based in the Community Relations Council.[13] On the literary front Hewitt's most significant legacy was to suggest for the first time that the North might be a distinct literary *locus* even if it faced in more than one direction. He wrote in 1953: 'It is obvious that the geographical situation and the circumstances of racial juxtaposition and intermingling must have had effects upon the literary arts practised in this area, which should to some degree have produced differences from and modifications of the same arts in the rest of these islands'.[14]

But Hewitt's proposition did not become obvious – nor would all critics assent to it today – until, to quote Seamus Heaney, 'poetry arrived' in Belfast in the early 1960s. The arrival of the generation of Heaney, Derek Mahon and Michael Longley was to prove more conspicuous than any previous flowering of poetry in Northern Ireland. What was the meaning of that arrival as we look back over thirty years later? I have said enough about sectarian divisions to indicate that, when the 1960s generation of poets met one another, they were aware of their separate histories up to that point. A colleague of mine who studies Ulster literary autobiographies says that they often contain sentences like 'When I was nineteen, I got to know my first Catholic/Protestant'. What distinguished the literary getting-to-know-you of the 1960s was that a sustained, recognisable and recognised literary focus began to develop in Belfast. Yet there was also a Dublin dimension. Longley and Mahon had cut their aesthetic teeth at Trinity College, Dublin. This contrasts with the importance of Philip Hobsbaum's 'Belfast Group' (a London dimension in that Hobsbaum came from London and had run his original Group there) for Seamus Heaney. You might also detect contrasts between a Dublin-Belfast and a Derry-Belfast axis.

The geographical, cultural and educational contexts of these poets are relevant in various ways. But the primary factor may be that they conditioned the variety of literary traditions brought into play. Close to home there were Anglo-Irish, Ulster regional, English and Gaelic precursors. Further away there were American and continental influences. However, without wanting to confine any poet within any notional Northern boundaries, I would say that Hewitt's 'differences' and 'modifications' came to pass; that they are still passing and to come. The first books of Heaney, Mahon and Longley, all published before the Troubles began in 1969, are very different in themselves, yet also notable for their shared interest in all the permutations of lyric forms at their most concentrated. This early aesthetic interchange, in my view, was not superseded by later events. It proved crucial to how poets imaginatively negotiated the crisis after 1969. Significantly, the generation born ten years later, that of Paul Muldoon, Ciaran Carson and Medbh McGuckian, has not opted for obvious subject matter either. These poets have absorbed the precedent of their elders while remaining fully alive to their socio-political environment. Carson has said, for instance, that his poetry is not *about* the Troubles, but may be *of* them. This second generation is well known for its deconstructive concern with language. One sphere of intertextual dialogue is the way in which Paul Muldoon deconstructs earlier poems by Seamus Heaney, and their aesthetic dialogue encodes epistemological and political issues. For instance, the end of Muldoon's poem 'The Boundary Commission' epitomises how his poetry alludes to socio-political conditions for which the term 'binary opposition' might have been coined: 'he stood there for ages/ To wonder which side, if any, he should be on'.[15]

I would propose that poetry's arrival, the intertextuality within and between literary generations, prefigured, and now symbolises, processes of articulation in the wider society, the effort to understand self and other. These processes, both in print and in action, are slowly manifesting what was repressed between and within the Ulster communities. But poetry does not only provide a symbol or model or precedent on the basis of dialogue between fixed identities. Rather, its intertextuality questions the simplified cultural package-deals which nationalism and unionism try to perpetuate and propagate. And intertextuality also goes deep into longer, wider cultural and literary histories. It is a matter of form and structure as well as of content. For example, poems by Northern Irish poets can be read in the *Penguin Book of Contemporary Irish Poetry*, the *Penguin Book of Contemporary British Poetry*, and Frank Ormsby's *Poets from the North of Ireland*.[16] All these contexts show off different facets of the poetry, and I stick by something that I wrote ten years ago: the apparent anthological confusion seems more accurate than any attempt to tidy it up. My reading of the aesthetic dynamics informs my approach to the issues of pluralism/diversity which are entering the foreground of Northern Irish politics. Here the long-term cultural agendas of both Yeats and Hewitt are still in process, still challenging ignorances and prejudices.

I must point out, however, that not every critic would agree with my intertextual, post-nationalist, post-unionist, culturalist readings. For instance, Seamus Deane's *Field Day Anthology* (1991)[17] promoted more or less nationalist canonical premises, and he would invoke other critical vocabularies and theoretical models. His criticism (like that of Declan Kiberd in *Inventing Ireland*, 1995)[18] stresses aspects of post-colonial theory, the historical role of Britain in Ireland, the power-relations exposed by nineteenth-century literature. In contrast, I have stressed religious differences, what political scientists term the internal model, what historians term British Isles history or archipelagic 'contexts of explanation',[19] and contemporary writing. Deane's 1995 Clarendon Lectures, published in 1997 as *Strange Country*,[20] present a very different perspective from mine. There he attacks so-called 'revisionist' historians who have complicated the nationalist ideology of history (I see myself as a revisionist literary critic). And he equates revisionism, ecumenism and cultural pluralism with colonialism. Ireland's culture wars intersect with culture wars elsewhere, but they are also shaped by the local ground on which they are fought.

So when I now commend an anthology, I recognise the theoretical issues raised by such compilations, and will mention one in a moment. The anthology contains many intertextual dialogues, including snarls and snags, which might bear out Paul Muldoon's contention that if you want to understand Northern Ireland you should read the poetry rather than all the historical, political and sociological studies. The anthology is Frank Ormsby's *A Rage for Order: Poetry of the Northern Ireland Troubles*, published by the Blackstaff Press in 1992. Ormsby includes poems written long before the Civil Rights movement and the eruption of open conflict in 1969. He includes poems whose relation to political violence outsiders might think obscure. He includes elegies, satires, topographical poems, poems that allude to other wars – World Wars I and II, Korea – poems of love and friendship, poems of country and city, poems about language and art, poems that draw on Greek, Celtic, Nordic, and native American myth. This suggests, firstly, that poetry is entangled with the Northern Irish conflict in a multi-dimensional way; and, secondly, that the conflict itself is multi-dimensional, that it touches every level of culture and community, everything that 'language' can signify. I find this myself when discussing poems with students from different backgrounds in the same classroom in Belfast. In what I see as a slow civil war, it is not only a matter of 'hope and history', to quote Seamus Heaney's *The Cure at Troy*, but of home and history. To imagine a civil war is as difficult a task as to commemorate one. The conflict involves as many layers of 'ethnic' complication as Bosnia, even if its scale is insignificant and its pursuit – in generally prosperous western European circumstances – self-indulgent.

A Rage for Order suggests, again, that intertextuality reigns: that no single poem or poet covers all the angles. Also, unlike politicians, many poems reflect on the perspectives from which they come. Not everything in the anthology is by a Northern Irish poet – for instance, Rudyard Kipling, Robinson Jeffers and Josef Brodsky make appearances. Jeffers spent some time where the Antrim coast faces Scotland, and his poem 'Antrim' seems right on the button: 'No spot of earth where men have so fiercely for ages of time/Fought and survived and cancelled each other,/Pict and Gael and Dane, McQuillan, Clandonnell, O'Neill,/Savages, the Scot, the Normans, the English ...' *A Rage for Order* proves the literary borders to be more positively permeable. But most poets included come from Northern Ireland, even if they no longer live there; and, I would like to make two further suggestions about their intertextual dialogues. Firstly, where poetry is concerned, religious differences do not only boil down – or up – to bigotry. Different theologies influence the ways in which poems conceive history and culture, word and image. This metaphysical complexity has contributed to the recent richness of poetry from Northern Ireland. My second point concerns lyric genre. I mentioned elegy: a genre which seems central to a civil-war poetry which draws into itself poetic models from other twentieth-century wars. Elegy is sometimes dismissed as a form of passive lament; but in a small-scale, slow-motion civil war, even the deaths of soldiers are not anonymous. To focus on the particularities of an individual death questions the grand narratives that may have conspired to produce it.

Before I return finally to art and peace, I would say that the self-image of poetry in *A Rage for Order* is not very confident about making anything happen or stop happening. There is little optimism that its intertextual dialogues, whether explicit or implicit, will be heard. The self-image of the Northern Irish poet is often that of a marginalised, ineffectual, silenced, wary figure whose fragile creations are overwhelmed by the tide of events. I have quoted Seamus Heaney's phrase for 'The Harvest Bow', poem as well as object: 'this frail device'. In the 1970s Derek Mahon saw his art as 'an eddy of semantic scruple/ In an unstructurable sea', Michael Longley saw his as 'leaving careful footprints round/ A wind-encircled burial mound'. This dialectic between poetry and history, art and peace, updates structures from W.B. Yeats's poetry of the 1920s. Yeats wrote in 'Nineteen Hundred and Nineteen': 'Now days are dragon-ridden, the nightmare rides/ Upon sleep'. To quote Paul Muldoon's 'Gathering Mushrooms': poetry again had to face 'a self-renewing gold-black dragon/ we push to the back of the mind'. All their poems became, in some sense or other, 'Meditations in Time of Civil War'.

Perhaps we could interpret 'The end of art is peace' as saying that art will have no function once universal harmony prevails. After the 1994 cease-fires, journalists would visit Belfast to ask poets: 'What are you going to write about *now*?' as if the entire corpus harped on a single theme in a single manner. Also, writers, like everyone else, have been wary of assuming that either art or history is about to end. One Belfast novel published in 1996 begins: 'Peace had settled over the city like the skin on a rancid custard. Everybody wanted it, just not in that form. The forecast remained for rain with widespread terrorism'.[21] The spring 1998 precarious 'talks', destabilised by unresolved social and cultural subtexts, as well as by violence, are a long way from the subtle dialogues of the poetry.

3. Four 'Peace' Poems

It may be significant that some 'peace process' poems revise earlier poems in the light of recent history, and that such revision contributes to their intertextual dialogues. The title of Ciaran Carson's 'Jacta Est Alea', of course, alludes to Julius Caesar crossing the Rubicon:

It was one of those puzzling necks of the woods where
  The South was in the North, the way
The double cross in a jigsaw loops into its matrix
  like the border was a clef

With arbitrary teeth indented in it. Here, it cut clean
  across the plastic
Lounge of The Half-Way House; my heart lay in
  the Republic

While my head was in the six, or so I was inclined.
  You know that drinker's
Angle, elbow-propped, knuckles to his brow like one
  of the Great Thinkers?

He's staring at my throat in the Power's mirror,
  debating whether
He should open up a lexicon with me: the price of
  beer or steers, the weather.

We end up talking about talk. We stagger on the frontier.
  He is pro. I am con.
Siamese-like, drunken, inextricable, we wade
  into the Rubicon.[22]

This poem also alludes, I think, to the climax of Louis MacNeice's long poem *Autumn Journal* (1939), which ends: 'Tonight we sleep/ On the banks of Rubicon – the die is cast'. *Autumn Journal*, like MacNeice's poetry in general, has been a major point of reference for Northern Irish poetry in its engagement with history. The structural significance of the *Autumn Journal* lies in its open-endedness to the flux of European events at the time of the Munich crisis. MacNeice says in his introductory note: 'It is the nature of this poem to be neither final nor balanced'.[23] This supplies a flexible model that much Northern Irish poetry has followed during the last twenty-nine uncertain years. Where Carson revises MacNeice is in his comic pessimism. The conclusion 'We wade into the Rubicon' suggests that no decisive watershed may ever be reached in the affairs of Northern Ireland. 'Jacta Est Alea' incorporates two ideas that recur in Northern Irish poetry: fixity or determinism and doubleness. The local polarities are represented by the split between heart and head, pro and con. If the image of Siamese twins heals the split, it does so ambiguously. Pro and Con are chiefly identical in their enmity. Twins appear in other Northern Irish poems. For instance, a sonnet in Paul Muldoon's sequence 'Armageddon, Armageddon' invokes the constellation of Gemini to figure the conflict: 'Were twin and twin at one another's throats?' In 'Jacta Est Alea' the bodily parts, throat and neck, carry further violent suggestions, even the notion of vampirism: 'arbitrary teeth indented in it'. If these are also the shapes of a political jigsaw, 'Jacta Est Alea' is less a complaint about the Irish border than a satire on how Northern Irish mentalities conspire to postpone peace for ever. The 'arbitrary' queries the pre-determined, as it does in Muldoon's 'Boundary Commission'. Both poems belong to a long line of poems about sides and otherness. One of these is Seamus Heaney's 'The Other Side', which ends with a question as to whether its Catholic speaker should engage the Protestant Other in talk – perhaps trivial, perhaps fundamental – about 'the weather/ or the price of grass-seed'. This precursor poem Carson again translates into comic mode, adding a touch of ominous thriller-idiom: 'He's staring at my throat in the Power's mirror,/ debating whether/ He should open up a lexicon with me: the price of/ beer or steers, the weather'. Besides functioning as a euphemistic cover for violence, the words 'debating' and 'lexicon' also challenge abstract and euphemistic ways of framing the language-questions that vex Northern Ireland. 'Talking about talk' is blunter, but still ironical. The phrase 'talks about talks' has become a cliché of failure to make progress. This poem, then, satirises political and literary vocabularies which exaggerate difference or minimise violence. Here self and other become 'inextricable'. They share the same body. Thus they are not only alike but interdependent. Carson's own ingenious language games prove the points he is making. Nonetheless, the obdurately divisive force of different languages, in the sense of institutionalised cultural codes, is highlighted.

A good many Northern Irish poems talk about talk. Michael Longley's sonnet 'Cease-fire' does so in a contrasting way:

I
Put in mind of his own father and moved to tears
Achilles took him by the hand and pushed the old king
Gently away, but Priam curled up at his feet and
Wept with him until their sadness filled the building.

II
Taking Hector's corpse into his own hands Achilles
Made sure it was washed and, for the old king's sake,
Laid out in uniform, ready for Priam to carry
Wrapped like a present home to Troy at daybreak.

III
When they had eaten together, it pleased them both
To stare at each other's beauty as lovers might,
Achilles built like a god, Priam good-looking still
And full of conversation, who earlier had sighed:

IV
I get down on my knees and do what must be done
And kiss Achilles' hand, the killer of my son.[24]

'Cease-fire' is a free-ish translation of a passage in the *Iliad*: the lull in the Trojan war while Priam is permitted to fetch the body of his son Hector, killed by Achilles, from the Greek camp. The last couplet, as the word 'earlier' tells us, is transposed from its position in the Greek narrative, where it precedes the events compressed into the quatrains of the sonnet. This implies that a pre-condition for 'conversation' between enemies is the kind of concession Priam has made. He has not exactly forgiven Achilles, but he has accepted the reality and fatality of what has happened. This generosity shifts the balance of emotional power in Priam's direction. His overture sets up the interchange whereby Achilles and Priam act out the roles of father and son. These doubles look into the mirror of each other. There are also images of common human bonds and rituals: tears, sexual love, funeral arrangements, feasting. Slow rhythms reinforce the ritual effect. And, here again, body language orchestrates progress towards a recognition of similarities, but in tragic rather than satirical terms. 'Cease-fire' is intertextual in many directions: most obviously with Homer, but also with a tradition of importing Homer into the Irish lyric. It is a war poem, too, and alludes to poetry of the first and second world wars, for instance the famous climax of Wilfred Owen's 'Strange Meeting': 'I am the enemy you killed, my friend'. Besides recalling previous poems in which Longley reworks themes from English poetry of the world wars, 'Cease-fire' remembers Paul Muldoon's poem 'Truce', inspired by the legendary fraternisation between the British and German forces on Christmas Day 1914. Muldoon's scenario also deploys images of shared humanity (singing, playing cards, smoking) in a context of difference. A sexual metaphor figures the end of the truce: 'As Friday-night lovers, when it's over,/ Might get up from their mattresses/ To congratulate each other/ And exchange names and addresses'. It should be said that neither 'Truce' nor 'Cease-fire' offers easy answers. Both poems take shape as remissions in a war that will resume – the Great War, the Trojan war. They ask questions and lay out choices: the makings of either peace or war.

There are no poems by Medbh McGuckian in *A Rage for Order*. Frank Ormsby considered McGuckian's language too far removed from wherever the front line is presumed to be. But that, it seems, is the point. Her poetry's approach to aesthetics and gender interprets its incapacity to speak in more direct terms. Women's voices play a very small part in the macho, territorial politics of Northern Ireland, unless to echo traditional stances. (A grouping called the Women's Coalition is trying to express, at the political level, what women have done to hold society together.) McGuckian took revenge for her omission from *Rage for Order* by choosing as epigraph to *Captain Lavender* Picasso's statement in 1944; 'I have not painted the war ... but I have no doubt that the war is in ... these paintings I have done'. In addition, the blurb promises that the collection 'addresses the politics of the author's native province'. But, as 'Credenza' indicates, McGuckian is still operating behind the lines:

A white melancholy sits in the lesser chair
at the front edge of time. In her moments
of cut radiance, colour runs all through her
like a hand-coloured paper Annunciation
in a gold-leaf frame. Then she has the sky-hook air
of here and there.

Not remembering him every day and every day
and every day has begun, the wet shoulders
of his breathing ending, the open rafters
of his inner nature little by little
never meeting again.

Her fingers explore the white keys only,
her fiery dress of tricolor ribbons
asks nothing from the low lights of the house,
where the piles of captured cannon
that had raised two pyramids
are being taken away.

Suddenly the all-black room sees everything
far down the street; war-talk sentences
act as if they had never been shot at;
a for-keeps winter inches wide
the voice of a wine the grapes
never belonged to.[25]

'Credenza' takes off from the last line of Michael Longley's poem 'The Civil Servant', an elegy for a murdered civil servant, which ends: 'Later his widow took a hammer and chisel/ And removed the black keys from his piano'. 'Credenza' is written from the widow's viewpoint. It dramatises a female madness that takes on the character of sanity. The title may combine cadenza – solo instrument – with credo, a system of belief. Cadenza questions credo, the aesthetic the political. The woman in the poem 'explores the white keys only'. They express her 'white melancholy' in the 'all-black room'. At the same time, McGuckian associates her with colour and radiance, 'a fiery dress of tricolour ribbons', that challenge the black and white binary opposition. The passionate spectrum of grief contrasts with the monotonous 'war-talk sentences' that 'act as if they had never been shot at'. (Here McGuckian may refer to *Autumn Journal* in which MacNeice indicts his countrymen 'who shoot to kill/ And never see the victim's face become their own'.) The war is 'in this poem' as absence of colour, armoured language, a broken body, mind and house, winter. The widow's mad playing may symbolise the necessity for a new kind of talk or 'voice' to come into political being.

All these poems, I think, process peace in different ways. Their revision of earlier poems is itself hopeful, but they still keep poetic and political options open. Seamus Heaney's 'Tollund' revisits his well-known poem 'The Tollund Man' – both its imagined ground of the 'old man-killing parishes', and its redemptive aspiration:

That Sunday morning we had travelled far.
We stood a long time out in Tollund moss:
The low ground, the swart water, the thick grass
Hallucinatory and familiar.

A path through Jutland fields. Light traffic sound.
Willow bushes; rushes; bog-fir grags
In a swept and gated farmyard; dormant quags.
And silage under wraps in its silent mound.

It could have been a still out of the bright
'Townland of Peace', that poem of dream farms
Outside all contention. The scarecrow's arms
Stood open opposite the satellite

Dish in the paddock, where a standing stone
Had been resituated and landscaped,
With tourist signs in *futhark* runic script
In Danish and in English. Things had moved on.

It could have been Mulhollandstown or Scribe.
The byroads had their names on them in black
And white; it was user-friendly outback
Where we stood footloose, at home beyond the tribe,

More scouts than strangers, ghosts who'd walked abroad
Unfazed by light, to make a new beginning
And make a go of it, alive and sinning,
Ourselves again, free-willed again, not bad.

The poem does not only revisit/revise Heaney himself. It also quotes from a pessimistic poem by Paul Muldoon and an optimistic one by John Hewitt. The Muldoon poem is 'Christo's', written during the hunger strikes when a number of IRA prisoners starved themselves to death. Muldoon uses the image of mounds 'draped in black polythene' to convey an oppressive atmosphere: 'By the time we got to Belfast/ the whole of Ireland would be under wraps'. Heaney's 'silage under wraps in its silent mound' evokes this ethos of deathly closure. In contrast, John Hewitt's 'Townland of Peace' offers an antidote to war. Written during the Second World War, it is consciously Arcadian in its escape from history and catalogue of idyllic images – 'crooked apple trees', 'dappled calves', 'netted sunlight' – that 'gave neither hint nor prophecy of change'. Heaney's revisions and self-revision again hinge on opposites or doubleness: on the two faces of Ulster in his own poetry and other poetry as 'dream farms' and territorial 'contention', as pastoral peace and landscape of death. Further oppositions in the poem are those between rural and urban, the traditional and the modern. These antinomies also pervade Northern Irish poetry, with Heaney's imagination often leaning towards the first two terms, rural and traditional. Here we have an ironically self-aware contrast between the scarecrow and the satellite dish, and an ironic landscaping of the tourist signs and resituated standing stone. Nevertheless, the poem enacts a thrust towards reconciliation of opposites, as the 'man-killing parishes' of 'The Tollund Man' are transmuted into the 'user-friendly outback' of 'Tollund'. This poem is more complex in its implied gloss on 'The end of art is peace' than is 'The Harvest Bow'. In talking to other poets, it brings aesthetic and cultural differences into the frame of what must be resolved before Northern Ireland becomes a townland of peace as opposed to a centre for conflict studies.

Yet the last five lines suggest, by default, that the cease-fire – and 'Tollund', like Longley's 'Cease-fire' belongs to the moment of the IRA cease-fire – has not yet brought new political language into being. Whereas Heaney successfully continues the revisions – the semantic scruple, that Northern Irish poetry brings to bear on its own structures – he cannot find new language at the socio-political level of his poem. It is unclear who 'we' are who 'stand footloose beyond the tribe'. Here reconciliation may be premature, and Heaney asks a lot of the word 'beyond'. Also his structure of transcendence, resurrection, absolution accords with a Catholic rather than Protestant approach to history. While the poem's aspiration towards 'a new beginning' is deeply felt, 'Ourselves again, free-willed again' begs further questions. For instance, 'Ourselves again' subliminally conflates two phrases from the Irish nationalist lexicon: 'ourselves alone' and 'a nation once again'. What I see as the weakness of the poem's conclusion – a weakness exposed by events – epitomises the gap between the complex language collectively developed by poetry and the rudimentary slogans on which Northern Irish politics has mostly relied.

Notes

1. See Warwick Gould, John Kelly and Deirdre Toomey (eds), *Collected Letters of W.B. Yeats* (Oxford, Oxford University Press, 1997), 27n, 70 n for relevant bibliographical information.
2. W.B. Yeats, 'Samhain: 1905', *Explorations* (London: Macmillan, 1962), 198-99.
3. W.B. Yeats, 'Ireland and the Arts', *Essays and Introductions* (London: Macmillan, 1961), 207.
4. W.B. Yeats, *Collected Poems* (London: Macmillan, 1950), 105.
5. See R.F. Foster, *W.B. Yeats: A Life*, Vol. I : *The Apprentice Mage* (Oxford, Oxford University Press, 1997), 460.
6. Seamus Heaney, *Field Work* (London: Faber & Faber, 1979), 58.
7. Paul Durcan, *A Snail in My Prime* (London: Harvill, 1993), 224.
8. Walter Pater, *Studies in the History of the Renaissance*, ed. Donald Hill (Berkeley and London: Macmillan, 1980), 213.
9. Dennis Kennedy, *The Widening Gulf: Northern Attitudes to the Independent Irish State 1919-49* (Belfast, Blackstaff, 1988), 166.
10. Sean Farren, *The Politics of Irish Education 1920-65* (Belfast, The Queen's University Institute of Irish Studies, 1995).
11. Julia Carlson, *Banned in Ireland: Censorship & the Irish Writer* (London, Routledge, 1990).
12. Seamus Deane, *Heroic Styles: The Tradition of an Idea* (Derry, Field Day, 1984), 10.
13. See a series of conference-based publications on culture and Northern Ireland (by the Institute of Irish Studies, The Queen's University, Belfast) starting with Maurna Crozier (ed.), *Varieties of Irishness* (1989). The most recent is John Erskine and Gordon Lucy (eds), *Varieties of Scottishness* (1997).
14. Tom Clyde (ed.), *Ancestral Voices: The Selected Prose of John Hewitt* (Belfast: Blackstaff Press, 1987), 64.
15. Paul Muldoon, *New Selected Poems 1968-1994* (London: Faber & Faber, 1996), 38.

16. *Penguin Book of Contemporary Irish Poetry* (Harmondsworth, 1990); *Penguin Book of Contemporary British Poetry* (Harmondsworth, 1982); Frank Ormsby, *Poets from the North of Ireland* (Blackstaff Press, 1979, revised edition 1990).

17. Seamus Deane, *Field Day Anthology of Irish Writing* (Derry, Field Day, 1991).

18. Declan Kiberd, *Inventing Ireland* (London: Jonathan Cape, 1995).

19. Steven G. Ellis, 'Writing Irish History: Revisionism, Colonialism, and the British Isles', *Irish Review* No. 19 (Spring/Summer 1996), 1-21.

20. Seamus Deane, *Strange Country* (Oxford: Oxford University Press, 1997).

21. Colin Bateman, *Of Wee Sweetie Mice & Men* (London: Harper Collins, 1996).

22. Ciaran Carson, *Opera et cetera* (Loughcrew, Oldcastle, Co. Meath, Gallery Books, 1986), 44.

23. Louis MacNeice, *Collected Poems* (London, Faber & Faber, 1966), 153.

24. Michael Longley, *The Ghost Orchid* (London: Jonathan Cape, 1995), 39.

25. Medbh McGuckion, *Captain Lavender* (Loughcrew, Oldcastle, Co. Meath, Gallery Books, 1994), 67.

Creating an Identity: John Hewitt and History

Britta Olinder

It is difficult, when writing about a poet who died over a decade ago in his eightieth year, to apply the theme 'Towards new identities': at least, if 'new' is taken as relating to the situation in 1998. However, if 'new' is taken to mean 'different', 'changed', 'invented', 'brought into existence', as *The Concise Oxford Dictionary* defines it, then it could very well be used about John Hewitt's creation of his identity as an Ulsterman of Planter stock. In this paper I will deal with the element of his identity that he relates intimately to history. In an attempt to do justice to a writer who is not read as much as he deserves, I will quote rather extensively from both his poetry and his prose.

There is no denying that history plays a vital part in the political life of Northern Ireland today, whether as an incitement to action or as a source of humiliation and, in Gerry Adams's words, of disgrace. Or should we rather say that history is exploited as a pretext? The questions we have to ask are: what parts and aspects of history are used? And for what purpose in the public discourse? And what difference do we find when we compare this use of history in politics with John Hewitt's view of history? It is the last of these questions that I will tackle here, since history was such an important aspect of Hewitt's own identity.

History was John Hewitt's profession. It was the subject he studied at Queen's (not English, as Ormsby has it in the biographical chronology of the *Collected Poems*[1]). As a museum man, he was surrounded by objects from the past. He has written the history of the art and artists of his province as well as that of the writing and writers of it. His view of society is coloured by his insights into history, and *vice versa*. His identity has to do with his family background and history, with changes in his region during different periods, and with the patterns of thought and action that he finds among dissenters throughout history. Thus history is an active dimension in Hewitt's work; and just as we can think of Hewitt as a landscape poet who has to do with place and geography, we can equally read him as a poet of history, one who blends the past with the present, seeing the present through the past, making the past come alive by comparison with the present.

This means that with Hewitt, we have to do with different areas or levels of history: his personal history and that of his family; branches of the discipline such as art history and the history of writing; the history of institutions such as schools, theatres or museums; and the history of his region, and of the dissenting tradition. In passing, we may note Hewitt's contribution to art history. Interestingly enough he presents, on the one hand, a very objective type of description, as he stresses in comments such as: 'in my own way a historian of the arts of my country, I have maybe an over-developed belief in the importance and the plain recording of such facts [as place and year of birth]';[2] and on the other hand we can follow the intimately personal story of the development of his individual taste and understanding of art, the latter especially in the autobiographical papers where he speaks of his favouring puritanism in art, as when he writes 'it has taken me a quarter of a century to acknowledge the power of the Baroque; and I still find that I do not readily think of Rubens among the great masters, and am positive that Renoir is grossly overestimated' (*ibid.*, 60). The story of the change in his estimation of Jack Yeats is also of great interest.[3]

As to literary history, this was the subject of his MA thesis, written more than twenty years after his first degree and focusing on 'Ulster Poets 1800-1870' (1951). Among other works in this field I would like to mention his editions of William Allingham's poems (1967) and of *Rhyming Weavers and Other Country Poets of Antrim and Down* (1974), with his claim that 'from their verses therefore we may learn a great deal about rural society and its structure'.[4] As late as 1982 he wrote an unpublished history of Belfast writing, called 'The Northern Athens and After'.[5]

As in the case of art history, his sense of the facts of literary history and its illumination of social and economic conditions are combined with his sense of aesthetic qualities. This combination of facts with value judgment comes out clearly in a poem called 'Gloss on the Difficulties of Translation'. After the three-line translation of a poem follows the comment that it is not a Japanese haiku but:

Ninth-century Irish, in fact,
from a handbook on metrics,
the first written reference
to my native place.

In forty years of verse
I have not inched much further.
I may have matched the images;
but the intricate wordplay
of the original – assonance,
rime, alliteration –
is beyond my grasp. (129)

Personal history – history to do with his own experiences, his family, the political events and developments he was able to witness or follow – is illuminated in many poems and occasionally in articles throughout his career. His family background is given full treatment in the prose of 'Planter's Gothic', his childhood autobiography, three chapters of which were published in *The Bell* in 1953. There is, however, at least as much of this kind still unpublished. The same period and the same people also come back in the sonnets of *Kites in Spring: A Belfast Boyhood* (1980). Occasionally the same incident, for example the story of the nurse who had to leave him because of her associates and her drinking habits, recurs in early poems, then in 'Planter's Gothic', and finally in *Kites in Spring*.

His twenty-five years in the Belfast Museum are covered in odd poems but particularly in 'A North Light', which consists of thirty-eight autobiographical chapters written at the end of the 1960s. There are also a number of other chapters from the same period and later, when he was director of the Coventry Art Gallery.

What Hewitt describes from his own life is history to us now. Take for instance this passage from 'No Rootless Colonist':

Easter Week 1916, without the immediacy of television or radio, seemed some distance away and unrelated to my circumstance. Hence it evoked no clear or deep reaction in a boy of eight and a half. The Armistice of November 1918 was more real, with the barefoot newsboys shouting their special editions, with the singing people in the streets and men in uniform carried shoulderhigh. I saw King George when he drove through Belfast to open the new Parliament in the City Hall in 1921, and the strife which came with Partition was shockingly close: curfew in the town, armoured trucks covered with wire-mesh passing along the street, a sniper at the corner, burnt-out public houses from the Crumlin Road to the Shankill. But again no political attitude was required of me. I pitied the victims, the hysterical woman, the young man shot in the entry.[6]

What I intend to look at in the following, however, is primarily what Hewitt himself regarded as history. At an early stage of 'Planter's Gothic' he gives his family this historical setting: '[The Hewitts], so far as I am concerned, stem from County Armagh. The name is on county hearth-rolls of 1610'. He adds playfully: 'There are other Irish [Hewitts] outside Ulster, but they are, I am sure, Cromwellian upstarts'.[7] In poetic form this becomes, in 'Sunset over Glenaan':

My breed is Planter also. I can show
the grey and crooked headstones row on row
in a rich country mastered long ago
by stubborn farmers from across the sea,
whose minds and hands were rich in husbandry,
and who, when their slow blood was running thin,
crowded in towns for warmth, and bred me in
the clay-red city with the white horse on the wall,
the jangling steeples, and the green-domed hall.

Inheritor of these, I also share
the nature of this legendary air. (113)[8]

He goes on to emphasize his dependence on his ancestors and his own role as inheritor of a tradition and as one link in the chain of generations. The strong ties of the region to Scotland are reflected in his family's Scottish connections:

The whole point of the ideal Ulsterman is simply that he must carry within himself elements of both Scots and English with a strong charge of the basic Irish.

When I discovered, not long ago, that the old Planter's Gothic tower of Kilmore Church still encloses the stump of a round tower and that it was built on the site of a Culdee holy place [older than Saint Patrick's mission], I felt a step nearer to that synthesis. It is the best symbol I have yet found for the strange textures of my response to this island of which I am a native. I may appear Planter's Gothic, but there is a round tower somewhere inside, and needled through every sentence I utter.[9]

His grandparents' flight to Scotland also becomes significant:

[L]ooked at now, when the [broad] social movements of the nineteenth century in these islands have been examined and charted, the choice of Scotland rather than England as a handy refuge must have been determined by the history of Ulster over the centuries. Long before the Plantation, there had been multitudinous comings and goings across the narrow waters since Mesolithic hunters came seeking the handy flints. In the nineteenth century and, in a measure since, there has, of course, been the seasonal flow of farm workers from the small crofts of Donegal and the Northwest. But in the mid-century there was a steady drift east, not merely of itinerant harvesters. (*Ibid.*, 9)

He goes on to exemplify from his store of biographical knowledge: 'Dr. Alexander Irvine's brothers left Antrim town to become miners in the Ayrshire pits. John Lavery the artist fled from Moira to become a leader of the Glasgow school. Thomas Eliott, one of the old Ulster poets, a little earlier took his trade of cobbling with him to that city' (*ibid.*). Among his family's Scottish memories he tells the story of

... a night of tremendous storm [when] John [his grandfather] was knocked up by the constable, a Highlandman, for the roof had been torn off the seed warehouse, and he had to hurry down under a fusillade of flying slates and tumbling chimneypots, to organise the salvage and the temporary repairs. This was the night of the Tay Bridge Disaster, 28 December 1879. But in folk memory this date has long since become Christmas Eve. (*Ibid.*, 10)

It is characteristic of him to note the mistake – but with understanding.

If the view is now extended from family history to the wider social perspective of the region, we find him arguing:

... for me, the main link [of Northern Ireland] with Scotland and the north-east of England is an industrial one. I see Glasgow, Liverpool and Belfast as being in a similar situation, in the attic of British industrialism ... Incidentally, the thing that people don't accept, stupidly, is that a river, or water, is not a border – it's a connection. And the people of the north-west of Ireland have used the 12 miles across to Scotland frequently. In the early days of the plantations, Presbyterians in County Down went over by boat to church services in Scotland, one Sunday a month. A regular steamer went from Belfast to Glasgow before there was a train from Belfast to Dublin. Our connection economically has been with that part of the British Isles and not with the rest of Ireland. We shared in the Industrial Revolution. Because we were building ships for British capitalism and making textiles for the British international market, our working people developed their loyalist ideology. So it had an economic basis; which is pure Marxism.[10]

Once, going to Donegal for a holiday, he discovers that 'I now could realise my area as the historical province and not as the politician's convenience'.[11] What he calls the historical province of Ulster is intimately connected with myth in people's perception of that history. Hewitt discusses the conflict between the Irish myth and that of the north of the island on the one hand, and the rough-cast myth of the Protestant colonizers on the other. 'Yet', he says,

Ulster takes up a long chapter of the Irish Myth, itself. Much that has happened in that province has gone to the making of the other Myth: Cuchulain, Deirdre, Oisin, Patrick, Colmcille, Shane O'Neill, Hugh O'Neill, Owen Roe O'Neill, Red Hugh O'Donell, McCracken, Mitchel ... Of Oisin the bard who came back from the Land of the Ever Young to debate with Patrick and die, there are the stone stumps of the gapped halfcircle on holly-hedged Lubitavish, called his grave.[12]

Apart from the great characters of myth and legend, Hewitt also had historical heroes of his own. They are listed in various places (with small changes), as for example here in his autobiographical papers:

From my reading of history and literature, directed towards England by the *curricula* of my various educational adventures, I had established that my England was not the land of kings and imperial proconsuls, but the England of John Ball, Jack Cade, Wat Tyler, and the Levellers, the Diggers, the Luddites, the Chartists, as my democratic and socialist enthusiasm had determined. Bunyan, Fox, Marvell, Blake, Cobbett, Morris were already preeminent among my fixed stars. (*Ibid.*, 2)

He comments on this in Damian Smyth's interview: 'That's one of the things that keeps me from being a 105% Irishman – part of my tradition is a British democratic tradition. That's why I'm on the side of miners, you see, which is not an Irish issue at all' (14).

A different aspect of Hewitt's historiography is the evocation of the classical Greek and Roman world. We find a doubtful attitude to the conquerors or other great men; for example, during a visit to Old Corinth:

we endured the harsh breath of Roman authority;
hung around the *agora* to hear if Paul should speak
once more of charity ...

What he is really interested in, however, is the older, anonymous history, the genuine history of the people. Instead of the big striking classical monuments of Corinth he lingers in front of the Perene Fountain:

and leaned for a long time over the low parapet,
gazing into the little caves under the arches,
listening for the liquid syllables
of an older oracle. (56-57)

The Greek island of Delos, 'awash ... with history' ('Mykonos', 54), conveys to him not specific memories of the different eras of glorious Greek achievement, which he puts into terms of the development of drama, but the idea of timelessness, eternity like 'the stone man and woman, headless, who must endure/ eternity together, pompously, with no comment', something that leads him on to evading the defined periods in favour of the total picture:

not the Helladic prelude, the Periclean opera,
or the Hellenistic epilogue,
but the whole saga of your kind. (55)

On board a ship in the Greek archipelago he comes across a man who attracts his interest. His experience in the living present opens up into the past as he finds himself trying to place the man in a homeric context on board one of Ulysses' ships ('To Piraeus', 108-9).

Hewitt's most significant use of classical history, however, is found in the poem 'The Colony', because here he considers Irish history in terms of Roman colonization. There is a marked transition from 'the legions', 'the colonists', *they*, to the first person plural:

We planted little towns to garrison
the heaving country, heaping walls of earth
and keeping all our cattle close at hand.

Now 'the barbarian tribesmen' come into the picture, the terror they inspire and the different policies envisaged to grapple with them:

Teams of the tamer natives we employed
to hew and draw, but did not call them slaves.
Some say this was our error. Others claim
we were too slow to make them citizens;
we might have made them Caesar's bravest legions.
This is a matter for historians,
or old beards in the Senate to wag over,
not pertinent to us these many years. (76-79)

It is extraordinary, Hewitt seems to say, to what extent history repeats itself. You catch the further irony from the way some of these words and concepts from the Roman Empire have been applied all along to the elements of power, i.e. Caesar, the Senate, the question of citizenship.

'The Colony' was written in 1949, a comparatively quiet period of Irish history. When we get to the troubled period beginning in 1969, however, Hewitt again writes in terms of Greek history, more specifically in terms of the relations with Thebes and with Thebans living within the city of Athens. From roughly the same period, the poem called 'The Roman Fort' (1971) tells us of the archeological investigation of a Roman camp and the reconstruction of it, and then suddenly switches to a comparison of the experience of a Roman and that of an English soldier 'in a beleaguered colony' surrounded by 'stubborn barbarians' (175-176). But in spite of the similarities between different periods of colonization Hewitt now finds this device hampering, as he makes clear in a poem from *An Ulster Reckoning* (1971):

Parallels Never Meet

Events in my native province now
twist my heart, threatening
any future I had planned.

To find focus for my taut feelings,
I thrust all back into a remote setting,
dressing the circumstances
in the properties of antiquity,
allegorising the actions and the actors
finding Peleponnesian parallels
for the arrogant soothsayer,
the time-server, the ambitious knave,
the stupid, the buffoon, the cynic,
the just man without courage.

But they trip and flounder in their togas;
the classical names are inappropriate,
deflecting by their associations and resonance,
giving a rhetorical inflation
to their ignorance and banality.
Reality is of a coarser texture;
the scene collapses absurd,
lath and canvas.

But the heartbreak remains,
the malice and the hate are palpable,
the flames authentic,
the wounds weep real blood
and the future is not to be foretold. (139-40)

In some poems the perspective is extended still further. There is a tension in Hewitt's poetry between on the one hand clearly expressed and defended feelings of home, of where his roots are, of where he belongs, and on the other hand the longing of his race (by which he sometimes means 'we Irish', and sometimes apparently includes the Scottish or English planters), a longing for somewhere else, an unsatisfied search. In this context we find the wider horizons, the larger sweeps of time. We are dealing with the waves of peoples from the east moving westwards. So in 'The Mainland', which here is England:

> The island people first were mainland people
> shouldered from crowded valley to the beach;
> some even afloat before the outsiders came
> with emblem and ultimatum of invaders
> heavily armoured in rumour, invincible.

He visualizes how the move must have taken place, and goes on to the realization of the discomforts and the tragedy of migration.He considers the gamble for life or death which it must have been to dare the completely unknown:

> And so departed while a drift of smoke
> from the torched thatches hung a day's march off.
> The only choice then was from the known landmarks
> into the sunset out of the fierce noon.

The certainty then grows when people have been settled for a good while that, as so often with Hewitt, the very earth has assimilated their flesh and blood:

> When seven generations had been buried
> in island earth and all was planted well,
> the hill tribes broken and the hill names kept,
> a long while since, the story should have ended,
> the island now a nation, its people one;
> but legends of the mainland still persist
> in hearthside talk and rags of balladry:
> and now and then a man will test their truth
> by sailing back across the ancient track
> to find it rich in all but what we sought. (96-97)

The parallel with the later plantation becomes gradually clear in the last section. At the end of the poem it comes back to the search, the ambivalent feelings about where the roots really are. It is worth mentioning that the poem was written during Hewitt's Coventry years. He could then be said to have sailed back himself the ancient track to England.

Another time Hewitt is more clearly Irish, even Celtic, in his attitude, as in the much earlier poem 'Ireland', written in 1932 and beginning on a highflown patriotic note:

> We Irish pride ourselves as patriots
> and tell the beadroll of the valiant ones
> since Clontarf's sunset saw the Norsemen broken ...
> Aye, and before that too we had our heroes:
> but they were mighty fighters and victorious.

Against these heroes of history he now sets in sharp contrast the anti-heroes of more recent times: 'The later men got nothing save defeat,/ hard transatlantic sidewalks or the scaffold'. From this point he goes on to undercut both pride and patriotic feelings. What else can he do at this point of disillusion than deny anyone's original claim to the island:

We are not native here or anywhere.
We were the Keltic wave that broke over Europe,
and ran up this bleak beach among these stones:
but when the tide ebbed, were left stranded here
in crevices, and ledge-protected pools
that have grown salter with the drying up
of the great common flow that kept us sweet
with fresh cold draughts from deep down in the ocean.

So we are bitter, and are dying out
in terrible harshness in this lonely place,
and what we think is love for usual rock,
or old affection for our customary ledge,
is but forgotten longing for the sea
that cries far out and calls us to partake
in his great tidal movements round the earth. (58)

What is remarkable here is Hewitt's identification with the Irish as Celts.

The same restlessness or wavering between the sensation of being at home and homelessness is expressed thirty-five years later, now written from England with a different historical perspective:

The Search

We left the western island to live among strangers
in a city older by centuries
than the market town which we had come from
where the slow river spills out between green hills
and gulls perch on the bannered poles.
...
But sometimes the thought
that you have not come away from, but returned,
to this older place whose landmarks are yours also,
occurs when you look down a long street remarking
the architectural styles or move through a landscape
with real wheat ripening in large fields.

Yet you may not rest here, having come back,
for this is not your abiding place, either.

The authorities declare that in former days
the western island was uninhabited,
just as where you reside now was once tundra,
and what you seek maybe no more than
a broken circle of stones on a rough hillside, somewhere. (160)

In the vast historical perspective places merge, and somehow the conclusion is
that nationality becomes – and should be – unimportant.

When it comes to pure history we see that Hewitt speaks now on behalf of all
Irishmen, now as an Ulsterman of Planter stock. At a distance, while in Coventry,
it is with rage and pity that he thinks of

... a people endlessly betrayed
by our own weakness, by the wrongs we suffered
in that long twilight over bog and glen,
by force, by famine and by glittering fables
which gave us martyrs when we needed men,
by faith which had no charity to offer,
by poisoned memory, and by ready wit,
with poverty corroded into malice,
to hit and run and howl when it is hit.
This is our fate: eight hundred years' disaster,
crazily tangled as the Book of Kells;
the dream's distortion and the land's division,
the midnight raiders and the prison cells. ('An Irishman in Coventry', 97-98)

In a poem entitled 'The Scar', written in 1971, Hewitt refers to an incident that
he has described in other poems both before and after, as well as in his autobiographical papers; an incident that symbolically has made him a partner in the
suffering of the Irish from the natural and political catastrophe of the Famine:

There's not a chance now that I might recover
one syllable of what that sick man said,
tapping upon my great-grandmother's shutter,
and begging, I was told, a piece of bread;
for on his tainted breath there hung infection
rank from the cabins of the stricken west,
the spores from black potato-stalks, the spittle
mottled with poison in his rattling chest;
but she who, by her nature, quickly answered,
accepted in return the famine-fever;
and that chance meeting, that brief confrontation,
conscribed me of the Irishry for ever ... (177)

So historical events and developments are naturally involved in the process of
definition, of establishing an identity, of finding out where he belongs. This is
seen very clearly in 'Once Alien Here': 'Once alien here my fathers built their
house,/ claimed, drained, and gave the land its shapes of use'. He recognizes that

his family were strangers asserting some right to the land but looking back to 'the ripe England of the mounded downs'. Their planting, however, means that they had forced away the 'sullen Irish limping to the hills [who] bore with them the enchantments and the spells'. Even so he is, he argues,

... because of all the buried men
in Ulster clay, because of rock and glen
and mist and cloud and quality of air
as native in my thought as any here,
who now would seek a native mode to tell
our stubborn wisdom individual ... (20-21)

He puts forward the idea that the fact that his ancestors were buried in the earth of Ulster, which he sees as 'a physical identification with the earth, with the climate',[13] gives him a right to it. So too does his unconditional love of the land and its climate.

As a direct reaction to the beginning of the latest period of troubles, these thoughts are repeated in varied forms in some of the poems in the collection *An Ulster Reckoning* (1971). A good example, which also illustrates the migrations caused by industrialisation, is:

An Ulsterman

This is my country. If my people came
from England here four centuries ago,
the only trace that's left is in my name.
Kilmore, Armagh, no other sod can show
the weathered stone of our first burying.
Born in Belfast, which drew the landless in,
that river-straddling, hill-rimmed town, I cling
to the inflections of my origin.

Though creed-crazed zealots and the ignorant crowd,
long nurtured, never checked, in ways of hate,
have made our streets a by-word of offence,
this is my country, never disavowed ... (132)

In a sequence of sonnets in the same collection, the view is widened by way of comparisons with the problems of Arabs and Jews, of Turks and Greeks in Cyprus, of Pakistanis and Indians. The poem 'Conversations in Hungary' then develops yet another historical parallel:

Our keen friends countered with ironic zest:
your little isle, the English overran –
our broad plain, Tartar, Habsburg, Ottoman –
revolts and wars uncounted – Budapest
shows scarce one wall that's stood two hundred years.
We build to fill the centuries' arrears. (130-131)

It is interesting to see what Hewitt makes of what is maybe the most symbolic event of Planter history, King William III's crossing of the Boyne. While recreating the situation from the inside, from the point of view of one of the king's followers, he marks his distance to it both by speaking of it as a legend and by reacting as a republican. The leader is 'a symbol only', 'a small man', 'lonely', it is his purpose that matters, no need to salute him, just follow the direction he gives and keep out of his way ('The Crossing', 68).

History is to Hewitt something real, concrete, something you have to relate the present to. He says about a visit to the Municipal Gallery, Dublin, that he 'stumbled into history unaware' when he suddenly found himself in a room of sculpture representing people who set a mark on the first part of this century: John O'Leary, George Bernard Shaw, James Stephens, George Russell, Jim Larkin, and Maud Gonne. He reflects on them as:

... emblems of the power
that wrought a nation out of bitterness,
and gave its history one triumphant hour ... (90-91)

Now, however, they seem forgotten in the present indifference to history. He looks around him at the contemporary scene and at what can be expected for the future, and despairs of the role and power of history.

When it comes to historical remains generally, we hear time and again – from the early poetry of the thirties, especially in 'The Return', to my latest example, which is from 1978 – that castles and fortresses, everything connected with kings and nobles and the glory of war, all this is uninteresting compared to the less obtrusive evidence of the lives and customs of the simple country people, or to the disastrous effects when power is concentrated on one side and frustration on the other. It is therefore interesting to compare Hewitt's view of history with a couple of famous pronouncements. Edward Gibbon, the author of *The Decline and Fall of the Roman Empire,* sees history as 'little more than the register of the crimes, follies, and misfortunes of mankind' (Chapter 3), while Hewitt emphasises the strength of the dissenters as well as what was built up by people working together. Thomas Carlyle, in his *On Heros, Hero-Worship, and the Heroic in History* (1841), states that 'The History of the world is but the Biography of great men',[14] whereas to Hewitt it is not only the great but also the small men who are important, ordinary people like the rhyming weavers or the sailor he observes in Greece who could have fitted in on board Odysseus' ship. In James Joyce's *Ulysses* we find Stephen Dedalus complaining: 'History ... is a nightmare from which I am trying to awake'.[15] This can be compared with Hewitt's search for roots and links in history as something that gives his own life a fuller meaning. In 'No Rootless Colonist', he writes 'I have experienced a deep enduring sense of our human past before the Lion Gate at Mycenae and among the Rolright Stones of the Oxfordshire border, but it is the north-eastern corner of Ireland where I was born and lived until my fiftieth year, where the only ancestors I can name are buried' (95). In an early poem, 'The Return' (13-19), he sums up his view of history; a view which is also his view of life and of humanity, and a view in which he finds his identity:

> ... life was eternal, involving every instant.
> ...
> Man has gone on, endured the incidence
> of Rome and Caesar, lived to see the end
> of woad and crucifixion, Thor and Zeus:
> if not men individual with these faces,
> jaws set so, brows this angle, eyes this colour,
> man has gone on, essential man, the Maker
> ... making something lovely;
> a bronze blade meant to kill, but leaf-precise.
> Always the touch of immortality
> upon the things of death; the mark of life
> on things with else no secondary meaning.
> For it is not the wars that we remember
> but the chiselled face, the brooch, the silver bugle,
> the temple, and the sonnet: these are Man. (18-19)

Whatever culture, whatever race or tribe, whatever period of history that constitutes his subject, Hewitt looks for the common denominator, the universal. He finds his identity in the human endeavour, persistent throughout history, to give shape and form to objects around us – in other words, in the aesthetic drive. John Hewitt's search for a definition of his humanity, his creation of an identity, combines his fascination with history and his love of the arts.

Notes

1. Frank Ormsby (ed.), *The Collected Poems of John Hewitt* (Belfast: the Blackstaff Press, 1991), xxxi. Page references to poems are to this edition and are given in the text.
2. MS of 'A North Light', 132.
3. *Ibid.*, 129-38. Other works of art history are: 'Some Observations on the History of Irish Painting', *Lagan* 1 (1943), 93-99; and 'Painting and Sculpture in Ulster' in Sam Hanna Bell, Nessa A. Rob and John Hewitt (eds), *The Arts in Ulster: A Symposium* (Harrap, 1951), 71-95.
4. *Rhyming Weavers and Other Country Poets of Antrim and Down,* edited and with an introduction by John Hewitt (Belfast: Blackstaff Press, 1974), 21.

5. See also 'The Course of Writing in Ulster', *Rann* 20 (June, 1953), 43-52.
6. 'No Rootless Colonist' *Aquarius* 5 (1972), 91.
7. 'Planter's Gothic: An Essay in Discursive Autobiography [1]', republished in Tom Clyde (ed.), *Ancestral Voices: The Selected Prose of John Hewitt* (Belfast: Blackstaff, 1987), 5-6. In the published version the family name is disguised as Howard.
8. Cf. 'Once Alien Here', 20.
9. 'Planter's Gothic', *Ancestral Voices*, 8-9. The words in square brackets are from the original manuscript.
10. Damian Smyth, 'So Much Older Then ... Younger Than That Now: An Interview with John Hewitt', *North Magazine* 4 (Winter 1985), 14.
11. 'A North Light', 111.
12. 'What is my Nation?', chapter in Hewitt's autobiographical papers, 4.
13. 'No Rootless Colonist', 94.
14. In Lecture I, 'The Hero as Divinity'.
15. (New York: Random House, 1946), 35.

Roots in the Bog: Notions of Identity in the Poetry and Essays of Seamus Heaney

Michael Böss

Seamus Heaney begins his essay 'Englands of the Mind' with a reference to T.S. Eliot's notion of 'the auditory imagination'. According to Heaney, Eliot defined the auditory imagination as 'the feeling for syllable and rhythm, penetrating far below the conscious levels of thought and feeling, invigorating every word; sinking to the most primitive and forgotten, returning to the origin and bringing something back', fusing 'the most ancient and most civilized mentality'.[1] Heaney presumes Eliot was thinking of the cultural depth-charges latent in certain words and rhythms. If so, one is close to the secret that explains how the words of a poem are bound together in a way that is not only delightful to the ear, but also pleases the mind and the body. For Eliot was probably 'thinking of the energies beating in and between the words that the poet brings into half-deliberate play; thinking of the relationship between the word as pure vocable, as articulate noise, and the word as etymological occurrence, as symptom of human history, memory and attachments'(151).

As an auditory phenomenon the poem is a distinct kind of music, and as such it reflects 'almost physiological operations' in the act of writing, Heaney observes in his essay 'The Making of a Music' (*Preoccupations*, 61). Both physiological operations are not only determined by the individual poet, however, but also by the culture and the literary conventions to which he has been exposed from his childhood:

> [I]n any kind of poetic music, there will always be two contributory elements. There is that part of the poetry which takes its structure and beat, its play of metre and rhythms, its diction and allusiveness, from the literary tradition. The poetry that Wordsworth and Yeats had read as adolescents and as young men obviously laid down certain structures in their ear, structures that gave them certain kinds of aural expectations for their own writings. ... But there is a second element in a poet's music, derived not from the literate parts of his mind but from its illiterate parts, dependent not upon what Jacques Maritain called his

'intellectual baggage' but upon what I might call his instinctual ballast. What kinds of noise assuage him, what kinds of music pleasure or repel him, what messages the receiving stations of his senses are happy to pick up from the worlds around him and what ones they automatically block out – all this unconscious activity, at the pre-verbal level, is entirely relevant to the intonations and appeasements offered by a poet's music. (62)

It is precisely because the music of the poem intones the 'sounds' from the unconscious levels of the mind that the poet's 'composition' may become a source of a deeper form of understanding of both oneself and of one's culture. Heaney feels spiritually related to Wordsworth, who writes in *The Prelude*:

My own voice cheered me, and, far more, the mind's
Internal echo of the imperfect sound;
To both I listened, drawing from them both
A cheerful confidence in things to come. (Quoted in *Preoccupations*, 63)

These lines are not only about writing poems in nature, Heaney points out. What is important is what they say about the 'activity of listening'. Listening to the sound of his own voice, the poet discovers that his spoken music is just 'the shadow of the unheard melody', 'the mind's internal echo': 'He is drawn into himself even as he speaks himself out, and it is this mesmerized attention to the echoes and invitations within that constitutes his poetic confidence'(63).

Thus, to Heaney the poetic act becomes a way in which the poet may make contact with his own creative powers; a way in which, by uncovering layer upon layer of the personal and collective unconscious, he may give words to unarticulated emotions and thereby be able to express a kind of existential authenticity. This aim is central to Heaney's own work as a poet. In his essay 'Feeling into Words', he describes his own aspiration to write

poetry as divination, poetry as revelation of the self to the self, as restoration of the culture to itself, poems as elements of continuity, with the aura and authenticity of archaeological finds, where the buried shard has an importance that is not diminished by the importance of the buried city: poetry as a dig, a dig for finds that end up being plants. (41)

Poetry, in other words, which although rooted in a past has the potential of breaking up the crust of surface realities to send one on a search for a continually evolving selfhood arising from one's contact with the deeper levels of mind and culture. As I will show in this essay, it follows that Heaney must see poetry as a complication of conventional notions of identity.

1. Culture and Language

Archaeological metaphors run through a great number of Heaney's early poems, for example, the well-known 'Bogland', which he wrote after a visit to his friend the painter T.P. Flanagan in the autumn of 1968. As this will be central to my reading, we need to be reminded of it in its full length:

We have no prairies
To slice a big sun evening –
Everywhere the eye concedes to
Encroaching horizon,

Is wooed into the cyclops' eye
Of a tarn. Our unfenced country
Is bog that keeps crusting
Between the sights of the sun.

They've taken the skeleton
Of the Great Irish Elk
Out of the peat, set it up
An astounding crate full of air.

Butter sunk under
More than a hundred years
Was recovered salty and white.
The ground itself is kind, black butter

Melting and opening underfoot,
Missing its last definition
By millions of years.
They'll never dig coal here,

Only the waterlogged trunks
Of great firs, soft as pulp.
Our pioneers keep striking
Inwards and downwards,

Every layer they strip
Seems camped on before.
The bogholes might be Atlantic seepage.
The wet centre is bottomless.[2]

Bogs are something Heaney knows well from his birthplace in Co. Derry. In one of his earliest poems he describes his grandfather cutting turf. When he wrote the poem, he later explained, he had felt as if he

had down a shaft into real life. The facts and surfaces of the things were true, but more important, the excitement that came from naming them gave me a kind of insouciance and a kind of confidence. I didn't care who thought what about it: somehow, it had surprised me by coming out with a stance and an idea that I would stand over. (41-42)

Thus, it was not only the grandfather – and father – who were digging but also Heaney himself in the act of writing, using his pen as a tool:

Between my finger and my thumb
The squat pen rests; snug as a gun.

Under my window, a clean rasping sound
When the spade sinks into gravelly ground:
My father, digging. I look down

Till his straining rump among the flowerbeds
Bends low, comes up twenty years away
Stooping in rhythm through potato drills
Where he was digging.
...

The cold smell of potato mould, the squelch and slap
Of soggy peat, the curt cuts of an edge
Through living roots awaken in my head.
But I've no spade to follow men like them.

Between my finger and my thumb
The squat pen rests.
I'll dig with it.[3]

The 'real life' which is brought up to the surface of memory in the poet's 'digging' with his pen is not only the father's and the grandfather's physical labour. It is also the poet's cognition that is brought about in his working with his pen as the smells from the mould and the sound of the slicing spade through the soggy peat 'awaken' in his head and make him find words with which to express the feelings to which memorised sense impressions give rise. The potato field and the bog, thus, are associated with the mind remembering, both on its conscious and its unconscious levels.

In 'Bogland' the perspective is wider. The poet no longer speaks as an 'I', but has become a 'we'. But the poem originally sprang from an attempt to fuse the personal and the collective. Heaney recalls how, originally, he had been 'vaguely wishing to write a poem about bogland', chiefly,

because it is a landscape that has a strange assuaging effect on me, one with associations reaching back into early childhood. We used to hear about bog-butter, butter kept fresh for a great number of years under the peat. Then when I was at school the skeleton of an elk had been taken out of the bog nearby and a few of our neighbours had got their photographs in the paper, peering across its antlers. So I began to get an idea of bog as the memory of the landscape, or as a landscape that remembered everything that happened in it and to it. (*Preoccupations*, 54)

The bog, thus, develops into a metaphor for – 'for want of a better word' – 'our national consciousness' (35). But although the past is being stripped layer by new layer, and the present is getting richer from new knowledge about what came before, there is no 'last definition', as he says in 'Bogland'. It is the mental digging process that matters in a world without essences. The wet centre of the bog, i.e. of Ireland, is 'bottomless' – 'our pioneers keep striking inwards and downwards'. Indeed, the centre of the bogholes may be 'Atlantic seepage'. It is not even a real centre, that is, but part of a lower level of connectedness.

It is the echo of this connectedness that Heaney hears in Irish place names, as, for instance, in the name of his family's farm, Mossbawn, in Co. Derry (17). The name is a derivative of a combination of a Gaelic and an English word which both have a common root in the Danish word *mose*, bog. The etymology of the word takes us back to the Ireland of the Vikings.[4] Heaney's point, however, is not that the farm originates in a Viking settlement but that language also has a 'wet centre'. Like the bog, words are 'bottomless', arbitrary, and without finite definitions.

In his essay 'Correspondences: Emigrants and Inner Exiles',[5] Heaney recounts a story he was once told by an Irish professor: One day a schoolmaster from Cork suspected two of his pupils had been copying from each other. But he was not sure who had copied from whom. In order to find out which of the two was the copyist, he kept both of them in the classroom at lunchtime one day. He placed them together at the same desk next to each other and asked them to write an essay about 'The Swallow'. After some time, he separated the two boys and made them sit each in their corner of the classroom. Shortly after he collected their exercise books. He was able to tell which of the two was the culprit after having read only two sentences of his text, which began: 'The swallow is a migratory bird. He have a roundy head'. Heaney adds his own conclusion to the story:

> When professor John Cronin first told me this story, I realised it was a two sentence history of Anglo-Irish literature. First comes the correct, stilted schoolbook English, a kind of zombie speech which walks shakily out of the evacuated larynx where Irish once exercised itself with instinctive freedom. *The swallow is a migratory bird.* Then into this undead English English there arrives the resurrected afterlife of the Irish and vigour is retrieved. The personality has found access to all its old reservoirs of sureness and impulse. Grammar goes wonky, vocabulary goes local, and an intelligence which had been out of its element in the first sentence gets right back into the second: *He have a roundy head.* I cite this as another example of the Irish psyche flitting like a capable bat between the light of a practical idiom and the twilight of a remembered previous place, alert as any linguistic philosopher both to the arbitrariness of signs and the ache of the unspoken. ('Correspondences', 25-26)

But the language shift from Irish to English is not the only thing which has caused a 'rift' in the Irish mind, Heaney adds. He refers to Dr. Proinsias MacCana, the medieval historian, who once inferred from a textual analysis of the heroic narrative *Táin Bó Cuailgne* that the introduction of Latin into the Irish church from the sixth century resulted in a clash between two cultures and world pictures: on one hand a mythopoeic culture ignorant of secular chronology and 'locating people and events in a past by reference to genealogical filiation or to the reigns of famous kings, whether legendary or historical', and on the other hand the Roman and international culture, which brought Christianity and Latin to Ireland and which put its mark on Irish culture from the first half of the sixth century and onwards.[6] Besides a new language and a new type of religion, this new international culture also brought new conceptions of time and history, of the sacred and the secular, and of artistic and religious categories, that were fundamentally different from those that existed in the native population.

This rift in the Irish consciousness has manifested itself ever since, Heaney claims. In fact, the language shift from Irish to English was a repetition of the same story. At that time, the Irish learned to speak English in order to be able to adapt to the modern, international world. But the shift implied far more than exchanging one language for another. Again, it was a matter of two cultures clashing, Heaney holds:

> ... between an international style of commerce and culture and the more indigenous conservatism and traditionalism of Irish life generally. Corresponding to the Old Irish immersion in the phantasmagoria of myth, we have the demure, frugal, admirably visionary if intellectually obscurantist world of de Valera's Ireland – pastoral, pure and Papist; and corresponding to the organisational, ecclesiastical, administrative Latin culture, we have the rational, international, pragmatic spirit of Sean Lemass, Dr. Ken Whitaker and the First Economic Plan. Need I go on? Of course I need not. ('Correspondences', 27)

It is the same kind of cultural and moral tension that Heaney hears in the Irish schoolboy's description of the swallow as a migratory bird with a roundy head. And it is the same tension which is felt whenever the ghetto-blaster is heard playing on the bog bank or which can be detected in the contrast between the 'Dallas architecture of Connemara bungalows' and the cabins in ruin on the hillside. It is a kind of 'spiritual and aesthetic violence' that is being committed, and yet '[i]t would be sentimental to expect the old world of season and custom and hallowed site and rite to have survived'. It is futile to distinguish between 'the traditional' and 'the commercial' (ibid., 28). Aran sweaters are no longer only worn by people living on the Aran Islands. They have become an international product. Mayo is no longer associated with its traditional hats but rather with computers. The old world no longer exists, and in this way the chances for the individual to experience a focus for his or her personal life have been greatly reduced.

2. Sensing the Past

Indeed, Heaney thinks that the old world has literally become 'unfocused'. He refers to the Latin etymology of the word *focus*, which means hearth, the domestic fireplace which once was the 'centre, the heat and the heart' of any Irish countryside home – that is both a physical and metaphysical centre in the life of the individual:

Any hearth was all the hearths there had ever been. Every morning the fact of fire was wonderful all over again as the primal flame was gratefully rekindled. Fast forward then, as they say in the video business, to the central heating system, and abruptly you have the cancellation of wonder. Your being is insulated from the physical and metaphysical life of flame. Your space has been made abstract by an imposed grid of pipe and radiator. You have comfort but you also have something inside you that is out of alignment. In a dumb old part of yourself you have left the world of roundy heads and entered the world of migratory birds. You are stumbling about in the international Latin and suppressing the hearth Irish. ('Correspondences', 28-29)

But then one day, one may suddenly and unexpectedly get one of these epiphanies which free energies and feelings from the unconscious and make one realise what life is all about, or which direction one's own life should take. One may run into

[a]n old house say, like the one I found myself in recently, where I lifted a latch for the first time in years; and there, in that instantly cold metal touch, in the pleasing slackness and scissor-and-slap of the latch mechanism, something unpredictably invigorating happened. My body awakened in its very capillaries to innumerable and unnamable rivulets of affection and energy. The moment that latch made its harsh old noise, a whole ancestral world came flooding up. And that inundation persuades me that in all of us (the lacuna in the midriff notwithstanding) there is a supply of dammed-up energy waiting to be released. In other words, a connection is possible between your present self and your intuited previousness, between your inchoate dailiness and your imagined identity. Your Irishness, to put it in yet another way, constitutes a big unconscious voltage and all it needs is some transformer to make it current in a new and significant and renovative way. ('Correspondences', 29)

Heaney claims it is possible, in the communication between the senses and the imagination, i.e. through one's auditory imagination, to find a source of mental energy 'in the ghostlife of a lifting latch', and designates this resource his own private 'Ireland', which is a state of mind rather than the mind of a state. But he does hope that it is from such experiences that future individual minds on the island will be inspired. It is his wish that it will be possible to 'base an intellectual and philanthropical project upon fidelity to some absent but intuited Ireland of the affections and the imagination'. However, his intent is not to recreate an Ireland of the past but a new 'work of meaning' ('Correspondences', 30).

It is as this lower level of connectedness, it appears, that poetry may have social significance as a source of new 'meaning'. Poetry is a potential means of healing a broken mind and a divided culture by drawing from the resources of the imagination. This is a perception that Seamus Heaney has gradually developed since the 'Troubles' started in Northern Ireland in 1969. At that time he came to realise that 'the problems of poetry moved from being a matter of achieving the satisfactory verbal icon to being a search for images and symbols adequate to our predicament', as we have often been reminded (*Preoccupations*, 65).

3. Poetry and Identity

When Heaney speaks of poetry as part of a process that may heal personal and cultural traumas, he does not speak in the way in which Irish peacemakers and politicians may speak of the urgency of reconciling cultural traditions. In an essay from the recent collection *The Redress of Poetry*, elaborating on an idea from 'Place and Displacement', Heaney explains himself with reference to the experience of young William Wordsworth.[7]

In 1791, when England declared war on France, Wordsworth was thrown into a serious personal conflict. At the time, Wordsworth sympathized strongly with the political ideals of the revolutionary cause in France. But his national loyalty rested with his native country. Never before in his life had he been in such a dilemma and felt so mentally split as he was in this situation. He felt deeply alienated and disaffected, for example, when in church he took part in prayers for English victory. As it turned out, however, writing a poem about his own trauma became part of a healing process, Heaney writes:

> *The Prelude* is about a consciousness coming together through the effort of articulating its conflict and crises. And the same could be said of much poetry from Northern Ireland. For the best efforts there have been evident in writing that is a mode of integration, of redistributing the whole field of cultural and political force into a tolerable order. (*Redress*, 189)

Poetry tends to be a kind of counterweight, a balancing force, a means of redress 'tilting the scales of reality towards some transcendent equilibrium' when something gets unbalanced, Heaney writes, borrowing an image from Simone Weil's *Gravity and Grace*. In poetic activity, a kind of 'counter-reality' is placed in the scales:

> A reality which may only be imagined but which nevertheless has weight because it is imagined within the gravitational pull of the actual and can therefore hold its own and balance out against the historical situation. This redressing effect of poetry comes from its being a glimpsed alternative, a revelation of potential that is denied or constantly threatened by circumstances. (*Redress*, 3-4)

But to effect the redress of poetry does not mean that the poet should deliberately aim at changing the social or political situation of his own time. The poet should not seek to adopt the language of politics, but should instead help 'set the world free to have a new go at its business' (*Redress*, 191). He should be both socially responsible and creatively free and strive towards being a 'source of truth' and towards offering 'a glimpsed alternative, a world to which "we turn incessantly and without knowing it"' (*Redress*, 192). Heaney illustrates his distinction between the poet as politician and the poet as source of truth by referring to the way in which his own generation of northern poets had felt 'called upon' to deal with the northern conflict:

Among the poets of my own generation in the 1960s there was a general feeling of being socially called upon which grew as the polarization grew and the pressure mounted upon the writers not only to render images of the Ulster predicament, but also perhaps to show solidarity with one or other side in the quarrel. Even if they preferred to avoid the redemptive stance, the writers could not altogether escape the myth of their own importance in an ongoing work of definition and transformation. We all experienced a need to get certain unique and almost subcultural realities of Ulster life into words, and we all learnt something from each other and from the example of other generations. (*Redress*, 193)

Heaney relates how he himself found inspiration in Patrick Kavanagh, John Montague and John Hewitt. They taught him that the question of cultural identity is more complicated than both the Celtic and Gaelic revivalists *and* unionists had claimed at the beginning of this century.

When, in the mid-eighties, Heaney found himself included in an anthology of 'British Verse', he belatedly responded by writing a poetic satirical pamphlet. In this 'open letter', in which he addressed 'Blake and Andrew, Editors, Contemporary British Verse, Penguin Books, Middlesex', he did not renounce his indebtedness to English culture, 'But British, no, the name's not right', for, as he wrote, 'My passport's green. No glass of ours was ever raised to toast *The Queen*'. Claiming an Irish identity, although living in the British state, was one of the freedoms of the citizen, he concluded.[8]

In *The Redress of Poetry*, he assents to an essay by Roy Foster, the Irish historian, who wrote in 1993:

Ownership of Irish history is claimed from all sides; the idea of a common stock, much less a universal scepticism, is not popular in all quarters. No one is exempt from this possessiveness; but we need not give up our claims on Irishness in order to conceive of it as a flexible definition. And in an age of exclusivist jihads to east and west, the notion that people can reconcile more than one cultural identity with their individual selves may have much to commend it.[9]

In the same essay, which is the introduction to his book of essays on 'connections in Irish and English history', Foster claims that today more attention deserves to be given to studying how people in the past have seen themselves as Irish 'than the awarding or denying of Irishness as a mark of good conduct, or embarking on self-justifying searches for uncorrupted "roots", or taking refuge in self-congratulatory conspiracy theories' (*Paddy*, xvi). If people stop focusing on the idea of an authentic 'Irishness', he hopes, a modernized nationalism might one day develop with 'tremendous relevance' for the tolerance of cultural diversity in the North, but also as something which might take some of the tension out of attitudes that still linger in the South (*Paddy*, 37).

Heaney supports this argument with some thoughts by the Irish philosopher, Richard Kearney, on an Irish sympathy for the dialectical idea of a both/and to the exclusion of a 'logocentric' either/or.[10] 'Two-mindedness' is indeed something I have had to live with all my life, writes Heaney:

There is nothing extraordinary about the challenge to be in two minds. If, for example, there was something exacerbating, there was still nothing deleterious to my sense of Irishness in the fact that I grew up in the minority in Northern Ireland and was educated within the dominant British culture. My identity was emphasized rather than eroded by being maintained in such circumstances. The British dimension, in other words, while it is something that will be resisted by the minority if it is felt to be coercive, has nevertheless been a given of our history and even of our geography, one of the places where we all live, willy-nilly. It's in the language. And it's where the mind of many in the republic lives also. So I would suggest that the majority in Northern Ireland should make a corresponding effort at two-mindedness, and start to conceive of themselves within – rather than beyond – the Irish element. Obviously, it will be extremely difficult for them to surmount their revulsion against all the violence that has been perpetrated in the name of Ireland, but everything and everybody would be helped were they to make their imagination press back against the pressure of reality and re-enter the whole country of Ireland imaginatively, if not constitutionally, through the northern point of the quincunx.[11]

It is evident that Heaney's notion of the multi-layeredness of Irish identities is as critical of traditional nationalist ideology, with its notion of an 'Irish' cultural authenticity, as it is of unionist claims of 'Britishness'.

In his essay 'Society and Authenticity' (1971), Lionel Trilling reminds us that the concept of authenticity is a product of 19th century romantic philosophy and poetry. Although Rousseau did not use the very word, it was clearly inherent in his idea of the uncorrupted state of society and of man, Trilling thinks. In aesthetic thought, the idea of authenticity came to be seen as the opposite of the neo-classicist ideal of beauty as nature perfected by art. The concept of authencity thus became closely associated with the idea of culture which has been predominant in the western world ever since, namely as a 'unitary complex of interacting assumptions, modes of thought, habits, and styles, which are connected in secret as well as overt ways with the practical arrangements of a society and which, because they are not brought to consciousness, are unopposed in their influence over men's minds'.[12]

This idea of culture as something organic and unitary, Trilling proceeds to argue, became more or less a substitute for the old biblical idea about the creation of the world. After the 'death of God', public national history – or 'narrative history' – supplied western man with new beginnings, so to speak, that counteracted the new existential 'weightlessness' with a 'sense of authority' and an 'assurance of destiny'. Historians would tell a tale that 'interpreted the sound and fury of events, made them signify *something*, a direction taken, an end in view'. 'To write the History of England as a kind of Bible' became one of the enterprises that Carlyle urged his own time to take up: 'For England too ... has a History that is Divine; an Eternal Providence presiding over every step of it ...; guiding England forward to *its* goal and work, which too has been considerable in the world!'(*Sincerity*, 138).

In the beginning was the genius of the Celtic race or the German race, or the French nation. Phrases like these expressed the typical ambition of nationalist

143

movements to maintain a fixed point of reference in an increasingly confusing, modern, and 'weightless' world. Seeing national authenticity as one such fixed point of reference, the modern individual might feel bound up with a people which was provided with a destiny and a mission, and which was writing its own chapter in the great narrative of the world.

But since the word authencity has become 'part of the moral slang of our day', as Trilling believed, it might be relevant to call attention to the etymology of the word, which had 'violent meanings' in the ancient Greek. *Authenteo* originally meant 'to have full power over', even to commit murder. An *authentes* is not only a 'master' and a 'doer' – that is a person who has the power to create something, but also a 'perpetrator', a 'murderer', even a person who commits suicide (*Sincerity*, 131).

This etymology tells us that the will to be authentic is a will to possess one's own world, i.e. to dominate one's own 'nation'. But at the same time it is a potential threat to this very world. The history of the twentieth century has given ample evidence of the possible murderous implications of the struggle to achieve so-called ethnic and cultural authenticity. Ireland is one the examples that at once comes to mind, of course.

But in the way Seamus Heaney defines 'Ireland' it is to be compared with a wet bog. It is a depth without any bottom, an identity without finite definitions or any real centre. Or rather, perhaps, its centre may turn out to be connected with an ocean across which one people after another have kept arriving in Ireland and whose waves have kept beating the coastlines of other European lands. Still, the lack of final definitions does not mean that one might just as well forget history, and that it is no longer possible to develop an understanding of oneself from a sense of the past in the present.

According to Heaney's idea of 'Ireland', identity is something that evolves in the process by which the individual engages in his or her own attempt of 'digging' downwards and inwards towards personal and collective depths. Identity is not a result, but is part of the process in which one probes into the layers and echoes of one's own world, and, during this experience, feels creative energy rising to the mind's surface. It is only in this sense that it is meaningful to talk about authentic identity. Striving for authentic identity in this sense is a personal and individual goal, not a national or a collective one. Nevertheless, one might say, it is a goal with, potentially, tremendous collective implications, both for Ireland and for the rest of the world.

Notes

1. Seamus Heaney, *Preoccupations: Selected Prose 1968-1978* (London: Faber & Faber, 1980), 150. Subsequent page references are to this edition and are included in the text.
2. From *Door into the Dark* (1969), here quoted from *New and Selected Poems 1966-1987* (London: Faber & Faber, 1990), 17-18.

3. From *Death of a Naturalist* (1966), here quoted from *New and Selected Poems 1966-1987*, 1-2.
4. Richard Brown, 'Bog Poems and Book Poems: Doubleness, Selftranslation and Pun in Seamus Heaney and Paul Muldoon' in Neil Corcoran (ed.), *The Chosen Ground: Essays on the Contemporary Poetry of Northern Ireland* (Chester Springs, Penn.: Seren Books, 1992), 153.
5. 'Correspondences: Emigrants and Exiles' in Richard Kearney (ed.), *Migration: The Irish at Home and Abroad* (Dublin: Wolfhound Press, 1989), 21-31.
6. For MacCana's article, see 'Early Irish Ideology and the Concept of Unity' in Richard Kearney (ed.), *The Irish Mind: Exploring Intellectual Traditions* (Dublin: Wolfhound Press, 1985), 56-78.
7. *The Redress of Poetry* (New York: Farrar, Straus and Giroux, 1995). Subsequent page references are to this edition and are included in the text.
8. 'An Open Letter' in Field Day Company, *Ireland's Field Day* (London: Hutchinson, 1985), 23-29.
9. Roy Foster, *Paddy and Mr Punch: Connections in Irish and English History* (Harmondsworth: Penguin, 1995 (1993)), xvi-xvii. Subsequent page references are to this edition and are included in the text.
10. Richard Kearney (ed.), *The Irish Mind: Exploring Intellectual Traditions* (Dublin: Wolfhound Press, 1985), 7-38.
11. *The Redress of Poetry*, 202.
12. Lionel Trilling, *Sincerity and Authenticity* (Cambridge: Harvard University Press, 1971), 125. Subsequent page references are to this edition and are included in the text.

European Past, Irish Present: Joyce's Modern Hells

William Pratt

'The loss of Satan was a tragedy for the imagination', Wallace Stevens once lamented in his poem, 'Esthétique du Mal', but what Stevens thought was lost can be readily found in the works of other modern poets and novelists. Perhaps the heroic figure of Satan, as Milton portrayed him in *Paradise Lost*, no longer occupies a central place in the modern imagination, but Satan still has his dominion in modern versions of the Myth of Hell, which is arguably as potent as ever. As long ago as 1857, in the Preface he wrote for the first book of truly modern poems, *Les Fleurs du Mal*, or *The Flowers of Evil*, Baudelaire declared: 'Everyone smells him and no one believes in him. Sublime subtlety of the Devil'. And not long after that, in the celebrated Grand Inquisitor episode of his novel *The Brothers Karamazov*, Dostoevsky imagined Satan as saying sarcastically: 'What's unenlightened, nowadays, is to believe in God, but it's all right to believe in me, the devil!' Clearly, Baudelaire and Dostoevsky both disagreed with Stevens, and so did Eliot in *The Waste Land*, Pound in the *Cantos*, and Faulkner in *The Sound and the Fury*, to cite other modern literary masterpieces. So all we need to do, if we want to be convinced of the continued relevance of Hell, is to read the masterpieces of modern literature. Most of all, we can read James Joyce, who portrayed Hell as vividly as any modern writer, and who, in his two most widely read novels, *A Portrait of the Artist as a Young Man*[1] and *Ulysses*[2], created images of Hell that rival those of his greatest contemporaries, and even compare with those of his greatest predecessors, from Homer to Dante to Milton.

There is no doubt that Joyce painted an unforgettable picture of Hell in *A Portrait of the Artist as a Young Man*, when he placed Hell at the centre of a young man's experience of growing up in Catholic Ireland. Stephen Dedalus, like Joyce himself, benefitted from a full Jesuit education, at Clongowes Wood College in the peaceful Irish countryside, at Belvedere College in the heart of the bustling Irish capital, and finally at University College Dublin. In Chapter 3, when the boys of Belvedere College go on a week's religious retreat, Stephen is forced to reflect on his sinful behaviour and is brought to an acute crisis of conscience. It is in the very middle of the novel that Stephen listens to a sermon on Hell which leads him to make a passionate confession of guilt, the beginning of a fuller self-understanding that leads him eventually to turn from the vocation of priest to that of artist.

Chapter 3 is the heart of the novel: it begins with Stephen's awareness of his sinful state, when he realizes that 'The chaos in which his ardour extinguished itself was a cold indifferent knowledge of himself'. He feels keenly that '[f]rom the evil seed of lust all other deadly sins had sprung forth', but he feels incapable of rising out of 'the swamp of spiritual and bodily sloth in which his whole being had sunk'.

When the retreat is announced to the boys of Belvedere College, Stephen is caught up in the fervour of a religious exercise shrewdly designed to lead step by step to guilt, repentance, and absolution. The priest, Father Arnall, starts his sermon by speaking of the 'four last things', which are 'death, judgment, hell, and heaven'. However, the four last things become telescoped into one, with more and more concentration on Hell, and in the end it is the fear of Hell which brings Stephen to make his confession.

Much of the rhetoric of the Hell sermon in *A Portrait* is drawn from the New Testament, from vivid accounts of the Last Judgment found in the Gospel of Matthew, Chapter 25, and in the Book of Revelation, Chapter 20, but Joyce adds potency to these apocalyptic visions of the end of time by drawing from a much later source, a 17th century Jesuit sermon by Giovanni Petro Pinamonti, written in Italian but translated into English, called 'Hell Opened to Christians, to Caution Them from Entering into It'.[3] The priest depicts God in his judgment seat and the Archangel Michael weighing souls from Revelation, and quotes with telling force Christ's pronouncement of a Last Judgment on sinners from Matthew 25: 'Depart from me, ye cursed, into everlasting fire which was prepared for the devil and his angels'. But Joyce has Father Arnall borrow many horrifying details of Hell from a later Jesuit sermon, which anticipates the New England Puritan sermons of Jonathan Edwards during the early eighteenth century, especially 'Sinners in the Hands of an Angry God', and he describes the fall of Lucifer, 'hurled with his rebellious angels into hell', in imagery close to Milton's *Paradise Lost*.

Joyce is thus traditional in his first fictional presentation of Hell, borrowing heavily from the Bible and from a Jesuit sermon, and echoing the language of English and American Puritans, but he is also modern, in some of the details of his description of Hell in the sermon, and in the response of Stephen Dedalus to what he hears, since Stephen goes through a sequence of emotions that amounts to a thorough psychological probing of his crisis of conscience, relieved only by his final desperate confession to an old priest in a strange church at the end of Chapter 3.

The description of Hell by Father Arnall begins ominously with the damnation of Lucifer, hurled down for defying God with his *non serviam: I will not serve*, and then goes on to declare that 'Hell is a strait and dark and foulsmelling prison, an abode of demons and lost souls, filled with fire and smoke'. The sermon uses each of the five senses to document a hell that burns with a dark fire, that gives off a terrible smell, that torments the sinner's body with heat so intense that '[t]he blood seethes and boils in the veins, the brains are boiling in the skull, the heart in the breast glowing and bursting, the bowels a redhot mass of burning pulp, the tender eyes flaming like molten balls'. In these phrases, Joyce has embellished the language of the Jesuit sermon with naturalistic images that make Hell even more repugnant. The awful howlings of the damned, filling the sinners' souls with disgust and humiliation, lead to the words of Christ repeated from the Last Judgment: 'Depart from me, ye cursed, into everlasting fire which was prepared for the devil and his angels!'

From the terrifying descriptive imagery of the Hell sermon, Joyce moves to the still more graphic portrayal of psychological terror inside the mind of Stephen Dedalus, who feels 'the scalp of his head trembling as though it had been touched by ghostly fingers', and as he passes along the corridor of the chapel he imagines, not without a touch of Joyce's black humour, that the coats hanging on the wall are 'gibbeted malefactors, headless and dripping and shapeless'. He thinks that every word of the sermon has been directed at him personally, and he imagines that he has already died and been condemned by Christ, just as the sermon foretold, for '[h]is brain was simmering and bubbling within the crackling tenement of the skull'.

But Stephen realizes with relief that he has not died, that he still has time to repent. In this receptive frame of mind, he returns for a further sermon on Hell at the retreat, and listens with a new consciousness of guilt to Father Arnall's description of the spiritual punishment visited upon sinners after death: the pain of loss, the pain of conscience, and the pain of remembered joy – the last echoing what Francesca's troubled spirit tells Dante in Canto V of the *Inferno*:

> Nessun maggior dolore
> che ricordarsi del tempo felice
> nella miseria. (V. 121-23)

> [There is no greater sorrow
> than to remember happy times
> in a time of misery.]

Finally, the priest describes the eternity of suffering in Hell in an extended metaphor which is Joyce's own invention and the most memorable of all his descriptions of Hell: he conjures up the image of a mountain of sand, each grain of which is carried in the beak of a bird through millions of years, and 'At the end of all those billions and trillions of years, eternity would have scarcely begun'.

Stephen responds wholeheartedly to the priest's appeal, as Joyce permits us to see into his mind: 'He had sinned so deeply against heaven and before God that he was not worthy to be called God's child'. He has a nightmare fantasy of slimy creatures crawling across a filthy field, and he hears an inner voice crying 'Confess, Confess!', but he cannot do so to any priest he knows, and so he seeks out a church far from the college, where he is a total stranger, so that he can confess freely without embarrassment. There, in a quiet chapel, he confesses to an old priest, who is astonished to hear the litany of sins a sixteen-year-old boy says he has committed, chief among them the 'sins of impurity' with women. The priest tells him, 'The devil has led you astray. Drive him back to hell when he tempts you to dishonor your body ... Promise God now that you will give up that sin'.

With great relief, '[b]linded by his tears and by the light of God's mercifulness he bent his head and heard the grave words of absolution spoken', and Stephen thinks to himself that '[h]e had confessed and God had pardoned him. His soul was made fair and holy once more, holy and happy'. Thus, with a feeling of peace in his heart, Stephen returns to the college and goes to mass, receiving the communion bread with gratitude: 'He knelt there sinless and timid: and he would hold upon his tongue the host and God would enter his purified body'.

Joyce finishes his first fictional image of Hell with Stephen convinced that it is horrifyingly real, but he does not continue in this redeemed state through the rest of the novel. However, he has had such a renewal of spirit at the retreat that he retains his capacity for self-criticism, and eventually he decides against the tempting religious vocation of the priesthood, choosing instead an artistic priestly vocation. His friend Cranley reminds him that he has never forgotten his Jesuit education, even in choosing to be an artist rather than a priest. The image of Hell has stayed in his mind, for at the end of the novel he is thinking of spiritual burning when he declares it is his high aim 'to forge in the smithy of my soul the uncreated conscience of my race'. And it is the gruelling memory of guilt, repentance, and absolution earlier in his life that has readied him to become the priest of art, who can later in life plan to create works of impersonal dramatic beauty, in his chosen role as 'a priest of eternal imagination, transmuting the daily bread of experience into the radiant body of everliving life'.

Since Joyce's irony permeates the novel, it is left to the imagination of the reader whether Stephen will finally have to pay for his rebellion and the pride of his artistic calling. He may, like Icarus, the son of Dedalus after whom Stephen is named, succeed in flying past what he calls the 'three nets' of family, church, and country, only to find he has flown too near the sun, till the wings of his imagination melt like the wax and feathers of Icarus's wings. He still remembers his indoctrination into the vision of evil, for near the end of the novel, he repeats the damning words of Satan, quoted by the priest in the Hell Sermon, *Non serviam*, and consciously runs the risk of incurring the same damnation as Satan. Stephen assures his friend Cranley that he is willing to face such a risk, that he has made up his mind to lose his soul eternally if it is necessary in order to become an artist: 'I am not afraid to make a mistake, even a great mistake, a lifelong mistake and perhaps as long as eternity too'.

But how seriously is the reader to take him? The question of Stephen's ultimate destiny remains, creating an ironic overtone that lingers after the last chapter of the novel is finished, leaving us, after Joyce's first fictional sally into Hell, with a troubling and ambiguous ending, despite the apparent resoluteness of Stephen's last diary entry, a prayer which he addresses to his mythical father Daedalus rather than to his real father Simon: 'Old father, old artificer, stand me now and ever in good stead'.

No reader can stop there, for Stephen Dedalus does not disappear forever at the end of *A Portrait of the Artist as a Young Man*: he reappears at the beginning of *Ulysses*. There, Joyce refuses to satisfy the reader's curiosity about whether Stephen will succeed or fail as an artist, or whether he is likely to suffer the pains of Hell after death, imagined possibilities in the first novel. In his second novel, Joyce shifts from the narrow but deep autobiographical focus of *A Portrait* to a much broader view of human nature, even though the setting is still his native city of Dublin. He chooses to paint a much larger picture of life in *Ulysses*, and to invent characters not modeled on those he knew, even if Stephen – that is, the dramatized figure of Joyce himself – remains in the centre.

In *Ulysses*, the autobiographical hero Stephen Dedalus is joined by two other main characters wholly of Joyce's imagination: Leopold Bloom, a Dublin Jew and a most unlikely hero, a foreigner to Ireland even though he is a native citizen, with a job as an advertising man for a Dublin stationer's firm, and his wife Molly (*née* Tweedy) who is unabashedly Irish, has a fine singing voice, and is a passionately full-bodied woman. Why would Joyce, who in his first novel seemed primarily interested in the most intelligent and cultivated members of the human race, have chosen to redirect his gaze to such a pair of fleshly vulgarians as Leopold and Molly Bloom, living in their modest house on Eccles Street and indulging sensually and not very discreetly in their extramarital love-affairs? Joyce was consciously expanding his knowledge of human nature by creating characters as much unlike himself and his fictional alter ego Stephen Dedalus as possible. Stephen now is a somewhat orphaned son seeking his lost father; no longer the soaring Icarus beside the 'hawklike figure' of his father Daedalus, he is cast in the subordinate role of Joyce's Telemachus to the Ulysses of Bloom and the Penelope of Molly.

Joyce's second novel thus differs greatly from the first in the role played by Stephen, and differs even more in its narrative technique, so that not only does Joyce invent characters unprecedented in his previous fiction, but invents a way of presenting them that goes far beyond any of the experiments he had tried in *A Portrait*. His radically new stream-of-consciousness method of portraying character made *Ulysses* much more than a sequel to *A Portrait*: Joyce's first novel, brilliant though it is, in retrospect looks almost like one of the last traditional English novels, while *Ulysses* seems the first great modern novel. So deftly does Joyce create the illusion that we are inside the minds of his three main characters – first Stephen, then Bloom, then Molly – that character differences come to matter less than character likenesses, and we have the sense of participating in a range of human experience that becomes all-inclusive. While Stephen himself changes little in character from *A Portrait of the Artist* to *Ulysses*, Joyce changes extraordinarily in his way of portraying him, so much so that it could almost be said that in his first novel Joyce shows us how Stephen decided to become an artist rather than a priest, with little of his art to prove it, while in his second novel he proves to us what a great artist Stephen potentially is, since the genius of poetry shines forth brilliantly from the mind of Stephen Dedalus: 'Ineluctable modality of the visible', he muses poetically to himself, 'Signatures of all things I am here to read ... Am I walking into eternity along Sandymount strand?' It would not be too much to say that Stephen's imagination has become even more metaphorical in *Ulysses* than it was in *A Portrait of the Artist as a Young Man.*

Still further differences separate these two fictional masterpieces, for if, in his first novel, Joyce effectively used Greek myth as well as Christian theology to tell a story of how a young man much like himself was initiated into the meaning of Western culture, in his second novel Joyce did something still more ambitious. *Ulysses* is a naturalistic work of fiction, so shocking in its scatological and sexual imagery as to be banned for years in English-speaking countries (Ezra Pound compared it to Swift and Rabelais), and yet it is built on one of the oldest myths in Western literature, the myth of Ulysses' voyage home from Troy to Ithaca, including the first imaginary journey to Hell, or Hades, the world of the dead. Joyce created a work of such import that Frank Kermode says of it in *An Appetite for Poetry* that it has 'two plots, one primordial and metaphoric and related to the true design of the world, the other modern and temporal and concerned with superficial connections experienced in time'.[4] Joyce himself said his intention was 'to render the myth *sub specie temporis nostri*', to retell the Homeric story in the language of his own time. The result is that one can read the novel without knowing anything about the *Odyssey*, as if Joyce were simply giving an account of ordinary people living in Dublin in the year 1904 – on one particular day, June 16, 1904, a single twenty-four-hour period that encompasses nearly everything his characters have thought or experienced in their lives. But one can also read the novel as Joyce himself conceived it, keeping the events of the *Odyssey* in mind as they parallel the daily events in Dublin, and then it becomes a much richer book, 'a spiritual encyclopedia', as Kermode calls it, 'the exemplary novel of our age', which enables us to see much more than our age, an 'inspired unity' like the Bible, 'concealing behind its stories an occult plot which is a master version of the plot of our world'(175).

This exalted opinion of Joyce's novel by a recent critic only serves to confirm what was said from the time *Ulysses* was first published. In 1923, a year after the book publication of Joyce's novel (it had been serialized a year before in *The Little Review*, but legal action against the magazine had blocked its completion) and in the midst of the scandal it created, T.S. Eliot wrote an essay on '*Ulysses*, Order, and Myth', declaring that 'I hold this book to be the most important expression which the present age has found; it is a book to which we are all indebted, and from which none of us can escape'.[5] Eliot went on to argue that 'the

151

mythical method' of Joyce, as he called it, which told a story about contemporary life parallelling the mythical adventures of an ancient hero, was 'simply a way of controlling, of ordering, of giving a shape and a significance to the immense panorama of futility and anarchy which is contemporary history' (177). Thus Joyce's novel was from its inception regarded as a work so original as to be, in Eliot's words, 'a step toward making the modern world possible for art'. What Eliot most praised was the way in which Joyce's novel brought the past and present forcibly together, making it impossible for the reader to understand the present without the past – though the contrast between them is continuously ironic, forcing the reader to guess exactly how the resemblance between Joyce and Homer can be understood, since it is nowhere obvious but always subtly present.

Of all the parallels Joyce drew between his *Ulysses* and Homer's *Odyssey*, none is more subtle or ironic than Chapter 6, the Hades chapter. This chapter is the equivalent of Book 11 of Homer's epic, but it follows the order of Virgil's epic, the *Aeneid*, where the descent into Hades is depicted in Book 6. Book 11 of the *Odyssey* is often called the *Nekuia*, or Rites of the Dead, in which Ulysses sails westward to the dark edge of the ocean and performs the rites prescribed by the enchantress Circe to call up the spirit of Teiresias and receive his prophecy, which alone will enable him to return to his native island of Ithaca. However, instead of Ulysses' epic voyage to Hell, as narrated by Homer, Joyce describes an ordinary funeral procession in Dublin to bury a dead friend of Leopold Bloom. Bloom rides in a carriage with Simon Dedalus, Stephen's father, and they pass young Stephen on the way, but the story is Bloom's, not Stephen's, and it is given to us through his mind, with the objectivity at times of an omniscient narrator.

As Chapter 6 begins, Leopold Bloom enters the carriage to go to the cemetery, joining Simon Dedalus, Martin Cunningham, and Mr. Power, all friends of the deceased Paddy Dignam. The funeral cortège, a horse-drawn hearse and three carriages, makes its way along the streets of Dublin, from Sandymount where Paddy Dignam lived to Glasnevin Cemetery where he is to be buried, east to west to north, crossing over four rivers as it goes, the Liffey and Dodder along with the Grand and Royal Canals, but Joyce mentions them in turn to suggest an unlikely correspondence to the four rivers of Hell – the Acheron, the Styx, the Phlegethon, and the Cocytus – which are all found in Classical accounts of Hell, in Homer as well as in Plato, Virgil, and Dante. Though the procession passes Stephen Dedalus at a distance, and Molly Bloom is mentioned, the Telemachus and Penelope of Homer are left out of Bloom's journey to Hell in Dublin, just as they were left out of Homer's account of Odysseus' journey to Hades.

Paddy Dignam's coffined body, at the head of the cortège, arrives at Glasnevin Cemetery before the mourners, just as, in the *Odyssey*, Ulysses meets first among the dead in Hades the soul of his old shipmate Elpenor, his former companion who had recently died on the island where the sorceress Circe had kept them. Elpenor died in a drunken fall, paralleling Paddy Dignam's death from too much drink, though the humor is much more evident in Joyce's account than in Homer's. In fact, the ironic tone of Joyce's novel is quite unlike the serious tone of Homer's epic, and the abundant graveyard humor in Joyce contrasts sharply with the epic seriousness of Homer. For instance, Bloom remembers silently to himself the florid face of Paddy Dignam: 'Blazing face: redhot. Too much John Barleycorn. Cure for a red nose. Drink like the devil till it turns adelite. A lot of money he spent colouring it'. Further ironic parallels occur in the funeral service at the mortuary chapel, for whereas Homer's Ulysses had performed the *Nekuia* solemnly, digging his pit and pouring his libations and making his blood sacrifices to invoke the spirits of the dead, it is the priest, not Bloom, who intones the Latin requiem mass while Bloom thinks to himself: 'Father Coffey. I knew his name was like a coffin. Dominenamine. Bully about the muzzle he looks. Bosses the show. Muscular christian. Woe betide anyone that looks crooked at him: priest. Thou art Peter'. It is evident that Bloom does not believe in the immortality of the soul, much less in the possibility of Christian salvation, and though he feels genuine sorrow for his friend's death, he hears the familiar words of the burial service without being moved, thinking to himself jokingly: 'The resurrection and the life. Once you are dead you are dead. That last day idea. Knocking them all up out of their graves. Come forth Lazarus! And he came fifth and lost the job'. To mock Christ's own words would be blasphemy, if Bloom were a believing Christian, but he clearly is not. When the body is taken to the freshly dug grave nearby and lowered into the ground, Bloom thinks irreverently: 'We are praying now for the repose of his soul. Hoping you're well and not in hell. Nice change of air. Out of the fryingpan of life into the fire of purgatory'. Outwardly, Bloom and his friends show the properly solemn behaviour of mourners at Paddy Dignam's funeral, but they share jokes on the way to the cemetery and even after the burial, and though Bloom broods on death, he refuses to hold out any hope that there is a state beyond it, remembering without any fear stories he has heard about ghosts, and declaring his own preference for life:

There is another world of death named hell. I do not like that other world she wrote. No more do I. Plenty to see and hear and feel yet. Feel live warm beings near you. Let them sleep in their maggoty beds. They are not going to get me this innings. Warm beds: warm fullblooded life.

The effect then of Joyce's consistently ironic contrast between Bloom's journey to the cemetery and Ulysses' voyage to Hades is that his modern Ulysses has become a figure of comic realism, not of epic heroism, and the modern Hell has become, not a place beyond the ocean where the living go to communicate with the dead, but a place on earth for the burial of bodies. In stark contrast with Homer, there is no prophecy of Teiresias to guide Ulysses homeward after his journey to Hell, no conversations with his mother's spirit or with dead heroes of the Trojan War to console him; there are merely trivial conversations with his friends on the way to the cemetery and irreverent musings about Catholic ritual as the funeral is being performed. So all the dark mystery of the Homeric voyage to the land of the dead seems to have been removed by Joyce in his jocular subjective account of the burial of Paddy Dignam through the mind of Leopold Bloom.

But although Bloom himself has no consciousness of his counterpart, Ulysses, the point is there for the reader to grasp: all this commonplace, matter-of-fact world of the modern city is being ironically contrasted with the mythical world of ancient Greece, which is somehow present in all that Bloom sees and does in Dublin on June 16, 1904, and the reader familiar with Homer is bound to be thinking of the parallels between the mildly comic actions of Bloom and the daringly adventurous actions of Odysseus.

And so we may read Joyce's modern version of Hell as a parodic rewriting of Homer, in which even Christian ritual is part of the parody, and which leaves us with the sense that what once was held sacred, whether by Greeks or by Christians, about the immortality of the soul and the existence of a place of dead spirits, is scarcely believed any longer – and there is the pity. Joyce thus forces us to see how much of what had once been the reality of human experience has been forgotten by modern man, reducing the heroic possibilities of existence to a mostly comic pathos. Bloom is as credible a figure as Ulysses, but the distance between them is the difference between a heroic journey into a visionary realm where the dead can communicate with the living and an ordinary ride through the streets of a shabby city to a graveyard where only the bodies of those we knew are buried. What Joyce accomplishes by his parallel, however, is the keen awareness of what has been lost: if a cemetery is all we have left of Hell, and if death is final both to the body and the soul, then we have plenty of reason to regret the diminished condition of man – a degenerate state which may be regarded as itself, perhaps, the modern equivalent of Hell.

And so Wallace Stevens was partly right, 'The loss of Satan *was* a tragedy for the imagination', since it is the tragedy of the loss which Joyce makes us experience in *Ulysses*, while he is entertaining us with the ironic comedy of the mythical parallels between Homer's classical epic of Ulysses' journey into Hell and Joyce's modern epic of the journey of Leopold Bloom through the everyday streets of Dublin. Hell in *A Portrait of the Artist as a Young Man* causes Stephen Dedalus to look deeply inside himself and decide to become an artist rather than a priest, whereas Hell in *Ulysses* causes Leopold Bloom to look inside himself and turn with relief from the world of the dead to the world of the living.

Stephen's conscience allows him to descend into Hell and come out again alive, absolved of guilt for his previous sins but willing to sin again if necessary to achieve artistic freedom, ready to share the fate of Icarus or of Satan and the rebel angels, risking eternal punishment after death to fulfill his chosen vocation as artist-priest. Bloom's conscience allows him to witness the burial of his dead friend with full Catholic rites as if it were a foretaste of Hell, to enter the graveyard and meditate on death and accept its finality, yet after the funeral to return to the world of the living gladly and go on with his itinerant journey through Dublin, which will end when he (Ulysses) goes with his adopted son (Telemachus) home to his wife (Penelope) in an unconscious re-enactment of the Homeric epic.

So Hell in Joyce's fiction takes two different and complementary forms, but in both, Hell is modern, not a place but a state of mind. Whether Joyce's Hell is portrayed in the originally submissive but ultimately defiant mind of Stephen Dedalus, or in the outwardly deferential but inwardly mocking mind of Leopold Bloom, it remains more subjective than objective, a probing of conscience more than a journey through space, and in both cases it is undeniably and admirably a *Modern* Hell, even while it consciously re-enacts the *Ancient* Hells long ago projected in the Bible and in Homer's epic.

Irish fiction after Joyce has been generally realistic and naturalistic, with no room for Hell, not even the Hell of Leopold Bloom who imagines it but doesn't believe in it. There is only one notable Irish fictional Hell since *Ulysses* in 1922, and that is the one depicted by Flann O'Brien in his novel, *The Third Policeman*, published posthumously in 1967. It is much nearer Joyce's second novel than his first, since it is a projection of Hell into the Irish countryside, and there is no recognition that it is happening after death until the end of the novel. The narrator is a murderer who is supposedly being punished by eternal damnation, but he is hardly aware of it; he shows no sense of guilt for helping to kill a poor old man and rob him, and imagines meeting him again in the underworld without remorse for his brutal deed. His tormentors are three policemen, two of whom he knows by Irish names, and a mysterious 'third policeman' who scarcely appears, though he gives his name to the novel. The descriptions are realistic but the atmosphere of the novel is fantastic, since the narrator and his victim go on living after their deaths. The point of the novel is that it has no point: there is an exact repetition, at the end, of a scene early in the novel, when the narrator first encounters what he thinks is a real police station, but which turns out to be Hell. O'Brien intended his plot to be circular, like *Finnegan's Wake*, but the idea was original with Joyce, and it is not convincing the second time around.

So indirect is Flann O'Brien's treatment of Hell in *The Third Policeman* that readers have been forced to rely on the author's own words about it, in a letter he wrote in 1940 to the American novelist, William Saroyan, long before it was published:

> When you get to the end of this book you realize that my hero or main character (he's a heel and a killer) has been dead throughout the book and that all the queer ghastly things which have been happening to him are happening in a sort of hell which he earned for the killing.[6]

There can be no doubt that O'Brien was influenced by Joyce when he chose Hell for his setting, since Joyce had given Hell its definitive Irish fictional treatment in his two earlier novels. However, the later Irish fictional Hell found in O'Brien's novel has none of the psychological reality or feeling of dread invoked by Joyce in his earlier modern Hells; and so the *locus classicus* of Hell in Irish fiction is still to be found in Joyce's two novels, which remain the greatest of the modern era.

Notes

1. Quotations in the text are taken from Chapter 3 of James Joyce, *A Portrait of the Artist as a Young Man* (New York: Viking Penguin, 1964).
2. Quotations in the text are taken from Chapter 6 of James Joyce, *Ulysses*, The Corrected Text, Hans Walter Gabler *et al.* (eds), (New York: Random House, 1986).
3. See James R. Thrane, 'Joyce's Sermon on Hell: Its Sources and Its Backgrounds', *Modern Philology* LVII (Feb. 1960), 177-98.
4. Frank Kermode, *An Appetite for Poetry* (Cambridge: Harvard University Press, 1989), 209.
5. T.S. Eliot, '*Ulysses*, Order and Myth', first published in *The Dial* (Nov. 1923), reprinted in Frank Kermode (ed.), *Selected Prose of T.S. Eliot* (New York: Harcourt Brace Jovanovich, 1975), 175.
6. Flann O'Brien, *The Third Policeman* (New York: Walker and Company, 1967), 200.

Aspects of Time and Identity in Samuel Beckett

Karl-Heinz Westarp

*From wild weird clime
that lieth, sublime,
out of space –
out of time*
(Edgar Allan Poe)

Edgar Allan Poe's lines express a wish common to mankind, known to us all, to be able to step outside of time and space, to transcend our often painfully experienced limits, to be omnipresent both in the spatial and the temporal sense of the word and to possess and fully grasp our identity in a single instant. This longing for transcendence also underlies Samuel Beckett's characters on their drab and meaningless way through the quagmire of life.

In the following I shall first try to describe our understanding of time, and of the past in particular for the shaping process of identity. Next I shall discuss Beckett's presentation of time and the past in some of his prose statements and fictions. Finally I shall look more closely at two of Beckett's short plays, *Footfalls* and *That Time*, and relate them to the question of identity.

1. The Concept of Time

The ticking away of seconds, minutes and hours is part of our daily human experience; constantly the hourglass of an unknown future is emptied out through the needle's eye of the present into an ever growing past. The Faustian wish 'verweile Augenblick, du bist so schön!' (Stay, moment, you are so beautiful!)[1] is not fulfilled, the moment will never be static. Cognitively it is very difficult to grasp 'time present', since the moment it *is* present and becomes conscious for us as such, it is already part of the past. In this light the hedonistic *carpe diem* motif seems absurdly empty and futile. Similarly the future does not exist, other than as expectation, for the moment it becomes present, it is already part of the past. 'Time', then, is with St. Augustine in book XI of his *Confessions* 'a kind of extension',[2] since we place events on an experientially irreversible time line and

157

thus time is, at least graphically, 'spatialized'. Since Einstein, 'science represents time as a line, alongside the three directions of space',[3] with the essential difference, though, that the three dimensions of space are reversible. For the interlinking of time and space Mikhail Bakhtin coined the concept of 'chronotope'.[4] Any printed text is a chronotope, because spoken language is a flow, is temporal, diachronic, whereas its printed representation is static, spatial, synchronic. The printed text attains as a visual object simultaneity, whereas its oral rendering can never obtain simultaneity, since the words 'fade as soon as they are uttered' (*ibid.*, 434) and become part of the past.

How does the past exist? As in the example just given, it may exist in texts, it may exist in other remnants of human activity, but none of these become consciously present *as* the past unless they are re-created, re-presented, in the sense of 'made present again' in our mind. Seamus Heaney poignantly formulated it in his poem 'Digging' (ll. 5-9):

My father, digging. I look down

Till his straining rump among the flowerbeds
Bends low, comes up twenty years away
Stooping in rhythm through potato drills
Where he was digging.

Similarly the future can only become present as wishes, hopes, expectations in our mind. The mind, therefore, measures the times.[5] St. Augustine says, 'when I think of [my childhood, i.e. the past] and tell about it, I consider a picture of it in the present time, because it is still in my memory'.[6] Or as one of Eudora Welty's characters in *The Optimist's Daughter* formulates it, memory is the 'continuous presence of the past'[7] or the 'presence of the past in the present' (*ibid.*, 178). This is true of our own life experience; we are always carrying our past – and our future – with us: 'Within the Child exists the Old Man; within the Old Man exists the Child'.[8] It is true also of the presentation of time in literature.

It seems, therefore, as Augustine says, that all our time conceptions converge on the present. 'There are three forms of time, the presence of the past, the presence of the present, the presence of the future: these three are certain and they are in the soul, and I see them nowhere else: the presence of the past is memory, the presence of the present is consideration/meditation, the presence of the future is expectation'.[9] For Rousseau the present moment was *arche*, 'where the soul can gather in the whole of its being without any need for recalling the past or encroaching upon the future: *where time is nothing to the soul, where the present lasts always*'.[10] But as I have stated earlier, this wish for permanence of the moment is futile. On the contrary, 'the present moment moves through time, and takes us with it' (Papineau, 14), irrevocably adding piecemeal to our identity, and we feel that time moves, and in one direction only, no going back, which seems indisputably clear, at least in the world of our macroscopic experience.

158

Two other conceptions of time, however, need to be mentioned here. Giambattista Vico attempted a description of the cyclical character of human history in his *Scienza Nuova* (1725), known to us from its many renderings in English literature, as for example in W.B. Yeats's *A Vision* (1925) and his poems of that period, and in J. Joyce's famous 'recirculation' in the cyclical 'ricorso' of *Finnegans Wake*'s (1939) 'Ordovico -Viricordo'.[11] The other time-conception is the modern chaos-theory, wonderfully orchestrated in Tom Stoppard's play *Arcadia* (1993). Recently Huw Price, in his book *Time's Arrow and Archimedes' Point*, has questioned the mono-directionality of the time arrow, since 'causation points both ways in time at the microscopic level' (Papineau, 14).

As a theological corollary it is worth mentioning here that this causation 'backwards in time' has for centuries been part of the Christian creed, for the redemption through Christ is believed to be effective also for those who lived before Christ.

2. Beckett's Presentation of Time

After these general remarks on the concept of time, I now turn to Beckett and ask how he understands and presents time. Beckett's most explicit non-fictional discussion of time is to be found in his early essay on Proust, which was seminal for the later fictional renderings of many of Beckett's major themes. In the essay he undertakes an examination of 'that double-headed monster of damnation and salvation – Time'.[12] Already at this point it is worth noticing the negatively loaded characterization of Time (with a capital 'T').

Proust's creatures ... are victims of this predominating condition and circumstance – Time; ... There is no escape from the hours and the days. Neither from tomorrow nor from yesterday. There is no escape from yesterday because yesterday has deformed us, or has been deformed by us. ... Yesterday is not a milestone that has been passed, but a daystone on the beaten track of the years, and irremediably part of us, within us, heavy and dangerous. (*Ibid.*, 12-13)

Humankind is helplessly caught in this Proustian imprisonment of Time, and the urge to escape this straightjacket grasp of Time in a longing for timelessness becomes all the more prominent, because the movement through time is experienced as a meaningless void. 'Time has become the "eternity" of unwanted existence, an invisible prison without walls and without exit' (Sebba, 308), perfectly visualized in the central image of the cylinder in Beckett's *The Lost Ones*. It 'eats voraciously into every second, hour, day, year, decade, century' (Knapp, 65). In 'Proust' Beckett formulates the individual's experience of movement through time as follows: 'The individual is the seat of a constant process of decantation, decantation from the vessel containing the fluid of future time, sluggish, pale and monochrome, to the vessel containing the fluid of past time'.[13] What is one to do when faced with this consciousness of an inexplicable, unbearable and indeed inescapable condition, since escape through suicide, as Gogo and Didi in *Waiting for Godot* come to realize, is no escape either? To avoid the experience of the void and the ever-present 'Time cancer' (*ibid.*, 18), Beckett and his characters do all they can to 'kill it'. Beckett's preferred mode of killing Time is to talk, to create words, thus creating the impression of some kind of existence, excluding the void. Critic Audrey McMullan writes in her analysis of *That Time*: 'The void has ... been present all along, only kept at bay by the production of the images or sounds, even though it is also the confrontation or the fear of confrontation with this void which perpetuates their production' (McMullen, 437). Fully aware of the profoundly Sisyphean task of continuing creation in words, Beckett nevertheless followed his father's deathbed advice to him in 1933: 'Fight, fight, fight'.[14]

It is striking that Beckett's characters continue their struggle through meaningless mud. So Malone in *Malone Dies*: 'I shall go on doing as I have always done, not knowing what it is I do, nor who I am nor where I am, nor if I am'.[15] Similarly in *The Unnamable*: 'You must go on, I can't go on, I'll go on' (*ibid.*, 418). Beckett himself formulated this impasse most strikingly in his 'Tal Coat' dialogue with Georges Duthuit: 'The expression that there is nothing to express, nothing with which to express, nothing from which to express, no power to express, no desire to express, together with the obligation to express'.[16] To fill the void and the empty identity-lacking self Beckett feels compelled to follow this obligation in an attempt to 'kill time'. As he told himself consolingly in 'Proust': 'Absence of mind is fortunately compatible with the active presence of our organs of articulation' (*ibid.*, 31). With more positive overtones the same attitude is to be found in James Dickey's wonderful phrase: 'In everybody at any time there is a hunger for the word'. So Beckett – and his characters – tell stories and anecdotes, compose inventories, create and hear voices for company, play games, recollect memories to pass the tedium, or simply wait; and in rare cases they are silent. Whenever silent, this silence is not void, as was well formulated by Klaus Reichert: 'Schweigen ist also nicht nichts, es ist festgelegt und bestimmt durch das, was es sagt, indem es das nicht sagt'. [Silence, therefore, is not nothing, it is fixed and defined by what it says by not saying it. My translation.][17]

Most commonly throughout Beckett's work, his characters talk. Thus, for example, Malone: 'While waiting I shall tell myself stories, if I can'.[18] 'That's it, babble. How long can it have lasted? Five minutes? Ten minutes? Yes, no more, not much more. ... In the old days I used to count, up to three hundred, four hundred, and with other things too, the showers, the bells, the chatter of the sparrows at dawn, or with nothing, for no reason, for the sake of counting, and then I divided, by sixty. That passed time, I was time, I devoured the world. Not now, any more' (*ibid.*, 202). Famous also are Winnie's inventories in *Happy Days* and Gogo and Didi's endless waiting for Godot with the final stage image:

Estragon: I can't go on like this. ...
Vladimir: Well? Shall we go?
Estragon: Yes, let's go.
They don't move.
Curtain[19]

3. The Past in the Present

Footfalls and *That Time* belong to the final period of Beckett's work, where he moved increasingly towards silence and his theatre was characterized by the use of minimal means. The original production of *Footfalls* and *That Time* at the Schiller Theater in Berlin in 1976 was directed by 60-year-old Beckett himself. Detailed notes of his directing process have been published, and they show Beckett's well-known concern for minute details of timing, blocking, sound and light. Two images of this production were remarkable: the restlessly pacing May in *Footfalls* and the ghastly face of the Listener in *That Time*.

3.1. *The Present in Memory and Stories:* Footfalls

The four sections of *Footfalls* are divided by a 'faint single chime'[20] which is almost inaudibly faint the last time round. Throughout the rhythm of the play is measured by the 'clearly audible rhythmic pad'(9) of daughter May's restless sleepwalk while invigilating her sick mother, who is present only in the form of a faint voice. Time is spatialized in May's seven steps from left to right and back again.

The first section of the play is a dialogue between mother and daughter, in which they first show concern for each other, next try to remember their age – both are uncertain – the mother being 89-90 and May in her forties, the mother being apologetic that she had May so late. This may have affected May's mental health, since the mother finally asks, 'Will you never have done . . . revolving it all? [...] In your poor mind'(10).

The second section is the mother's interior monologue – a voice which she thinks is present in the daughter's mind (11) – while she, together with the audience, watches May move. Then follows the mother's dialogized memory of the time when the daughter was 'still little more than a child'(11) and wanted to be able to hear her feet fall. Finally the mother expresses her concern for the sleepless May who '[t]ries to tell how it was. (*Pause.*) It all. (*Pause.*) It all'(11).

In the third section we are inside May's head. She first remembers a vision of a person 'when she was quite forgotten'(12) walking in front of the alter 'at certain seasons of the year, during Vespers'(12). May's description of the figure resembles herself now: 'A faint tangle of pale grey tatters'(12). The middle part of this section is May's dialogized story of old Mrs Winter and her daughter Amy at church 'one late autumn Sunday evening'(12), exactly parallel to May and her mother, where Amy denies having observed anything strange at Evensong. Though there are details which might suggest character identity between Mrs Winter and the mother and between Amy and May, Beckett leaves this question open for interpretation. In the last four lines of the play May replays the dialogue with her mother which ended the first section of the play. Here 'the Speaker becomes the Listener without ceasing to be the Speaker'.[21]

After the chime for the fourth section there is '(*No trace of May*)'(13).

In *Footfalls* the present of the two women is there through the mother's voice, May's pacing and her voice. Their past is present through their partly dramatized memories of crucial past events, and May's remembered story of Mrs Winter and her daughter Amy (an anagram for 'May'), which may throw light on what 'it all' means. 'So as well as pacing out the eternal round of time, May appears to be seeking to resolve something that cannot ultimately be resolved'.[22] The empty stage at the end of the play makes it clearly open-ended, and no answer to the riddles of the past, the present and identity is indicated.

3.2.   The Present Informed by the Past as a Means of Identification: That Time

In *That Time* the stage present is even slighter than in *Footfalls*: on the dark stage we only have the Listener, or rather his 'old white face, long flaring white hair as if seen from above outspread'.[23] His breath can be heard and his eyes are open, and though they are closed when the three monologue voices A, B, C begin.[24] The play has three sections. The end of a section is indicated by ten seconds of silence with the Listener's 'breath audible, slow and regular'(9) and his eyes opening three seconds later. After the third section the play ends as follows: 'After 5 seconds smile, toothless for preference. Hold 5 seconds till fade out and curtain'(16). The Listener has no other identity, yet the opening and closing of his eyes – and the final smile – indicate that he reacts to the three sets of voice monologues, which are memories in the Listener's own mind. 'Voices A B C are his own coming to him from both sides and above'(9). They give him company and comfort and make out his identity, in much the same way as in *Krapp's Last Tape* where Krapp listens to tapes of earlier stages in his life, whereas his last tape runs on – recording silence. The Listener 'identitiless ... exists only in terms of the succession of voices echoing from the past' (Knapp, 65). The Listener has access to his past and his identity only through the words of the monologues. The title of the play *That Time* occurs time and again in the monologues, each of the voices trying to establish a more clearly defined point for 'that time', possibly even in relation to the other voices' 'that time', yet ending in Voice C's last comment: 'Come and gone no one come and gone in no time gone in no time' (16). The three voices seem to establish in the present – simultaneously in the mind of the Listener – three different pasts, in that way giving the Listener a present which is nothing but memories of the past, which nevertheless are 'in no time'.[25]

Through collation of the voice fragments in the single sections, the audience is able to establish some kind of time-identity relation between the three voices which are heard three times in the same order in each section: ACB; CBA; BAC; to which section 1 adds CAB and section 2 BCA – only the combination ABC is missing. Piecing the fragments together we see A, a middle-aged man journeying back to Dublin, the city of his birth; C is the same man, aged, visiting public buildings for shelter, where diachronic and synchronic perspectives are juxtaposed; B is the same agent, now a young man, who gives a descriptive recollection of his loved one and past feelings for her. Based on James Knowlson's recent life of Samuel Beckett, *Damned to Fame*, John Taylor states that 'tellingly, [Beckett] did turn to his own past for solace or to recover scenes uncontaminated by adult elucubration' (Taylor, 4). His past is present in B's monologue 'on the stone in the sun gazing at the wheat or the sky or the eyes closed nothing to be seen but the wheat turning yellow and the blue sky vowing every now and then you loved each other'(11).

The Listener experiences his past – or rather his 'pasts' – through the words of the voices. Therefore his 'past can be seen simply as a function or a construct of the language system, ... deployed in the present moment of utterance' (McMullen, 427), as McMullen phrased it. In connection with his discussion of, among other texts, *That Time*, Bert O. States introduces Gaston Bachelard's concept of the 'image of intimate immensity',[26] which I consider very helpful in concluding my remarks on that play. States takes his starting point in the figure of the Listener's white head against the dark empty stage. He says, 'when you put a finite shape, or figure, against what amounts to pure space, you achieve a representation of limitlessness' (*ibid.*). The finite present shape of the Listener achieves identity, as we have seen, through the voice memories in his mind. That way 'space becomes epiphanic by virtue of something temporal culminating within it'. The late plays thus achieve 'their peculiar intensity by the way they fill up empty space before us with time' (*ibid.*, 456-57). 'Spatial and temporal, visual and verbal categories as well as notions of identity, merge into a dimension where all difference is dissolved' (McMullen, 437).

4. Conclusion

To conclude, in the discussion of time and identity it seems that the presence of the past in fiction and in reality are indistinguishably the same: through words and images, fiction makes present in the reader a world built upon an author's past experience, often spiced with hopes and visions; similarly in real life our past spiced with expectations for the future is present in our minds in pictures, words and phrases, which make this present moment the most intense yet also the most fragile part of our life.

Notes

1. Johann Wolfgang von Goethe, *Faust I*, 'Studierzimmer', ll. 1699-1700.
2. E.P. Meijering, *Augustin Über Schöpfung, Ewigkeit und Zeit* (Leiden: 1979), 85; Augustine's *Confessions*, XI, 23; my own translation.
3. David Papineau, Review of Huw Price, *Time's Arrow and Archimedes' Point* in the *Times Literary Supplement*, June 13, 1997, 14.
4. Audrey McMullen, 'Beckett's "Cette Fois"' in *French Studies*, 44/4 (1990), 429.
5. Cf. Meijering, 97; Augustine's *Confessions*, XI, 27.
6. *Ibid.*, 86; *Confessions*, XI, 18.
7. Eudora Welty, *The Optimist's Daughter* (London: Virago, 1984), 195.
8. Bettina Knapp, 'Beckett's *That Time*: "That Double-Headed Monster ... Time"' in *Études Irlandaises*, XV-2, December 1990, 66. Cp. Wordsworth's line in 'My heart leaps up when I behold': 'The child is the father of the man'.
9. Meijering, 73; Augustine's *Confessions*, XI, 20.
10. G. Sebba, 'Time and the Modern Self: Descartes, Rousseau, Beckett', *Studium Generale*, 24/3 (1971), 315.
11. James Joyce, *Finnegans Wake* (New York: Garland, 1971), 215.
12. Samuel Beckett, *Proust* and *Three Dialogues* (London: Calder & Boyers, 1965), 11.
13. Samuel Beckett, *Proust* and *Three Dialogues*, 15.
14. John Taylor, 'I can't go on, I'll go on', *Times Literary Supplement*, September 27, 1996, 4.
15. Samuel Beckett, *Molloy, Malone Dies, The Unnamable* (London: Calder & Boyers, 1966), 226.
16. Samuel Beckett, *Proust* and *Three Dialogues*, 103.
17. Klaus Reichert, 'Geschriebene Sprachlosigkeit' *Frankfurter Allgemeine Zeitung*, 15.2.1997, no. 39, 'Bilder und Zeiten', 2.
18. Beckett, *Molloy, Malone Dies, The Unnamable*, 180.
19. Samuel Beckett, *Waiting for Godot* (London: Faber & Faber, 1966), 94.
20. Samuel Beckett, *Footfalls* (London: Faber & Faber, 1976), 9. All further references in the text are to this edition.
21. Bert O. States, 'Playing in Lyric Time: Beckett's Voice Plays' *Theatre Journal* 40, 4, (December 1988), 460.
22. James Knowlson, '*Footfalls*', in S.E. Gontarski (ed.), *On Beckett: Essays and Criticism* (New York: 1986), 352.
23. Samuel Beckett, *That Time* (London: Faber & Faber, 1976), 9. All further references in the text are to this edition.
24. The black stage is reminiscent of the even less 'dramatic' stage with an open red mouth against the black backdrop in Beckett's *Not I*.
25. Cf. McMullen, 430, 433.
26. States, 456. The concept is taken from Bachelard's *The Poetics of Space*.

Irish Theatre:
The State Of The Art

Fintan O'Toole

John Millington Synge, writing about Goethe, felt that his weakness was that he had: 'no national and intellectual mood to interpret. The individual mood is often trivial, perverse, fleeting, [but the] national mood [is] broad, serious, provisionally permanent'.[1] The relevance of this view to his own work and to that of his co-workers in the creation of the modern Irish theatre is obvious. But, at the same time, it raises a question about contemporary Irish theatre. If the greatness of the artist is dependent on the greatness of the times, if artistic originality is in some sense conditioned by time and place, then what can be said to be distinctive about this particular time and this particular place, and how do those distinctions help to shape the theatre? What national or intellectual mood is there to be interpreted? Is it, indeed, possible to talk at all of either the nation or its moods in the singular?

Synge's view is useful at least as a reminder that contemporary Irish theatre cannot be interpreted as a mere lineal descendent of Synge's. The fact that Synge's theatre, the Abbey, still exists and is still at the core of Irish theatre lends a superficial appearance of continuity, but like most superficialities in Ireland, it is deceptive. The playwright Denis Johnston, writing in the 1950s, identified four distinct Abbey acting companies and he thought that the Irish-speaking Cumann ... had no more to do with the past than the Holy Roman Empire had to do with Hadrian. He compared the Abbey to a knife that had had four new blades and five new handles and still insisted that it was the same knife. Synge usefully reminds us that what is true of actors is just as true of writers – that they give shape to and are shaped by their own times and places, and that times and places change.

Yet it strikes me that anyone looking at the theatre in Ireland in the 1990s would find more similarities with the theatre of Synge than they would have done even a decade earlier. Neither Synge's language nor his peasant world remain at the heart of Irish theatre, yet the theatre of the last few years shares much with Synge's. It is strongly marked by a concern with language for its own sake. It is primarily poetic rather than naturalistic. It has an angular rather than direct relationship to Irish society. It works, as the Synge of *The Well of the Saints* works, through evocation rather than dramatisation. What I want to try to do is to suggest, in broad strokes and with a concern for woods rather than trees, why

165

this should be so, keeping in mind at all times, of course, that every generalisation can be contradicted by particulars.

What I want to suggest in essence is that we have been through a particular movement in our theatre and in our society over the last 30 years, and that movement is now at a close. If we want to trace broad patterns, we can say that in this century we have had in Irish theatre three quite distinct movements. The first is the theatrical revival centring on Synge, Yeats, Lady Gregory and O'Casey. That revival effectively terminated at the end of the 1920s, its end marked by the Abbey's failure to produce either Johnston's *The Old Lady Says No!* or O'Casey's *The Silver Tassie*. It was followed by a long period of decline and decadence, the counter-currents to which are too scattered, too marginalised and too isolated to be called a movement.

A second revival, in my own view no less powerful, began in the late 1950s and continued well into the 1980s. It is marked, obviously, by the work of Tom Murphy, Brian Friel, John B. Keane, Thomas Kilroy and Hugh Leonard. And we have now entered into some kind of third phase, a phase that is too new to be fully defined, but whose outlines can be at least tentatively suggested. As I have already suggested in some important respects this third phase has more in common with the first revival than with the second, yet it is important to stress that it includes the later work of two of the most important writers of the second revival, Murphy and Friel.

I realise that these distinctions are crude and schematic, yet I think we have to make them if we are to understand where we are now. This is particularly important because the process of transition from the second phase to the third has been a confusing and difficult one for audiences and critics. We have become used to a theatre of conflict, a theatre of doubleness, and those expectations were met in ever more spectacular ways in the 1960s, 1970s and 1980s. We have had in recent Irish theatre great, highly wrought, intensely dramatic, and in a real sense classical works. What I want to suggest is that we will not get such works in the immediate future, that something has shifted and that criticism needs to come to terms with whatever that something is. The drama which has been present in our society has moved on, and the theatre is moving on with it, moving away from that conflict, that doubleness. If this is true, then we have to find new ways of talking about it, of evaluating it, even of defining what is and is not dramatic.

One of the striking things about the world of John Synge is precisely that it was to him a world – a unified nexus of time and place. His seeking out of the Aran Islands, of the sharp spatial definition that an island affords, is symbolic. *The Aran Islands* begins by asserting a control over place and time that are impressive in their rigour. The book's first sentence – 'I am in Aranmor, sitting over a turf fire, listening to a murmur Gaelic that is rising from a little publichouse under my room'[2] – is dense with the specificities of place. The next sentence – 'The steamer which comes to Aran sails according to the tide, and it was six o'clock this morning when we left the quay of Galway in a dense shroud of mist' – is alive with the imperatives of time. And these essential fixtures remain in place throughout the book. He excluded matters relating to the past and the future of the Aran Islands, except as they arose in thought and conversation during his visits. The frame of the book, as of the plays, is classical in its preservation of unities – time, place and action each remains essentially singular.

To travel around Ireland with Synge in his prose works is to encounter a society that is certainly not simple – on the contrary, it is full of subtle gradations of class and region, and of the infinite colours of human personality – but it is, broadly speaking, a single cultural entity. It is a world whose borders are already leaking as people continue to make their way to the New World, but within those borders, the people are in essence one people. In the theatre of the first revival, there is a substratum of nationalism: Irishness is what defines the cast of characters, 'Ireland', a single thing which does not need to be spelt out, is the oil that makes the plot run.

The societies of the great early Irish plays, Synge's included, are patently bounded, close, sharing a common ground that is so clear that it hardly needs to be marked at all. It is not that outsiders do not play an important role in these plays. It is precisely that in order for outsiders to play the role they do, they need to be set against a bounded and closely-knit society. It is essential to *The Playboy*, for instance, that Christy Mahon is so patently an outsider. The play works by setting the closeness of the tribe, manifested in the forthcoming wedding of Pegeen to her cousin Shawn Keogh, against the threat of the outsider. Pegeen, at the start of the play, talks about the loose, uncontrolled, unbounded men who might be abroad and threatening.

Or think of *The Plough and the Stars*. Again, the outsiders are immediately and overwhelmingly obvious as outsiders. The society of the play is so obviously *one* that it can incorporate the political or personal oddities of a Bessie Burgess or a Young Covey without difficulty. In the discourse of the play, those who are outside the discourse can literally hardly be spoken to. The Woman from Rathmines or the British soldiers who occupy the stage at the end, cannot, in a play where conversation is the very stuff of life, be engaged in conversation.

This assumption that society is essentially single, that even its divisions are divisions *within* rather than *between*, reflects the reality of the vestigial Gaelic culture, a peasant culture in which class distinctions tended to be obscured by the general poverty and the common sense of a far greater division between native and foreigner. What is striking in that culture is the way in which every action, every word, every person, has meaning only in relation to a whole, a whole that is defined by the timeless truths of custom. The view of reality is never a personal view. At no time is it at variance with the values and customs of the society as a whole. To be out of step with a custom is to be all but sub-human. One feels a strange sense of timelessness: that actions that require months or years are so reduced that they seem to take on the rhythm of the day. This, of course, is precisely what Synge sought to immerse himself in on the Aran Islands.

It seems to me to be no accident that McGahern's idea that in Ireland all places are brought in and reduced to the island frame and that all action fills one day regardless of what went before or will come after could also be applied to Samuel Beckett's *Waiting for Godot* or *Happy Days*. Nor is it any accident that it could *not* be applied to the work of any serious Irish playwright *after* Beckett. For, in the great gulf that separates the Irish playwrights who began to write before the late 1950s from those who began to write after the late 1950s, Beckett, the exiled Parisian post-Proustian protestant atheist, is closer to Tomas O Crohan, the Catholic, Gaelic peasant, seldom off the Blasket Islands in his life, than either are to the mental world of a Brian Friel, a Tom Murphy, or a Thomas Kilroy.

The mind-set of Beckett and O Crohan, of Synge and Yeats, is that of a single world: Beckett's endless days and continual present tense, Synge and O'Casey's close-knit, well-defined societies, Yeats's notion of Unity of Being, a state in which all doubles become single, are, in spite of the vast differences in their styles of theatre, in this respect all of a piece. For the playwrights of the second revival, on the other hand, all vision must be double vision. This, in essence, is what differentiates one period from the other.

If we go back to O Crohan for a moment, one of the striking things is that although members of his family go to the New World, the USA, that new world can still be perfectly encompassed within the frame of the old. For him, America is *deor allais* the land of sweat. Far from threatening the rule of custom, America serves only to reinforce that rule, for O Crohan is able to complain that America coarsens manners, that its emphasis on self-seeking endangers custom, and that this obviously makes no sense. In the balance between the old world and the new, the new world is found wanting, is self-evidently *less*. In the Ireland whose national mood the playwrights of the second revival had to interpret, nothing could be less obvious. Their Ireland is shaped by America, a place in which the new world is superimposed on the old, like a colour print that's out of key. It is from this that their characteristic double vision comes.

From the late 1950s onwards, 'Ireland' as a single, simple notion which might underlie and give formal coherence to a work of theatre began to seep away. This happened because we were no longer merely going to the New World. The New World was also coming to us, in the form of six billion pounds of investment from multinational corporations, four and a half billion of it from the USA. Government policy of trying to protect a unified, predominantly rural, Catholic and conservative society collapsed, and the floodgates holding back Yeats's filthy modern tide were opened. The society became complex, no longer definable as a single reality. Theatre, too, was no longer able to operate with single realities either. The theatre of naturalism, the theatre in which every effect has a cause, in which every action has a motive and in which every character has a fundamental substratum of coherence, became virtually impossible. The very notion of character as something given, something singular, as a vessel within which words, ideas and emotions could be contained, became highly problematic.

Old worlds don't just become new worlds, and Ireland didn't just become another state of the union. It became a double world, a slippery state in which the traditional and the modern jostled for the status of reality, in which every truth was equally untrue, in which past, present and future seemed to melt into each other, in which the borders of reality and of personality became permeable. Such a place is both a good ground in which to be a playwright, since the clash of cultures is inherently dramatic, and also a difficult one, since the sense of unity which underlies the work of a Synge or an O'Casey is no longer available. The combination of social opportunity and formal challenge gave us an extraordinary generation of theatrical creators, one which is, amazingly, still restlessly active.

John B. Keane's important plays, the ones written between 1959 and 1966, gave the new sense of doubleness and of objective and external – and therefore formally unadventurous – expression. They dramatised the causes, if not the psychic consequences, of the kind of breakdown of the notion of a single, defined, bounded, personality that is found later on. They present us clearly with two opposed moral and psychological environments in which their characters have to live. The people of *Sive, Big Maggie, The Field,* are drawn between a customary world of rights and duties, of fixed forms of family, sexuality and property, on the one hand, and a world of freedom, sexual, financial and moral, on the other. The world of Keane's central figures, Meena Glavin, Big Maggie, the Bull McCabe, like the world of Tom Murphy's great early play *A Whistle in the Dark,* is essentially a tragic one. Doomed to live by old values in a new world, they can literally do nothing right, for what they perceive to be right is no longer, by the lights of the new world, so. There is a fundamental disjunction between actions and their consequences, as there always is in tragedy. The times are out of joint.

With the emergence of Brian Friel, the doubleness begins to be internalised, to infiltrate the borders of personality itself. In Friel, doubleness is characteristically located in the notion of exile, but equally characteristically, even that very notion of exile itself is double. There is the physical exile of the impulse to leave Ireland, most obviously of Gar O'Donnell in *Philadelphia, Here I Come!,* but also, and more profoundly, of Frank Hardy in *Faith Healer.* There is also, though, the sense of being an exile in one's own country that is rooted in Friel's status as a Northern Irish nationalist. This double doubleness of exile leads to a kind of theatre in which character, personality and language themselves become slippery, and constantly threaten to divide, as Gar O'Donell divides between a public and a private self, or as Hugh Leonard's Charlie in *Da,* and the entire cast of characters in *A Life,* split into past and present selves. In a slightly different configuration, Tom Murphy in almost all of his plays divides the self between two characters, often brothers, sometimes friends or mortal enemies, who appear to be separate but who emerge as two halves of the one whole.

In Friel, too, memory is utterly problematic. The relationship between the past and the present is thrown into such doubt by the speed of change that no version of the past can ever be trusted. There is no stable point in the present from which one may look at the past and say with certainty: this is what happened. Gar O'Donnell's sense of himself and of his father is founded on the memory of a happy day they spent together, but the day may never have happened. In *The Freedom of the City* and *Making History* official versions of what happened are seen to be invented, to be an exercise in the impossible. In *Faith Healer* we get three versions of the events which the play narrates, but instead of confirming memory as something shared and communal, it merely confirms it as something which has collapsed as a public phenomenon into a private fiction. And if the past is unreliable, then not only does the naturalistic law of cause and effect become unworkable, but also the whole notion of character as the sum of all the things that happened to it becomes untenable.

Characters become open, permeable, unbounded. Frank Hardy, the faith healer, is literally permeable. He lays on his hands, and sometimes, when he touches someone, something flows out of him and heals. He has no essence, no fixed nature. He is nothing except what he can sometimes, mysteriously, cause to happen in others. And he can neither comprehend nor control this power. The power itself does not even provide a fixed centre: it is either miraculous or ludicrous, either magical or a piece of sheer charlatanism. That other cod magician, Tom Murphy's J.P.W. King in *The Gigli Concert*, is also utterly permeable, except in the opposite direction. Instead of things flowing out of him, they flow in, in the form of the dreams, obsessions and impossible desires of the Irishman who comes to seek his help. Likewise, the invented, fictional self of Tom Kilroy's Brendan Bracken in *Double Cross* gives way under extreme pressure to another, dormant self of his past life.

The essential point about all of this is that in this second revival of Irish theatre, we had an extraordinary period in which formal adventurousness and the desire to reflect and reflect on one's immediate society were not contradictory impulses but complementary ones. The doubleness of the society, the co-presence of contradictory worldviews, made it necessary for the theatre to evolve forms in which the collapse of personality, the instability of character, the failure of the naturalistic laws of cause and effect, were not just *avant garde* experiments but also necessary forms of social realism. In essence, realistic theatre in Ireland was, for 30 years, *avant garde* theatre. The society simply could not be encompassed within the singular vision of naturalistic theatre.

It is not, of course, that there was anything unique about Irish theatre's concern with the disintegration of personality, with the essential doubleness of contemporary life, with the notion of a radical discontinuity between past and present. It is that Irish theatre had a particularly direct and concrete route to these universal concerns, and that, because they could deal with these things and at the same time be dealing with a society, they could grapple with fundamental aspects of the human condition in the late 20th century without becoming abstract, without losing contact with the social and the political. This was a position of enormous privilege and one which a number of great theatrical imaginations exploited to the full.

If the basis of this broad paradigm is right, and the second phase of Irish theatre from the late 1950s to the late 1980s was driven by the intensely dramatic conflict between tradition and modernity, then it should also be true that the collapse of that conflict should mean the end of that phase and the opening of a new one. This is, I think, broadly what is happening.

There is no dramatic conflict between tradition and modernity in Ireland any more. If we take Daniel Corkery's famous definition of traditional Irishness as being constituted by three things – '(1) The Religious Consciousness of the People; (2) Irish nationalism; and (3) The Land'[3] – then it is clear that each of the parts is under immense stress. In relation to land, even rural Ireland now is either more or less industrialised or more or less marginalised. More profoundly, land itself has lost its economic value, since, under the reform of the EU's Common Agricultural Policy, land itself is virtually worthless without a production quota attached. Nationality has become more a question than an answer, more a quest than a point of departure. Religion, far from being a serene guarantor of traditional values, is itself the site of a bitter battlefield. Insofar as it still exists, traditional Ireland is alienated, angular and embattled, as strange, with its moving statues and paranoid visions, as any *avant garde* has ever been. Its image in the theatre is no longer John B. Keane's proud, confident, dangerous Bull McCabe, but Sebastian Barry's odd, sad, comic, encircled Boss Grady's Boys, imagining themselves as foot-soldiers.

Such a vision of traditional Ireland cannot be the source of great, sweeping dramatic confrontations. What we have instead are fragments, isolated pieces of a whole story that no one knows. Ireland is not one story any more, and we cannot expect single theatrical metaphors for it. Instead of one story and many theatrical images of it, we are moving towards a dramatisation of the fragments rather than the whole thing, the whole society. In the plays of the emerging third phase there are isolated worlds, closed entities, in which we move away from the doubleness of the second revival and back to the singleness of the first, with two very large differences. In the first place, this new singleness no longer assumes a single country underlying the drama, a single social world to which the action refers. In the second, it retains and builds on the key elements of the second phase – the disintegration of personality, the permeability of character, the discontinuity between cause and effect.

In this latter respect, Friel's *Faith Healer*, which looked at first like a glorious oddity in Irish theatre, with its self-conscious lack of dramatic conflict, now looks like a great exemplar, like a key bridge between the second phase and the third. Its evocation of a suspended time and a purely theatrical space, of a dramatic world that is radically discontinuous with the social world outside the theatre, is an essential discovery for the plays of the third phase. In the ultimate refusal to inhabit fixed categories, Frank Hardy himself is neither dead nor alive. He is, in the narrative, a dead man, but in the drama before us on stage, he is alive to tell his tale. This metaphorical withdrawal from the social world, this creation of a theatre of suspended animation, is followed directly by some of the important works of the third phase. The same device is used in Tom Murphy's *Too Late for Logic*, in Dermot Bolger's *The Lament for Arthur Cleary* and *One Last White Horse*, in Frank McGuinness's *The Bread Man*.

Perhaps symbolic of the way in which this third phase is both close to and radically unlike the first revival is the use of an island community in Sebastian Barry's *Prayers of Sherkin*. In Synge's *The Aran Islands,* in Michael Collins's vision of Achill Island as the essence of Irish nationality, in the writings of the Blasket Island authors, the uniformity of island life stands as a microcosm of the life of the nation, acting by analogy as an image of an assumed fixity and purity. In *Prayers of Sherkin,* staged in 1990, Irish theatre returns to the island; and it is indeed a remarkably certain, unified culture that is on display. Whereas in the only play of the second revival to use the island metaphor, Friel's *The Gentle Island*, the allusion is bitter and sardonic, the isolated island a site for savage and violent conflict, in *Prayers of Sherkin* conflict is almost entirely absent. It is also, like the great plays of the first revival, essentially poetic, relying on its power to evoke a world through language rather than assert it through action.

But, on the other hand, the meaning of the island's community is almost directly opposite to the meaning that Aran or the Blaskets or Achill had for the first, nationalist, revival. The island community is not pure native but 'angular' foreigner, an English sect settled on Sherkin. And the island itself is not proof against time, but unstable and unfixed. This isolated community, this world to itself, is repeated in various forms in the plays that mark the move into the third phase. In Tom Murphy's *Too Late for Logic* it is the self-enclosed underworld of a certain sort of middle-class Dublin, a world into which no light enters from any other source. In Brian Friel's *Dancing At Lughnasa* it is a single house, a single family, both so single indeed, that the entry of a new thing can lead only to the collapse of the entire world of the play. In John McGahern's *The Power of Darkness* we are given a world so cut-off, so much without a single point of outside reference, that as soon as the doubleness of reflection enters at all, the action can only and literally stop, refuse to continue and collapse in on itself. In much of the work of Frank McGuinness the singleness is a matter of gender, men and women existing in different zones whose borders cannot be crossed.

You can mark the shift I'm talking about simply by noting that when outsiders intrude on the worlds of these plays, they are immediately obvious as outsiders, just as they would be in Synge and O'Casey. We are back with Christy Mahon and the Woman from Rathmines. Patrick Kirwan in *Sherkin*, coming from the mainland, represents almost literally a different world when he comes to woo Fanny Hawke. Father Jack in *Lughnasa* trails a whole continent and a whole different culture behind him when he enters. Paddy in *The Power of Darkness* seems to come from a entirely different story, even a completely different play. In each case, the outside represents a different country (the mainland, Africa, the war in the Pacific) and speaks a different kind of language. As with Synge or O'Casey, the coming of the outsider serves to emphasise the singleness, the highly bounded nature of the world into which he comes.

Yet that bounded place is not Ireland. In the plays after the late 1980s, Ireland as a bounded place has ceased to exist. Africa and Spain seep into the Ballybeg of *Lughnasa*. The ocean that laps against the shores of *The Power of Darkness* is the Pacific. Sebastian Barry's *White Woman Street* is set in the American West, Sligo a distant, angular and elusive memory. Dermot Bolger's *The Lament for Arthur Cleary* and *In High Germany* are dominated by Germany. Schopenhauer's Germany of the early nineteenth century is an important presence in *Too Late for Logic*. The bounded fragments which are the worlds of these plays are fragments not of a coherent whole called Ireland, but of a mixed-up jigsaw of the continents.

It is too soon to say what the full shape of this change is, but two particular changes are immediate and obvious. One is that conflict is no longer of the essence. The theatre of the second revival was a theatre of conflict enacted through the clash of large forces. Action – what happens moment by moment on stage – was crucial because it is through action that the conflict moves towards resolution. But this is not the case with the new work. In it, there is little conflict and there is little tension or suspense. It is striking the degree to which we know in all of these plays what is going to happen before it happens. In each of the plays, the question *what happens next?* is not the appropriate one. In *Sherkin,* we know as soon as we know the characters that Fanny will leave the island and that the play is an enactment of that inevitability. Nor is there any choice between good and evil – all the characters are remarkably sweet. The plot is slight and could be summed up in a sentence.

In *Too Late for Logic, The Lament for Arthur Cleary, The Bread Man* and *One Last White Horse*, we know from the start that the protagonist is dead. The end is at the beginning in a way that deliberately removes the notion of an open-ended conflict. In Murphy's case this is truly remarkable, for he is a writer whose sense of not knowing how a play is going to end, of ending a play being a matter of forcing the impossible to happen, is crucial to his work.

In *Lughnasa,* famously, we are told what is going to happen to the sisters long before the play ends, undercutting the whole sense of drama, of something evolving through action or even through narrative suspense. In Friel's most recent play *Wonderful Tennessee* there is virtually no plot at all, just a group of characters waiting for something that we know is not going to happen.

In *The Power of Darkness,* a narrative of suspense and action is set up only to collapse completely. The story and the action – an exaggerated story and melo-dramatic action – stop in their tracks, and the whole second half of the play is about the impossibility of the play going on.

In Vincent Woods's *At the Black Pig's Dyke,* plot and action are replaced through the medium of mumming by a ritual invocation of an inevitable death.

Related to this loss of tension and suspense is the second obvious change, the re-emergence of poetry in the theatre. If drama cannot be created out of conflict, then it must be evoked through language, though by no means only through verbal language. Again, *Faith Healer* is the obvious forerunner, but it is still striking that the re-invention of a dense theatrical language has involved a virtual obliteration of the fixed distinctions between narrative fiction, poetry and dialogue. The emergence of broken narrative forms in a play like Murphy's *Bailegangaire*, Murphy's own turning to the novel, the fact that key plays like *Prayers of Sherkin* and *The Lament for Arthur Cleary* actually began life as poems, the surge of interest in writing for the theatre by poets like Seamus Heaney and Brendan Kennelly, and novelists like John McGahern and John Banville: all of these are evidence that there is a third phase of Irish theatre in which the specificity of theatre itself – expressed in concepts like conflict, drama, action, character – is on the wane. These plays are all extraordinarily linguistic creations, concerned to evoke or conjure up a world rather than to create one. They have to do so because the worlds they are concerned with are so particular, so angular, that an audience cannot share in them through naturalistic convention.

Because we no longer have one shared place, one Ireland, we can no longer have a naturalistic theatre of recognition in which a world is signalled to us through objects and we tacitly agree to recognise it is as our own. We must instead have a theatre of evocation in which strange worlds, not our own, are in Yeats's phrase 'called to the eye of the mind'. Our theatre now is about the business of calling up rather than recreating, and this will demand of us new ways of seeing and new categories of criticism. This is hard, and it is because it is still living that the Irish theatre is marking itself in new ways.

Notes

1. As quoted in Robin Shelton, *J. M. Synge and his World* (London: Thames & Hudson, 1971), 60.
2. J.M. Synge, *Plays, Poems and Prose* (London: Dent, 1964), 249.
3. Daniel Corkery, *Synge and Anglo-Irish Literature* (Cork: The Mercier Press, 1966), 19.

Notes on the Contributors

Marie Arndt is a lecturer in English at the University of Kalmar, Sweden. She is a member of the Executive Committee and the Bibliographical Sub-Committee of IASIL, and initiator and co-founder of NISN, the Nordic Irish Studies Network.

Michael Böss is a lecturer at Aarhus University, Denmark, where he teaches British history and cultural studies. A specialist in Irish Studies, he has written and edited a number of books, most recently *Den irske verden: Historie, kultur og identitet i det moderne samfund* (1997).

Lissi Daber teaches British and Irish literature and history at Aalborg University, Denmark.

Darlene Erickson is an associate professor of English at Ohio Dominican College, Columbus, Ohio, U.S.A. She is author of *Illusion Is More Precise Than Precision: The Poetry of Marianne Moore* (1992).

Tom Garvin is professor and head of the Department of Politics at University College, Dublin. His most recent books are *Nationalist Revolutionaries in Ireland* (1987) and *1922: The Birth of Irish Democracy* (1996).

Edna Longley is professor of English literature at The Queen's University of Belfast, Northern Ireland. Her latest book is *The Living Stream: Literature and Revisionism in Ireland* (1994).

Britta Olinder is a lecturer in English at Göteborg University, Sweden. She has published research on seventeenth century drama as well as on the literatures of Ireland and the Commonwealth countries.

Fintan O'Toole is a theatre critic and columnist. In the 1980s O'Toole established himself as one of the most influential critical observers of contemporary Irish politics and culture as editor of the magazine *Magill*. In the early 1990s, he was artistic director of the Abbey Theatre. His most recent books are *The Ex-Isle of Erin: Images of a Global Ireland* (1997) and *A Traitor's Kiss: The Life of Richard Brinsley Sheridan* (1997).

William Pratt is professor of English at Miami University of Ohio, Oxford, Ohio, USA. He has published poems, translations, critical essays and reviews, as well as books, among them *The Fugitive Poets: Modern Southern Poetry in Perspective* (1965, revised edition 1991). In 1996, he co-edited *The Big Ballad Jamboree*, a newly discovered novel by Fugitive poet Donald Davidson, and published a collection of his essays called *Singing the Chaos: Madness and Wisdom in Modern Poetry*.

Ruth Sherry is professor of English Literature at the Norwegian University of Science and Technology, Trondheim, Norway. She has specialized in writing on Irish literature and society.

Colm Tóibín is a journalist and writer who has won special critical acclaim for his prose style. His first novel was *The South* (1990) and his most recent novels are *The Heather Blazing* (1993) and *The Story of the Night* (1996).

Karl-Heinz Westarp is head of the English Department at Aarhus University, Denmark. He has written or edited studies in a wide range of fields, most recently *Flannery O'Connor: The Growing Craft* (1993), *The Literary Man* (1996) and *The Novels of Eudora Welty* (1998).

Abstracts

Tom Garvin
The Slow Triumph of Politics: Irish Endgame

This essay argues that a tradition of militant insurrectionist nationalism wedded to violence is being slowly eroded by a general Irish commitment to democratic politics in both parts of the divided island. Crucial events in this historical development have been the failure of the 1798 rebellion, the success of Daniel O'Connell's democratic politics in the 1823-1840 period and the hesitant but real development of electoral democracy in Ireland since 1886, despite the revolutionary interlude of 1913-23. The campaign for a nationalist and socialist revolutionary settlement in Ireland waged by the Provisional IRA since 1970 has been a failure and is being supplanted gradually by democratic mechanisms.

Colm Tóibín
New Ways to Kill Your Father: Historical Revisionism

Against a background of elements from his intellectual autobiography, Tóibín enters into a critical dialogue with historian Roy F. Foster and so-called historical revisionism. He acknowledges the need for judicious historical scholarship and he rejects his own early attraction to the notion of being relieved from the burden of the past.

Ruth Sherry
The Uses of the National Anthem

The Irish national anthem, 'The Soldier's Song', originally written ca. 1907 as a republican rallying song, has always been controversial. It was adopted as the Irish national anthem by the Free State government in 1926. The anthem had symbolic significance in marking the Free State's separation from the United Kingdom, but its political content has effectively been toned down by the ways in which it has been presented in recent years.

Marie Arndt
Sean O'Faolain as Biographer and Commentator

In Sean O'Faolain's biographies of Constance Markievicz, Hugh O'Neill, Daniel O'Connell and Cardinal Newman, the author juxtaposes fact and fiction. He often constructs an ideal Irish past in order to make critical comment on present Ireland in the guise of history. O'Faolain makes the biographed subjects his mouth-pieces, and this often reveals more about the author himself than about the individuals he is writing about.

Darlene Erickson
With Skill, Endurance, and Generosity of Heart:
Frank McCourt's *Angela's Ashes*

Frank McCourt's award-winning memoir, *Angela's Ashes*, describes the life of an Irish family in Brooklyn during the Great Depression, their ill-timed return to Ireland and the slums of Limerick, and the author's journey to America. The essay presents major issues in the book, which is a 'tough read', but also reverberates with Irish songs and laughter.

Lissi Daber
Nationalism and Unionism in Northern Ireland in the 1990s

The article accounts for the importance of group identities in Northern Ireland, where living with difference, and frequently defining yourself by what you are not, is typical. Identity is difference in this border country. However, political events of the Spring of 1998 may lead to a future weakening of the significance of difference.

Edna Longley
Northern Ireland: Poetry and Peace

Since Yeats's early adage that 'the end of art is peace', the 'intertextuality' between poetry and peace has become more complex for poets to handle. Though pacifism is not the beginning of art, peace and with it civilization can be the consequence of processes modelled by poetry. Edna Longley considers mid twentieth-century Ireland as a kind of Dark Age on the painful way from cultural nationalism through cultural regionalism to 'civilization'. She argues that poetry has contributed to processes of articulation of self and other in Ireland and thinks that northern Irish poets now have reached a post-nationalist stage, which she exemplifies by close readings of four poems by Ciaran Carson, Michael Longley, Medbh McGuckian and Seamus Heaney.

Britta Olinder
Creating an Identity: John Hewitt and History

What is special about John Hewitt's view of history? Taking as its starting point Hewitt's writing on the history of literature and the arts in Northern Ireland, this essay examines the history of Hewitt's own family and the way this relates to his view of the history of both his native region and the rest of the world. What and whom Hewitt considers important in ancient and more recent history are always determined by his socialist viewpoint. His comparisons of trends in ancient history with the series of migrations to Ireland and with contemporary events can be seen as a means of delineating his own position in the great flow of events.

Michael Böss
Roots in the Bog: The Notion of Identity in the Poetry and Essays of Seamus Heaney

Seamus Heaney's poetics and poetry have often dealt with questions of identity. One of his concerns is to affirm how important it is for the individual to develop a sense of connectedness with the past. But Heaney also wants to avoid the pitfalls of the claims to single-minded collective identities that have been voiced so often in Ireland, North and South. This essay demonstrates that it follows from Heaney's conception of the relationship between language and mind that authentic identity is a personal goal, not a national and collective one. In an 'intuited Ireland of the affections and the imagination', Heaney hopes, Ireland will be an island where people may be prepared to acknowledge a multi-layered sense of identity.

William Pratt
European Past, Irish Present: Joyce's Modern Hells

Hell is still a potent image in Modern Literature. There are two Hells in Joyce: the Hell of the sermon in Chapter 3 of *A Portrait of the Artist as a Young Man* and the Hell of Chapter 6 of *Ulysses*, where Joyce parodies Homer's narrative of Odysseus' voyage to Hades in Book XI of *The Odyssey*. Joyce's two Hells are superior to and more serious than any other fictional Irish Hell written later, such as Flann O'Brien's *The Third Policeman*.

Karl-Heinz Westarp
Aspects of Time and Identity in Samuel Beckett

Our general perception of time leads to difficulties in defining ourselves in terms of past, present and future. Samuel Beckett perceived time as a prison from which there is no escape. Therefore it must be 'killed' through words, games, inventories, or simply by waiting. His plays *Footfalls* and *That Time* (1976) are examples of re-presenting past memories in an attempt to reach self-identification.

Fintan O'Toole
Irish Theatre: The State of the Art

Twentieth century Irish theatre, O'Toole argues, has been through three distinct phases. The first revival centred around Yeats, Synge, Gregory and O'Casey. After a period of decline a second revival started in the late 1950s with the work of Murphy, Friel, Keane, Kilroy and Leonard. At the end of the century Irish theatre now seems to have entered a third phase which has a great deal in common with the first revival. Apart from late plays by Friel and Murphy it comprises Bolger, Woods and Barry. This latest phase marks the end of a theatre of conflict and doubleness with little emphasis on action. Instead the authors evoke drama through a dense theatrical language that involves a virtual obliteration of the fixed distinctions between narrative fiction, poetry and dialogue. O'Toole explains this movement to a drama of evocation by the social and cultural changes Ireland has been through in the past 30 years. The new theatre demands new ways of seeing and new categories of criticism.